CRAFTING DIGNITY

CRAFTING DIGNITY

HOW IMMIGRANT DAIRY WORKERS
TRANSFORM RURAL COMMUNITIES

ALISA GARNI

UNIVERSITY PRESS OF KANSAS

Published by the University Press of Kansas (Lawrence, Kansas 66045), which was organized by the Kansas Board of Regents and is operated and funded by Emporia State University, Fort Hays State University, Kansas State University, Pittsburg State University, the University of Kansas, and Wichita State University.

This book will be made open access within three years of publication thanks to Path to Open, a program developed in partnership between JSTOR, the American Council of Learned Societies (ACLS), University of Michigan Press, and the University of North Carolina Press to bring about equitable access and impact for the entire scholarly community, including authors, researchers, libraries, and university presses around the world. Learn more at https://about.jstor.org/path-to-open/.

Library of Congress Cataloging-in-Publication Data

Print LCCN: 2025032295 (hardback)
ISBN 978-0-7006-4088-1 (hardback)
ISBN 978-0-7006-4089-8 (paperback)
ISBN 978-0-7006-4090-4 (ebook)

British Library Cataloguing-in-Publication Data is available.

EU Authorised Representative Details: Easy Access System Europe
Mustamäe tee 50, 10621 Tallinn, Estonia |
gpsr.requests@easproject.com

To everyone struggling for dignified, holistic, sustainable, and inclusive futures.

CONTENTS

ACKNOWLEDGMENTS

Many people helped me with this project over the course of ten years. I give my deepest thanks to everyone who agreed to participate in the study. Many people let me hang around, gave me tours, invited me into their homes and workplaces and to important events, answered questions, and shared detailed work and life experiences. I hope to have done justice to those experiences in this book.

I owe an additional debt of gratitude to the people at the heart of the book who traversed a variety of borders to struggle against multiple sets of injustices. I admire and appreciate them and the enormous positive contributions they make. I hope this work makes a positive contribution to their lives in some way. I am inspired to always keep trying.

Marcus Dominguez, Jill Applegate, and Zaira Ruiz provided outstanding research assistance over the course of many years. All three conducted interviews, observed, recorded, transcribed, and engaged in countless discussions with me. Zaira additionally provided feedback on a draft of the completed manuscript. Lynsey Aikin and Citlally Orozco provided additional invaluable assistance. Getting to carry out this research alongside such talented, passionate, conscientious, and meticulous people was extraordinary.

I'm grateful to everyone I got to collaborate with in the language classes and workshops—both from within Dairy City and beyond. To maintain confidentiality, I avoid identifying people by name. I appreciate everyone.

Mario Cano and Mary Kohn, two colleagues and friends, spent time in Dairy City at different times over the years. They provided me with great advice and insight. Mary Kohn also gave me feedback on early drafts that was informed by her scholarly expertise and direct knowledge. Erynn Masi de Casanova provided invaluable feedback on the proposal and several early chapters, as well as a draft of the completed manuscript. She asked incisive questions and made very helpful suggestions. Her own work served as a model and an inspiration. Margaret Gray provided extensive critical comments on drafts of early chapters as well as a draft of the completed manuscript. She was tireless in her attention to detail and in encouraging me to bring my voice to the fore while remaining grounded in the data and relevant scholarship. Margaret's own work also served as a guide and an inspiration.

At the University Press of Kansas (UPK), David Congdon took on this project with expert care. He read multiple drafts, synthesized feedback from reviewers, fielded questions, provided feedback, and offered excellent advice. Andrea Laws, Kelly Chrisman Jacques, Nick Walther, and several additional people at UPK also provided invaluable support, which I really appreciate.

Wiley & Sons, and the editors of *Rural Sociology*, provided permissions for portions of work that first appeared *Rural Sociology* in 2018 to appear in the book, primarily in Chapter 3. "Permission was conveyed through Copyright Clearance Center, Inc."

Many thanks, as well, to Jessica Falcone for excellent methodological advice. Nicolette Manglos-Weber read and provided critical feedback on an early draft of Chapter 4. Theresa Selfa and Cecilia Menjívar engaged with me in helpful conversations about the work as it developed. My program, department, and university supported two sabbaticals (for this project and another) and provided multiple undergraduate research awards for my research assistants. Collegiality from colleagues was a great help. A special thanks to Kevin Steinmetz, who donated used laptops.

Ethan Blue and Cari Coe, through many conversations about the project over the years, showered me with intellectual and moral support. Frank Weyher, my wonderful husband and colleague, read and commented on multiple drafts of every chapter. Frank supplied tough and stellar feedback informed by his in-depth knowledge of an astonishingly broad range of scholarship, an unerringly sharp attention to detail, and a kind and loving respect for me and my ideas. He spent hours, days, weeks, months, and years listening to and encouraging me.

As always, all errors and omissions are mine.

Last, but not least, thank you to my family and friends for supporting me in a lifetime of learning.

INTRODUCTION

On a cold fall evening, Paloma Hernández stepped into the doorway of her weathered two-story farmhouse, located half a mile from the heart of "Dairy City," Kansas.[1] Wearing a denim shirt, sturdy work boots, and a blue bandana around her chestnut brown hair, Paloma resembled Rosie the Riveter and the women workers of World War II. Paloma was returning from a shift at one of three local dairies where she provides veterinary care for thousands of heifers. She is well-known, at the dairy and beyond, for maintaining excellent herd health and extremely low death rates. Paloma moved from Mexico to Dairy City in 2011 after she miraculously dissuaded attackers from raping her and killing her husband when they were ambushed on a remote highway in Veracruz. Paloma believes her attackers knew who she was and targeted her for her relative wealth. After a series of escalating robberies and assaults, she felt she would never be safe in Mexico. In rural Kansas, Paloma feels safe but exhausted, though she rarely admits to the latter. "When I'm around, there are no deaths," she says with a smile. Paloma knows she is essential. The dairy owners know it, too.

At a public town picnic a few months earlier, Owen Bauer—a fifth-generation descendant of German homesteaders and the third generation of his family to operate the Bauer farm—boasted to hundreds of feasting locals that Paloma is one of his star employees. He used a microphone connected to elaborate DJ equipment that Paloma's nephew, a former police officer in Mexico City, had set up in Dairy City's public park to play cumbia, salsa, and US country music. Owen's voice boomed through the large speakers in the thick, hot afternoon air. "We just don't know what we would do without her." Hundreds of people, white and Latinx/e, applauded.

Paloma is among approximately two hundred people from Mexico, Central America, Eastern Europe, and South Africa who immigrated to Dairy City in the past twenty-five years to work on one of three local dairy farms.[2] Immigrants in the United States are overrepresented among essential workers in agri-food production (Lichter 2012; Jordan 2020). In the dairy industry alone, immigrants constitute 51 percent of the labor force and produce 80 percent of the country's milk (Adcock, Anderson, and Rosson 2015, 2, 12; Mercier 2014; Panikkar and Barrett 2021). The egregious exploitation of immigrant workers who labor under brutal conditions in food-producing industries is well-documented in the scholarly literature (Bonanno and Constance 2001; Huffman and Miranowski 1996; McMichael 2013).[3] By contrast, rare industrial farmers like the Bauers who seek to retain immigrant employees like Paloma by attempting to eschew the degrading labor practices of other agricultural employers remain largely invisible in scholarly work, and they raise a crucial question: What happens to employees, companies, and communities when an employer resists pressures to degrade work and instead tries to promote dignity?

Dairy City presents a fascinating case study of how independent rural dairy farmers in Kansas and people from mostly urban places abroad were brought together in their respective struggles with globalized social changes.[4] While dairy farmers contended with pressures to grow/industrialize their operations to stay in business, people who recently immigrated contended with multiple intersecting violences linked to deindustrialization, harsh immigration regimes, and declining means for attaining or preserving middle-class lifestyles (Alvarez 2019). However, the ways in which two of three sets of farmers mutually sought security with people immigrating from abroad are atypical in Dairy City. The two sets of dairy farmers at the heart of this story gradually learned that stabilizing their farms while taking significant risks to grow them meant deepening their commitments to employees who took risks in relocating to a remote rural community that had suffered decades of demographic and economic decline. People who hadn't imagined doing dairy work in a remote rural town found themselves building tenure on farms where employer commitments to them opened surprising avenues for local integration, household cohesion, and intergenerational mobility. *Crafting Dignity* explores how these interactions unfolded and what significance they hold for individuals, the town, and broader social change.[5] The two farms at the core of this book serve as important reminders that degradation is not inevitable—a critical insight at a time when "widespread notions of the inevitability of insecurity protect US employers [and governments] from responsibility" (Pugh 2015, 196).

Variable Labor Practices

In the past twenty-five years, three sets of farmers in Dairy City recruited people from abroad to help them expand production and capture growing shares of global markets, but they each pursued distinctive labor practices. The first farm, the Hoffman dairy, adopted commonly documented labor practices typical of advanced finance capitalism, in which companies "exist to create shareholder value, not to provide stable employment" (Davis 2009, v; Sennett 2008, 35). Practices included "lean" labor organization, or temporary work arrangements with "strict task regimens" and management by "fiat" (Sennet 2008; Crowley 2016; Crowley and Hodson 2014).[6] When problems related to this form of labor organization led to employee attrition and declining milk production, the Hoffmans replaced employees with robots that, despite costing approximately 200,000 dollars each, neglect tasks essential to the operation.[7]

The second farm, the Bauer dairy, took a different tack. The first in their family to recruit immigrant employees, Gail and Wayne Bauer used craft-like labor organization. They worked alongside employees, swapping skills and tackling problems together. Having accumulated over a decade of job tenure, many immigrant employees with no previous farming experience use "embodied skill," or knowledge gained through practical experience/applied skill (Schwalbe 2010; Sennet 2008),[8] to search for and fix problems known to plague industrial dairy farms. The Bauers learned that committing to employees builds tenure, which is crucial for employees to innovate and stave off costly and life-threatening mistakes. People who immigrated from abroad and took dairy jobs brought invaluable experience in personnel management, marketing and sales, accounting, and machine/equipment repair. Craft-style labor organization on the farm facilitated "sharp mutual exchanges" (Sennett 2008), meaning employees voice concerns and work with managers, and other employees, to fix problems. These dynamics have important implications for individuals, the farms, and the broader community.

The third farm, the Pleasant Valley Dairy (PVD), initially used bureaucratic management that fragmented work and created tensions among employees who had few means for communicating or collaborating. With little room for maneuver, frustrated employees were more likely to "pass on rather than solve problems" (Crowley 2016, 92; Crowley and Hodson 2014). As problems multiplied, including cows running into the street and employees accusing one another of negligence, the lead manager, Peter, sought employees' recommendations for reform. He blended financial rewards with a more craft-like style that supported more work-life balance, open communication, and pathways for training and promotion into a greater variety of positions. Peter devised ways to build flexibility into people's schedules so they could attend school events with their children and pursue other interests and errands as needed. PVD scheduling and compensation packages became popular.

Suddenly under pressure to keep up with PVD, the Bauers then improved their compensation practices after employees complained about pay per shift and lack of overtime pay.[9] PVD and Bauer now pay between fifteen and twenty-five dollars per hour. When I began my research in 2015, however, wages were eight or ten dollars per hour, with raises starting at six months. Pay restructuring was bumpy, as managers raised wages for new hires and then had to remedy wage suppression for more tenured employees. Bauer and PVD offer paid vacations—ten days per year, significant support for in-town housing in single-family homes, and other financial incentives, like production bonuses and/or tickets to professional sporting events. PVD has long offered 401(k) accounts for full-time employees, and Bauer recently began doing the same. In the past few years, the two farms added health insurance for full-time employees, including dental and vision. Bauer then added disability insurance. PVD pays time and a half for overtime and double for holidays.

Several years ago, local service and farm implement manufacturers began competing with Bauer and PVD for immigrant employees. According to Owen Bauer, by 2016, such competition had driven up average local wages, including benefits, to twenty dollars per hour. He noted that while farmers can't raise the price of milk, they must boost compensation to compete for employees. Hans Hoffman, by contrast, claims to have "very low labor costs," but both the Bauer farm and PVD have outgrown the Hoffman farm. Bauer is now a series of farms employing a growing number of people in an ever-broader array of positions—milking, herding, insemination, maternity, veterinary, hauling, construction, machine repair/maintenance, safety oversight/management, personnel management, cattle ranching, and more, while PVD is experimenting with improved feed sources and converting waste (methane) into energy.

Similar to "the high-end niche garment market where quality and turnaround are key," quality and efficiency in dairy farming are essential, and they are achieved "not *in spite* of the increased cost of labor but *because of* it" (Plankey Videla 2012, 191). Competition driven by quality supports farm and job/community growth. Net positive labor practices encourage recently immigrated employees and their families to access local institutions—like the school, which was on the brink of closing before recent immigrants began arriving in 2000, as well as health-care services, civil services, and other local businesses—making Dairy City a more viable and interesting place to live than it was prior to the renewed onset of immigration in 2000.

Paloma's resemblance to a woman worker of World War II, however, is both fitting and ironic. It is fitting because Paloma challenges restricted citizenship as a recent immigrant and woman to support her family and drive the local economy through industrial employment. She works at a large modern dairy that must mass-produce milk efficiently to survive, but which uses craft-style management and a twentieth-century corporate welfarist logic to enhance production, including long-term employment, on-the-job training, upward mobility, benefits, and relatively high wages (Davis 2009; Edwards 1979; Fine 2006). Then, however, powerful unions reinforced welfare for workers engaged in mass production (Edwards 1979; Davis 2009; Zeitlin and Weyher 2001).[10] It is thus ironic because today, advanced shareholder capitalism has deprived most managers of their authority to raise productivity by collaborating with employees (Davis 2009). Instead, most managers antagonize employees. They perpetually reduce their commitments to workers, making work even more precarious, fragmented, and mechanical than it was before the labor and civil rights movements of the mid-twentieth century (Davis 2009; Edwards 1979).[11] They also exploit people's precarious immigration statuses to extract more unpaid labor power from them, often by "managing in the shadows," or taking advantage of people's structural vulnerabilities to intimidate and control them (Keller 2019; Gray 2014).[12] In this "tumbleweed society," people experience high rates of burnout, turnover, and degradation (Pugh 2015; Davis 2009; Stull et al. 1995).[13]

Confronting Multiple Intersecting Violences

The globalized degradation of work, in which many employers and governments reduce their commitments to workers in pursuit of ever lower costs of production (Davis 2009; Pugh 2015; Wright 2001),[14] is the context in which people like Paloma made fraught decisions about immigrating to Dairy City. It also affects people's assessments of dairy work and life in Dairy City, and thus their decisions about whether to stay. People who arrived in Dairy City during the past twenty-five years lost livelihoods and jobs abroad through the twin structural violences of deindustrialization and declining access to health, education, housing, and retirement. They fled the collapse of peripheral Fordism in Mexico and the rise of neoliberalism there and in war-torn Central America, Eastern Europe, and South Africa. The rise of neoliberalism and the fall of peripheral Fordism—or Fordism in the "global periphery/global south"—entailed the downsizing or dismantling of firms, the reorganization of work to disempower workers, and the decline of social welfare (Hernández-León 2004, 426; Shaiken 1995; Bernard 2004). They and thousands of people who were "members of the formerly protected skilled and semiskilled working class" were thrust into "the international labor market" (Hernández-León 2004, 425;

Massey, Arango Hugo, Kouaouci, and Pellegrino 1999; De Haas, Castles, and Miller 2019). People also experienced multiple intersecting violences in their displacements across borders (Alvarez 2019). Their structurally rooted suffering was "normalized" through symbolic violence that spuriously places blame for declining life chances on individuals rather than governments and employers, where it belongs (Alvarez 2019). Legal violences then eliminate access to rights and protections that would empower their struggles against injustice (Alvarez 2019). They face anti-immigrant rhetoric, sentiment, and treatment (Golash-Boza and Hondagneu-Sotelo 2013; Golash-Boza 2015; Gonzales 2013).[15]

Leaving mostly urban areas abroad, people recently immigrating to Dairy City joined the ranks of people immigrating from rural areas abroad to rural US places—revealing the extent to which insecure employment and uncertainty for workers are proliferating beyond what has previously been documented by scholars studying rural-to-rural international migration and "new destinations" immigration (Lichter 2012; Sexsmith 2019; Harrison and Lloyd 2012).[16] While recent immigration to Dairy City in some ways resembles new destinations immigration, which largely refers to people seeking rural industrial employment when US urban economies become unstable (Zúñiga and Hernández-León 2005; Hirschman and Massey 2008), Dairy City, as I will show, is an *ancient* destination (West 1998),[17] and people moved mostly from urban (post)industrial or commercial areas *abroad* to a remote rural US town dominated by agricultural production.[18] What's more, many people who immigrated in the past twenty-five years to take jobs at Bauer and PVD have stayed for a decade or more. Several households include the third or fourth generation (children and either parents and/or children's children). This counters trends of people leaving rural towns as soon as they find better opportunities elsewhere (Lichter 2012; Sexsmith 2019; Harrison and Lloyd 2012)[19] but supports a broader recent pattern of people avoiding the risks of family separation under a hostile immigration regime by settling in the United States rather than returning to countries of origin after a few years of working and saving, or to retire (Durand and Massey 2003; Massey, Durand, and Pren 2016; Massey 2020).[20]

As part of their efforts to promote employee retention, the Bauers and

PVD managers learned that they needed to recruit employees with their families, rather than targeting lone immigrants who were cut off from their families. This contrasts with farmers in other parts of the country who equate "employee reliability" with isolation and entrapment (see especially Sexsmith 2019; Keller 2019; Gray 2014). Instead, the Bauers and PVD managers realized, after making several mistakes, that fostering tenure and recruiting the next generation required encouraging immigrant employees and their families to stay in Dairy City. Dairy owners began using their local influence—as board members and owners of other local businesses, city council members, relatives of the mayor (past and present), and friends and relatives of the school principal, local teachers, hospital workers, and law enforcement officers—to encourage settlement. With improving services for recent arrivals, Dairy City itself has become something of a recruitment tool. In addition, people who have not recently immigrated come to depend on those who have: Without recent immigration, local businesses and institutions would have further withered following economic and demographic declines of the 1980s and 1990s. At the same time, recent immigrants have been focused on helping their children attain formal advanced degrees and pursue *non*-farm careers. Most of the 1.5 generation is going to college, and a couple have returned to Dairy City to work both farm and non-farm jobs (e.g., a Bauer ranch manager and an EMT).[21] How these tensions play out may hinge on the extent to which the Bauers and PVD managers develop craftwork, as well as the relative significance that "craft" takes on in the broader social context.

Currently, immigrant parents and children in Dairy City are concerned that the costs of higher education are rising and outpacing both compensation and housing costs across the US.[22] Simultaneously, the "portfolio" or tumbleweed society "is bulldozing the career path" (Sennet 2008, 265; Pugh 2015; Davis 2009).[23] Many corporations have divested of their physical assets, community ties, and commitments to workers (Davis 2009, 3, 7; Sennett 2008). "Rewards for service" continue to wane as employers increasingly treat tenure as a liability rather than an asset (Wright 2001; Sennet 2008; Davis 2009).[24] Workers who attempt to protect themselves from un- or under-employment by developing a "portfolio" of skills that they can apply to any existing jobs (hence the term "portfolio society") are perpetually at risk of losing jobs to similarly qualified people abroad who are paid less for the same work (Sennett 2008, 35; Davis 2009; Tough 2023).[25] Even people in jobs once thought of as "safe"—in auto manufacturing, computer programming, securities, acting, and engineering—are fighting replacement by robots, artificial intelligence, and/or people in other countries who are paid lower wages (Bradsher 2023; Davis 2009; Sennett 2008).[26] As I show, it is against this context that people evaluate working at Bauer and PVD in the long run.

Although most children of recent immigrants are graduating college and are likely to move and pursue non-farm careers, more people across the US economy are turning to trade or craft jobs that provide a decent living and may be more resistant to outsourcing or "insourcing," or the replacement of existing employees either with technology or with "fresh" employees who are less likely and/or less able to complain (Ocejo 2017; Tough 2023; Schwartzman 2013).[27] Some of these jobs—including brewing, distilling, barbering, and butchering—are even considered "hip" (Ocejo 2017). Dairy farming is not considered hip, but when it is organized in a craft-like manner, it may provide social and economic stability. I explore how this may affect patterns in Dairy City now and into the future.

Crafting Dignity

Bauer and PVD decisions to use variable degrees of craft-style labor organization, including supporting employee autonomy both on and off the farms, are highly strategic. They provide a strong case for why and how employers on other farms, and across all industries, would be much better off promoting dignity at work instead of participating in the degradation of work and community that has become so pervasive. The volatility of dairy farming magnifies the power of positive managerial practices for creating ecologies of growth.

Since the early 2000s, US dairy farmers have been under pressure to produce ever larger volumes of quality milk to survive, and thousands have failed (Clay, Garnett, and Lorimer 2020; Kardashian 2012; Hendrickson et al. 2001).[28] They must "get big" to effectively negotiate transportation costs with truckers and market positions with powerful corporate milk processors and retailers (Hamilton 2008; Kardashian 2012).[29] Getting big means confining ever larger herds to reduce feed, energy, and real estate costs while breeding and milking cows as frequently as possible to raise income (Jackson-Smith and Buttel 1998; Kardashian 2012; Clay et al. 2020); however, the more that cows are confined, bred, and milked, the more vulnerable they become to stress and illness, which threatens production and income (Jackson-Smith and Buttel 1998). Keeping herds calm and healthy thus requires that people perform complex and well-coordinated sets of tasks at all hours of the day and night, every day of the year (Amaral-Phillips 2014). Although robots and software can collect data on cows' habits and condition (Holloway, Bear, and Wilkinson 2014), they are unable to invent, design, or solve most of the problems they detect—people are needed for that. To this end, a veterinarian observed, "in the [dairy] industry we all have the same feed trucks, the same vaccines. What sets one operation apart from the other? It's the people, and it's the way they treat the animals" (Ford qtd. in Runyon 2016). Annual labor turnover rates of even just under 10 percent can critically reduce milk production and raise herd mortality rates (Adcock et al. 2015, 11; Rosson 2012, 273). "The last thing you want to do is bring a new worker into your barn every six months" (Duval qtd. in Laca 2016, 1).[30]

Whether farmers bring new workers into their barns every six months, however, and how people are able to treat the animals, depends on how farmers treat the people doing the work. Labor organization is the difference between Paloma's decade of experience mastering near-zero death rates and Perez's (2020) documentation of Maria, a Wisconsin dairy employee with a law degree from Mexico who burned out and quit after working fourteen-hour days—with few days off—for four years. The farmer in Perez's (2020) account reportedly "wept" when Maria left, and rightly so. Maria and her sister had helped boost quality milk production, enabling the farm to grow; such growth was now under threat (Perez 2020). And while Maria's work, like Paloma's, contained elements of craft, in that she developed "heightened awareness of how materials respond to our efforts to make them comply with our design . . . to invent, solve problems, and learn new things" in the effort to make "things well," it lacked the core component, which is employers "thinking about how to design work to make it good for human beings" (Schwalbe 2010, 109; Perez 2020). Like the Wisconsin farmer (Perez 2020), most dairy employers design work to take advantage of people facing adversity, instead of thinking about how to "design work to make it good for human beings" in the face of adversity.

Adversity comes not only in the form of economic restructuring and hostile immigration regimes—as well as the interactions between the two, which place immigrant farmworkers in particularly precarious positions—but also in the nature of dairy work itself. While craft work generally "is often hard and dirty, requiring one to work in foul weather (freezing or boiling), breathing dust, and being soaked to the skin by rain or snow," it also involves "winning out over the elements and showing persistence in the face of adversity" (Applebaum 1981, 109 in Hodson 2001, 153–154). On industrial dairy farms, workers battle the elements, the stench of thousands of cows living in close quarters, and a variety of safety hazards that can threaten their lives and those of the animals they tend. Rarely is this work organized as craft on US dairy farms (Keller 2019; Harrison and Lloyd 2012; Sexsmith 2019).[31] As a result, most people burn out, get injured, feel diminished or demoralized by the work, and/or they may be forced to leave (Perez 2020; Sexsmith 2019; Keller 2019).[32] Even when people struggle on, poor work experiences cause people to withdraw from community (Sennet 2008, 36; Pugh 2015; Gibson and Gray 2019). The declining quality and quantity of face-to-face interaction, driven largely by people's demoralizing work experiences, reduces opportunities for people to build connections, to struggle together through difficult circumstances, and to grow social and political capital (Gibson and Gray 2019; Pugh 2015; Sennet 2008).[33] By contrast, when employers think about how to support their workers, they better position people to prevail through hardship, both at and beyond work.

Building on these ideas, I use the notion of "crafting dignity" to explore how "sociable forms" of craft-style management—emphasizing communication and collaboration (Sennet 2008)—combine "managerial citizenship behaviors" (Crowley 2016; Crowley and Hodson 2014; Hodson 1999, 2001)[34] with craftwork (Sennet 2008; Schwalbe 2010) to promote dignity at work (Bolton 2007; Casanova 2019; Lucas 2015), even under the most extreme conditions (Sayer 2007; Ackroyd 2007).[35] Crafting dignity is thus my way of describing the application of managerial citizenship behaviors and sociable forms of craft-style management to craftwork. Ideally, it contributes to the development of dignity at work through a people-centric model of production that extends from the workplace to the community and back again. Crafting dignity thus refers to a process of raising the quality of relations at and beyond work in a reciprocal fashion.

Crafting dignity, when it is achieved, works through the intersection of managerial citizenship behaviors and dignity at work. Managerial citizenship behaviors mean managers behaving ethically, listening to employees, sharing information reliably and quickly, recognizing and respecting employees as whole human beings (not just workers), and exchanging skills (Rubin and Brody 2011; Crowley and Hodson 2014). Dignity at work requires that managers provide employees with meaningful and interesting work, "responsible autonomy," "recognized esteem," and "expectation for respectful treatment by bosses, peers, subordinates, customers, and other individuals salient to one's work roles" (Lucas et al. 2017, 1507; Roscigno, Yavorsky, and Quadlin 2021, 567; Bolton 2007, 2011).[36] Dignity at work also involves "equality of opportunity, collective and individual voice, safe and healthy working conditions, secure terms of employment, and just rewards" (Bolton 2007, 8; Lucas 2015; Roscgigno et al. 2021; Casanova 2019).[37] Under these conditions, even when work is considered "dirty," the people doing it may be regarded as "tough," "respectable," and "honest" for doing it: "Work of heroic proportions can dignify" (Sayer 2007, 35; Ackroyd 2007; Hodson 2001).

Dairy work is dangerous, complex, and demanding. Employees trim thousands of cows' hooves to prevent lesions that would "suppress estrous behavior" and make pregnancy difficult and costly (Amaral-Phillips 2014). They artificially inseminate heifers with expensive sex-selective semen to keep them lactating. If insemination fails, farms lose the expensive semen *and* future milk production. Employees feed cows carefully apportioned diets at designated times, which vary according to heifers' reproductive stages. Failure to feed properly inhibits cows' livers from producing the glucose needed for milk, and the abomasum for the rennet for cheese (Amaral-Phillips 2014). Metabolic disorders caused by improper feeding inhibit milk production (Amaral-Phillips 2014). Employees milk thousands of cows three times a day by stimulating lactation through careful teat handling, keeping teats clean to prevent mastitis while ensuring that pumps are attached securely (Amaral-Phillips 2014). (According to a local veterinarian, for robots to milk cows, cows' udders must be uniform. Cows with unusual udder conformation are often sold or culled.)[38] When cows' temperatures are elevated, employees restrain cows for evaluation, but not for too long, lest cows develop digestive problems and foot lesions (Amaral-Phillips 2014). They regulate the moisture content of cows' bedding (Amaral-Phillips 2014), herd cows according to their varying stages of reproduction to meet their distinctive vaccination and veterinary needs (mix-ups can cost lives and infect milk), monitor cows' labor and help deliver calves, feed and care for calves, vaccinate and provide veterinary care both regularly and at a moment's notice, repair and operate large farm machinery and software, maintain strict sanitation for frequent farm inspections (Amaral-Phillips 2014), and much more (see also Garni 2018).[39]

Management practices are paramount in how complex work happens. They affect both firm productivity and broader social relations. The social relations in which the farms are embedded, in turn, affect the farms and the people working on them. Using ethnography, I detail the experiences of immigrant employees on local farms as well as their settlement experiences in, and impact on, Dairy City. I follow immigrant families from work to school, church, doctors' offices, hospitals, holiday parties, family celebrations, informal gatherings, staff meetings, and home. In detailing how people's work lives are woven into the broader social fabric of rural America, I aim to provide critical new insight on the connections between work, immigration, and community.

"Natural Laboratories"

Despite the growing scale of international migration to small rural towns in the twenty-first century (Marrow 2012; Lichter 2012; Johnson and Lichter 2020), both the towns and the people moving there are "typically ignored or downplayed in current public policy debates about immigration reform and the incorporation of new immigrants (Hirschman and Massey 2008; Okamoto and Ebert 2010)" (Lichter 2012, 6). Rural communities, however, provide excellent "natural laboratories" for studying how people experience and respond to the pressures of globalization (Lichter 2012). Their relatively small size emphasizes the phenomena of interest to great effect (Merton 1987; Lichter 2012). At the same time, scholars to date have focused on a significant but incomplete set of labor and migration patterns in rural communities, creating opportunities to explore the more unusual managerial patterns in Dairy City and their implications for broader social change (Lichter 2012). Qualitative research is ideal for explaining outliers, not just cases that cluster around the mean (Stinchcombe 2005; Katz 1997, 2001; Timmermans and Tavory 2012). Having to account for outliers strengthens explanations of predominant patterns, such as the ways former employees described labor relations on the Hoffman farm, while also providing deeper insight into unique and rare phenomena, like managerial efforts at PVD and Bauer to boost production by committing to workers (see also Zúñiga and Hernández-León 2005, 254, 253).

Dairy City, Kansas, is a small town with a variety of actors responding to historical change in different ways. The population is less than 1,000 residents.[40] About 25 percent of residents identify as Hispanic (US Census Bureau 2024).[41] While most local farm owners are white descendants of nineteenth-century European immigrants who were granted full citizenship rights, most people who immigrated from Latin America, Eastern Europe, and South Africa in the past twenty-five years have faced hostile national immigration and labor regimes. Until the 1990s, Dairy City had approximately thirty small dairy farms, with around a dozen cows, plus a variety of other farm animals and crops. Today, the three remaining dairies—Bauer, PVD, and Hoffman—each have roughly between 1,000 and 5,000 cows, and counting.[42] All three dairies expanded their operations and began recruiting immigrant employees in 1999 or 2000, but they used distinctive managerial strategies. I used relational ethnography (Desmond 2014) to closely examine variations in employer and employee relations under the pressures of globalization. Using relational ethnography to closely examine these variations enabled me to make fruitful comparisons and theoretical generalizations (Katz 1997, 2001).

Rather than studying groups or places, per se, the goal of relational ethnography is to study relational dynamics and processes (Desmond 2014). I focus on how "differently-positioned people" became locally "bound . . . in a relationship of mutual dependence or struggle," and what resulted from these "dynamics" (Desmond 2014, 555).[43] In Dairy City, people who risked trading mostly urban professional or service jobs abroad for dirty and dangerous work on remote rural Kansas dairy farms are situated differently from—and interwoven with—white US dairy farmers trying to grow family businesses in a volatile production-based industry. I used this form of relational ethnography to study how they were drawn together and what resulted from the "dynamics that emerge[d] between them" (Desmond 2014, 554).

As part of my research, I spent more than five years conducting interviews and periodic observation on two farms and throughout the community and its surrounds. I and three research assistants—Marcus Dominguez, Jill Applegate, and Zaira Ruiz, with additional help from Lynsey Akin and Citlally Orozco—interviewed employees and their relatives, dairy owners and managers, extension officers, veterinarians, farm experts, clergy, teachers, staff, school administrators, service providers, health-care workers, residents and community members, public or town officials, and local leaders. We interviewed sixty-nine people, some of them multiple times. Interviews were a mix of semi-structured and more informal conversations. We attended staff meetings at PVD, PVD and Bauer "office" (dairy) holiday parties, birthday celebrations, religious confirmations, weddings, quinceañeras, school events, doctor consults, informal gatherings, and even accompanied a worker and his family to the emergency room. We wrote field notes for our visits. We also followed well-established traditions of conducting community engaged research through regular volunteer work in the community (Falcone 2018; Garcia 2010; Plankey-Videla 2012).[44] This enabled me to observe how people experience changing social structures, what is important to them, and how relational dynamics develop and change over time (Duneier 2001; Desmond 2014). I followed Becker's (2001, 65) advice in "trying to find out something about every topic the research touches on, even tangentially."

Marcus, Jill, Zaira, and I had ready access to the Bauer and PVD dairies, and a mix of secondary and primary data on the Hoffman farm. The Hoffmans declined to speak with us. The first few times we requested interviews and visits with the Hoffmans, they were several weeks into their implementation of robots that milk and feed cows. They and dozens of volunteers were spending twenty-four hours a day with the cows, acclimating cows to the robots so they would eat and produce milk. Even after this period, however, the Hoffmans declined to speak with us. I interviewed and spent time with (former) Hoffman employees and professionals who knew or worked with them, and I have read interviews the Hoffmans gave to reporters, but I never met them. As a result, and because my primary interest is in the more unique Bauer and PVD experiences—based on what people told me, the Hoffman farm is more in line with the "lean" labor practices already well-documented in the literature, I focus my analysis on Bauer and PVD. I am also interested in the organization of work and community in relation to immigrant workers; since the Hoffmans largely eliminated their workforce, their case is most useful as a contrast to the other farms, to illuminate the broader context, and to represent the sort of practices already documented and analyzed by others. I include the Hoffman case accordingly. To maintain strict confidentiality, when I cite the secondary research on the Hoffman farm, I change the wording (but not the meaning) of original quotes the Hoffmans gave to reporters or the public so the quotes cannot be searched or identified. Quotes from interviews with former employees, colleagues, and people familiar with the farm are original (but still deidentified to protect everyone's confidentiality).

The size and structure of the three farms affects how work is organized, as well as the array of positions available. The Hoffman and Bauer dairies are family owned and operated, and PVD is incorporated, meaning that one hundred members of various local families own it. To serve on PVD's board of directors, which includes seven of the one hundred owners, members must live locally and visit the farm regularly. All members must be invited. The lead manager at PVD and the owner-managers on the Bauer and Hoffman farms have autonomy to manage work as they wish. PVD has thirty-six permanent immigrant employees, just under half of whom are women. Several more people work part-time at the dairy. Immigrant employees occupy positions ranging from milking to herding, maternity, and shift management. It is a more limited range than the one found at the Bauer dairy. At the Bauer dairy, the three lead managers are brothers who bought shares in the aughts.[45] Four generations of Bauers currently live on the farm. At the time of my research, the Bauers employed thirty-two immigrant employees, approximately 40 percent of whom are women, but they are expanding their operations and hiring more employees. Like PVD, the Bauer farm also employs part-time workers to support their full-time ones when the latter want or need time off.[46] Immigrant employees at Bauer occupy a somewhat broader range of positions than those at PVD, from milking and pushing (where nearly everyone starts) to herding, maternity, medical, feed/feeding, mechanics and equipment maintenance, machine operation, welding, pen and structure maintenance, personnel management, and the development and oversight of farmworker safety. As yet, no immigrant employees on either farm have bought ownership shares (something I address in Chapter 5). The Hoffman dairy is in its fifth generation. The owner-operators are a husband-and-wife team, plus four of their children. Until 2015, the Hoffmans employed an estimated six immigrant workers—first South African and Eastern European, and then Latin American. An estimated 15 percent of the employees were women. The Hoffmans then implemented multiple robots and retained, at least for a time, two part-time immigrant employees, both Hispanic men.

In addition to visiting the Bauer and PVD farms and conducting interviews, observations, and conversations with a variety of participants over the course of five years, research assistants and I also spent time with employees from all three dairies via English as a Second Language (ESL) classes two nights a week, every week from June 2015 through October 2017, and then once a week from November 2017 through December 2019, plus a couple of sessions in early 2020. The paraprofessional at the school requested that we help her extend classes for adults who wanted to practice English but had fewer opportunities than their children do via the local school. She had been offering classes to adults for years but was overextended. All participants knew that we held the classes in conjunction with our research and repeatedly consented to participate (see Thorne 1980). They also knew that participation in the classes was not in any way contingent on their participation in research. At the ESL classes, we practiced language skills and discussed issues related to work and community. This provided me with a clearer sense of what is significant to them, rather than me imposing my own assumptions (see McCorkel and Myers 2003). It also gave me the chance to regularly ask people about their days and hear details about work, family, and community. They trusted me with many confidences and have come to know me and my family, as well. Several monolingual English-speaking members of the community who had requested Spanish classes from the paraprofessional—she declined, due to time constraints—asked me and my research assistants to teach Spanish. We offered Spanish classes for nine months in 2018–2019. We were set to continue through 2020 until the COVID-19 pandemic scuttled our plans. Over the course of this research, my research assistants and I spent most of our time with recent immigrant families in Dairy City.

People who had recently immigrated also asked me and my research assistants to participate in organizing community workshops on specialized health care (e.g., women's health and cancer prevention), banking and finance (e.g., savings and investments, including for college educations and retirement), college visits, and immigration issues. These workshops were a continuation of workshops the paraprofessional had been hosting for years. In fact, I first met people who had recently immigrated in 2015 via a workshop on immigration that the paraprofessional held at the local school on a Saturday. She had arranged for an attorney from Kansas City to make two presentations and meet with families throughout the day. For the workshops that we helped to organize by request, we collaborated with families, farm owners, school principals, paraprofessionals, and/or city officials to use public space and advertise. These experiences gave me further insight into people's interests and concerns, as well as how they experience local social life (Katz 2001; Duneier 2001; Geertz 1973). People's efforts to find a role for us—and to fit us into an existing structure—taught me a lot about how they viewed and experienced that structure (Katz 2001; Duneier 2001). Absent such opportunities, I might have missed key aspects of people's everyday lived experiences and relational dynamics within the community (Katz 2001; Desmond 2014; Duneier 2001).

My research assistants and I are fluent in Spanish. One of my assistants and I are in the first generations of our families to be born in the United States (in my case, this refers to my father's side of the family). Each of us has spent considerable time in Latin America and the Caribbean. I have lived and studied in Costa Rica and El Salvador (starting when I was sixteen), and I have done qualitative research in Guatemala and Nicaragua. In college and for two years after graduating, I worked in public interest law, which included regularly organizing free workers' rights and immigrants' rights clinics. These experiences facilitated rapport with people in Dairy City. Even the Bauers, the lead PVD manager, and two PVD board members gravitated toward our experiences and backgrounds because, they said, they often feel frustrated by most people not understanding how hard it is to immigrate to the United States.

To make sense of the patterns I encountered through fieldwork and interviews, I turned to theories of immigration, work, and labor markets. I analyzed the ways in which emergent patterns conformed with and deviated from these theories and concepts. I revisited the field to check facts, test, refine, and retest theories. This process is referred to as "analytic induction" or "abduction" (Katz 2001; Timmermans and Tavory 2012; Small 2009). It involves working back and forth between theory and empirical data to generate an explanation that fully accounts for nuances and variances in empirical patterns (Katz 2001; Timmermans and Tavory 2012; Small 2009). It also involves seeking disconfirming evidence to challenge theories and build nuance (Katz 2001; Small 2009). In the process, I combined and extended theories of "managerial and employee citizenship," "craftsmanship," and dignity at work to illuminate the connections between labor and community development (or underdevelopment) in rural places, while at the same time contrasting my findings with the more common research findings and theory regarding "lean production" sites.

Chapter Outline

I organize the book to explore how rural dairy farmers and (mostly) urban immigrant employees came together, the variable dynamics of crafted dignity that developed between them, and how these dynamics affect individuals, households, farms, and the broader community.[47] This involves charting farmers' move from small to large dairies and recent immigrants' moves from mostly urban industrial and/or commercial areas to rural Kansas, farmers' recruitment practices, the labor relations that developed on the farms, how on-farm relationships interact with off-farm relationships, and how the emerging dynamics reflect and inform broader social change.[48] Each chapter delves into different aspects of these relationships. In the conclusion, I tie together the details of these relationships to show how they "hang together in a web of mutual influence" (Becker 1996 in Desmond 2014, 554; see also Becker 2001).

In Chapter 1, I explore how the ancientness of immigration to Dairy City juxtaposed with its decline in the late twentieth century situated dairy farmers and immigrant employees in a paradoxical dynamic as they came together in the twenty-first century. The Bauers and PVD owner-managers drew on multiple historical, structural advantages to face risks in expanding their farms in the 1990s and early 2000s. However, since they were attempting to expand their operations following decades of demographic and economic decline, they were challenged to recruit people in ways that would simultaneously grow the farms and the town. As owners of multiple local businesses, the Bauers and PVD managers seemed to realize that recruiting permanent employees and encouraging their local integration best served the full range of their interests. I explore how managers' early recruitment mistakes caused attrition, forcing them to improve their practices. The roots of crafted dignity on the Bauer and PVD farms can be seen in these farmers' early learning curves. They learned that they nominally needed to recruit whole families, respect work-life balance, and mind employees' interests. I compare their practices with those documented among farmers in other parts of the country.

In Chapter 2, I explore how the consolidation of a destabilizing portfolio society compelled people recently immigrating to seek stability and household or family cohesion in a "peaceful" rural community. While these patterns have some features in common with previously documented cases of "new destinations immigration," in that many people immigrating to rural communities in the twenty-first century seek greater stability than what they have found in traditional gateway cities, the difference is that by trying to improve quality of work and life in Dairy City, rather than capitalizing on a shrinking array of alternatives, the Bauers and PVD managers enhanced their powers of recruitment. I explore how the tensions built into their efforts relate to people's decisions about moving to Dairy City. I recount several people's stories of moving to Dairy City and taking dairy jobs to explore their recruitment experiences and the range of their backgrounds. Heterogeneity in people's backgrounds is often mentioned but more rarely described in studies on twenty-first-century immigration to rural areas with production-based industries (see also Zúñiga and Hernández-León 2005).

In Chapter 3, I focus on the impact of variable managerial strategies on dignity at work, or lack thereof, and farm performance. The Bauer farm adopted the greatest degrees of sociable forms of craft-style work organization. PVD initially pursued a more bureaucratic style of management paired with high compensation in an effort to retain employees before incorporating more craft-like practices within the bureaucratic framework. The Hoffman farm reportedly relied on "lean flexibility" with high compensation for temporary positions before replacing most of its employees with robots that milk and feed cows. I detail how the differing forms of organization affect people and firms before considering how these practices affect immigrant incorporation and community development in subsequent chapters.

In Chapter 4, I follow immigrant families from work on local farms to school, church, doctors' offices, hospitals, and encounters with local law enforcement officers. I consider how local farmers attempt to influence the settlement context for recent immigrants, as well as how employer commitments to workers affect immigrant incorporation and prospects for economic development more broadly. I focus on farm owners' power to broker (or undermine) trust between people who have recently immigrated and those who haven't. The Bauers and PVD owner-managers have significant ties to local civic leaders, public servants, service providers, and business owners. They have used these ties to help immigrant employees build connections with local institutions, organizations, and businesses. Formal and informal networks developed to support a broader ecology of institutions/organizations. This ecology provides a more positive settlement context for recent immigrants, a stronger local economy, and a more inclusive community. It also shows how people who have not recently immigrated depend on those who have.

In Chapter 5, I explore the relationship between immigration and mobility via dairy farms. I analyze how people who traded professional jobs abroad for work on dairy farms in Dairy City, as well as people who were denied advanced formal educations, develop farm careers in Dairy City. The stories of people who moved from both rural and urban contexts abroad to rural US communities illustrate the extent to which insecure employment and uncertainty for workers are proliferating. Such insecurity and uncertainty affect people's long-term assessments of dairy work, as well as whether to stay in Dairy City. I also explore the tension between Dairy City farmers' desires to recruit the children of immigrants, parents' aspirations for their children, and educational experiences and career development among the 1.5 generation. I consider how these tensions relate to a refrain that is common among PVD and Bauer dairy owner-managers: "imagine this is your farm." This refrain represents both a way forward and a core contradiction, because immigrant employee ownership is currently only symbolic, and to that end, exploitative. Making employee farm ownership a reality could help build on virtuous circles of dignity at work and community growth. Included in this chapter is a discussion about the impact of US immigration policy on (im)mobility.

In the conclusion, I use evidence from Dairy City to examine connections between positive managerial practices, employer commitments to workers, firm productivity, and the growth of social capital within and beyond the worksite. Most studies document negative managerial practices, a lack of employer commitment to workers, a narrow focus on firm productivity, and transience. The unexpected positive synergies found on two Dairy City farms facilitates analysis of how sociable forms of craft-style management tie dignity at work to heightened community vitality. I discuss how craftwork in rural industry affects day-to-day interactions and relationships that extend beyond the worksite. Analyzing the interaction between respect for immigrant workers at the worksite and in local communities broadens existing theoretical conceptions of the relationships between work, immigration, and community. I discuss how mandating positive labor, agricultural, and immigration policies is essential for generating and replicating ecologies of growth, as well as where efforts toward these ends currently stand as they relate to US farm work. I address how the emergent cycles of growth fostered by two of the farms in Dairy City require the implementation and enforcement of legislation at state and federal levels that meaningfully protect workers and people who immigrate. People in Dairy City who challenged insecurity by crossing borders, barriers, and entrenched labor practices provide powerful reminders of employers' and governments' responsibility to unite people in forging healthy, equitable, and sustainable futures.

1

One hundred and fifty years before Paloma came to Dairy City to escape violence in Mexico, Kathrina, a German homesteader, set out in the tall grasses surrounding Dairy City to guide her cattle home. As the sun set, Kathrina lost her bearings. Hearing a rustling in the grass, Kathrina's neighbor mistook her for a wolf. He promptly shot her dead. Kathrina's death was documented in reports of German homesteaders who built mud and sod homes in what is now Dairy City. They traveled to land offices to secure homestead or preemption papers and formed mutual aid societies to assist one another in growing their farms. They also contended with fatal lightning strikes, devastating prairie fires, bull gorings, failed harvests, and long days traveling over fifty miles to get supplies for their farms. Returning from the supply runs, many people reportedly became "benumbed and bewildered," completely losing their sense of direction and "wandering aimlessly about" until they perished "in sight of their homes, [only] to be found by their neighbors and buried" (Kansas Historical Society).

Many of the places that scholars would today call "new immigrant destinations" are actually among the oldest in the country.[1] Immigration to contemporary Dairy City predated Kathrina's arrival in the 1800s, and Paloma's arrival in 2011, by several thousand years. According to Elliot West (1998, 31–32), "white pioneers who moved onto the plains east to west believed they were leaving the old country for the new. They had it exactly backward. Before the first human habitation on the eastern seaboard—and 5,000 years before the first Sumerian writing and 7,000 before the Old Kingdom was established in Egypt—plains[people] had fashioned flourishing economies." For many centuries, Dairy City was part of a "multicultural borderlands" where people from across the Americas met via elaborate systems of trade and exchange (West 1998, 27). Twenty-first-century immigration to Dairy City is only "new" in the sense that it followed an unusual demographic and economic decline triggered by white settler colonialism in the nineteenth and twentieth centuries (see the appendix).[2]

In this chapter, I explore how the ancientness of immigration to Dairy City juxtaposed with its decline in the late twentieth century situated dairy farmers and immigrant employees in a paradoxical dynamic as they came together in the twenty-first century. The Bauers and Pleasant Valley Dairy (PVD) owner-managers were able to capitalize on multiple historical-structural advantages that enabled them to take risks and expand their farms in the 1990s and early 2000s. However, given that they were attempting to grow their farms following decades of demographic and economic decline, and since they owned multiple interconnected businesses that depended on a local clientele, they were challenged to recruit people in a manner that would grow the farms and keep the town afloat. The Bauers and PVD seemed to realize that recruiting permanent employees who were thus positioned to become "rooted" locally best served the full spectrum of their interests. I consider how variable degrees of crafted dignity at the Bauer farm and PVD relate to current farm owners' decisions about how to grow their operations.

Farmers' decisions about how to grow demystify employers' role as "the organizing structure for economic and social life . . . The employment practices of . . . firms [form] the careers and broader life chances of individuals and households, [employers'] choices about how and where to expand [shape] regional economies, and their charitable donations and community involvement [determine] the character of cities" or towns (Davis 2009, 2). When done positively, this could resemble a people-centric model of production that reciprocally raises the quality of relations at and beyond work, a central concern for crafting dignity. While

Davis (2009) was writing about twentieth-century industrial corporations that acted as "benevolent elites," disciplining one another to commit to workers and invest in communities (in contrast to today's "arm's length" global investors), I update his language to emphasize that employers are still a principal "organizing structure for economic and social life" in the twenty-first century. The Bauers' and PVD managers' "choices about how and where to expand" have directly observable consequences on "regional economies" because they are so locally embedded, but the fact that most employers today are "arm's length" investors does not obviate their responsibilities—it only veils them (Davis 2009, 2, 7).

Turning Points

In 2003, when the dairies had only just begun recruiting people from abroad—and the Bauer farm had only six people on staff who had recently immigrated from Mexico—Dairy City's then mayor said, "with declining populations and challenging economic conditions, strong cooperation will be even more important in the future." He was reflecting on the challenges faced by interconnected local businesses that were losing customers. These included three local banks, two insurance companies, a funeral and nursing home, a local newspaper, emergency and health service providers supported by a waning number of volunteers, a grocery store, locksmith, educational cooperative, the public school—typically one of the largest employers in town—a real estate company, a trucking company, a local branch of a rural telecommunications company, two small agricultural equipment manufacturers, a variety of other service providers and small businesses (e.g., construction, appliance sales and repair, drilling, auto repair, a local bar/restaurant that replaced a failing pool hall), and non-profit organizations, such as booster and rotary clubs. Owen Bauer told me,

> It's all family-owned farms and businesses in [Dairy City]. Businesses are incredibly connected. The grocer sells to bar/restaurant, which my parents own [they later sold the bar/restaurant to a family that immigrated from Mexico in the early 2000s]. My uncle is mayor. He owns

a bed and breakfast, a [cattle breeding genetics company] and a [cattle ranch/company]. He also works at [Dairy City] State Bank. Another uncle does tractor repair and my aunt owns a farm.

Owen's brother owns a share of the Bauer dairy and two other local businesses. The lead manager of PVD owns a cattle ranch, is married to a local health-care provider, and lives next door to the manager for a financial services provider. PVD board members own farms and related businesses in and around the area. This situation is common and has a long history. The roster of owners, managers, and employees running local businesses reflect the surnames of families that arrived in the late 1800s. In a striking example, archives show that ninety years after Sofia Newcomb (pseudonym) and her children arrived in Dairy City and claimed several homesteads, Sofia's grandson, who was killed by an angry bull on one of his family's farms, had enjoyed a successful career as a rural reporter and agricultural extension assistant. He was survived by another two generations of his family who remained in Dairy City as farmers, teachers, and businesspeople (Kansas Historical Society, n.d.). White European immigrants' ready access to clearly titled land and citizenship positioned them and their descendants to develop diverse business interests that remained fairly strong until the onset of renewed farm crises and rural depopulations in the 1980s and 1990s.

In the 1980s and 1990s, rising interest rates led to farm foreclosures and crippling depopulation that threatened the town. Owen Bauer said, "the 1980s were horrible for farmers, and we lost a lot of people." He emphasized that the depopulation crisis had been so severe that the town subsequently nearly lost its school. If they had lost the school, Owen noted, they "would have lost everything." He wasn't wrong. Rural schools are typically the heart of remote communities (see also Gibson and Gray 2019). Not only are they major employers—teachers, staff, administrators, bus drivers, custodians, cooks, health-care providers, and so on—but they are also the primary institutions bringing people together via regular sporting events and the performing arts (Gibson and Gray 2019). School staff and faculty buy homes, boosting local real estate and financial services. School employees patronize local businesses—telecommunications, groceries, insurance, hardware/appliance, construction; in short, all the businesses the mayor in 2003 was so afraid of losing. Schools are also a major recruiting tool for towns. People with children often make decisions about where to live based on the quality of local schools. Had the dairies not recruited people to move to Dairy City with their families, in the hopes of encouraging employees to build tenure on the farms, 20–25 percent of the school's student body would not exist. Without them, there would likely be no school at all. Further, and despite a dramatic increase of the Latinx/e population in Dairy City in the past twenty-five years (US Census Bureau 2024), it would still take a great deal more immigration to restore Dairy City to its pre- nineteenth and twentieth-century population and diversity.

The Bauers decided to expand their dairy operation amid the farm and depopulation crises of the 1980s and 1990s. Owen's mother, Gail, and his grandmother, Olivia, explained:

GAIL: Yeah, because the eighties were tough here, a turning point.

OLIVIA: Yeah, that was a *turning point* [*adding emphasis*]. Interest rates were so high.

GAIL: . . . Interest rates went up to 15 percent! It was unreal.

OLIVIA: Yeah, because we looked that up—the first farm we bought [a farm that had gone out of business], because we have one loan from [names local lender] at a good rate, at 7.5 and 8 percent on part of it and then the rest of it was through the bank at like 14 percent, it was expensive.

ALISA: Were you looking to expand in the 1980s?

OLIVIA: [*Nodding*] That is when we took off, that is when we started. We formed a partnership with [Gail and Wayne, Olivia's son].

The context is notable. The Bauers were looking to expand at a time when farm crises were driving other farmers out of business and younger generations of people were leaving Dairy City. The Bauers had begun specializing in dairy in the mid-1960s when the "milk market was fairly good," Olivia said. Olivia and her husband, Anton Bauer, liked dairy cows. By contrast, "I didn't like chickens that well and there wasn't big money in them." Olivia and Anton began investing in upgraded milk parlors in the 1960s, so that by the 1980s, when they sought to expand, "we had some things that had kinda been grandfathered in, you know, that we still had to make changes, of course, but that's the way that we decided to go." She added that "for some people, it was too expensive [to upgrade] or they were too old and they were not going to spend that money to make those changes." Such challenges were exacerbated by younger generations starting to move away from Dairy City, leaving only older generations to farm and maintain the town. Olivia noted that the number of farms in the area started to decline precipitously.[3] She and her husband had to fend off people's "skepticism" that they could succeed, despite their advantages.

A new set of opportunities and challenges arose in the 1990s and early 2000s. Wildly fluctuating milk prices compelled dairy farmers to scale up their operations. To increase profits when prices were high and staunch losses when they plummeted, dairy farmers—often referred to as "producers"—needed to quickly achieve scale to negotiate with powerful retailers and milk processors (i.e., companies that buy milk to make cheese, yogurt, ice cream, whey, and more) (Hamilton 2008; Kardashian 2012).[4] Large producers also have more leverage in negotiating transportation costs with truckers and feed prices with crop farmers (Kardashiam 2012; Hamilton 2008).[5] They are more likely to secure bulk/discounted prices and create efficiencies—like reducing real estate costs by confining large herds in consolidated barns that lower utility costs—and they receive more state and federal subsidies than small farms (Kardashian 2012). Thus, by 2010, the "cost of production per litre of milk was more than three times higher for farms with fewer than 50 cows than for farms with more than 2,000 cows, a substantial gap that meant negative net returns for farms with fewer than 1,000 cows" (Clay, Garnett, and Lorimer 2020, 37; Gillespie 2024; appendix). Achieving scale, however, is both costly and risky, as it involves significant capital investments.

While the Bauers and PVD owners lacked access to a labor force for their growing farms, they were well positioned to grow in other ways. Their farms are located far enough from densely populated areas to avoid complaints about water and air pollution from large local populations, but close enough to one of the country's largest producer cooperatives to efficiently transport milk and receive good value for advertising and sales, because the cooperative is powerful. They also have substantial support from local and state politicians. The Kansas Department of Agriculture (KDA) even tries to recruit farmers from other states by enacting farm-friendly policies. Rather than relocating and having to make new capital investments, the Bauers and PVD owners built on growth in a state friendly to large-scale industrial agriculture (see the appendix).

Territorialized Growth with People

Growing exponentially meant that the Bauers and PVD owner-managers needed to recruit new employees. They were not alone. By 2015, immigrant employees had become so essential on US dairy farms that losing them "would reduce the US dairy herd by 2.1 million cows, milk production by 48.4 billion pounds and the number of farms by 7,011. Retail milk prices would increase by an estimated 90.4 percent . . . [It would also] reduce US economic output by $32.1 billion and reduce employment by 208,208 jobs" (Adcock et al. 2015, 2). This is because large herds of sedentary cows yield high volumes of milk, but only if they are bred, fed, and cared for properly. Producers can mechanize some tasks, but they still need people to do what machines cannot. Many dairy farmers implement lean labor organization (Keller 2019; Sexsmith 2019; Harrison and Lloyd 2012, 2013),[6] but high labor turnover reduces milk production and raises calf and cow mortality rates (Adcock et al. 2015, 11; Rosson 2012). Both strategies also displace people from farming communities, forcing farmers to rely even more on expensive technology (Gibson and Gray 2019). To compensate, farmers must then boost production with fewer people and more technology—a sort of treadmill. They may become so busy managing complex technologies with little help from other people, who have been displaced, that they refrain from participating in any remaining local social institutions after depopulation (Gibson and Gray 2019). Communities become "deterritorialized," opportunities for people to build common ground through in-person interactions diminish, and people are less likely to struggle together to confront structural challenges (Gibson and Gray

2019). Profits become increasingly deterritorialized (Gibson and Gray 2019). This is the opposite of crafting dignity.

Owen, by contrast, told me he wants "to keep people around, reduce turnover, and create more of a community. I want to create growth." (Since the Bauers were the first to recruit permanent immigrant employees, and because their practices influenced PVD, I feature the Bauers heavily in this section.) Owen talks about encouraging youth to "raise show cows together." He also wants to build duplex homes in which people with young families who have recently immigrated live next door to older residents who are lonely. This stems in part from the recent saturation of the local housing market, due largely to the Bauer's and PVD's housing practices, as I explain below, but also from Owen's desire to assist with people's social and economic integration. Owen's economic interests are best served through coordinated growth. He told me he thinks every dollar one of his employees spends in Dairy City "generates seven for the town." Owen estimates, in other words, that when a person spends one dollar earned at the dairy at another business in Dairy City, like the locally owned grocery store, the other business owner (e.g., the grocer) spends that dollar at another locally owned business, the owner of that business spends it at another local business, and so on. This is more likely when people live in integrated communities where they consume goods and services.[7] Owen told me he'd like more studies on multiplier effects so he could publicize the results, which he thinks are strongly positive. Coordinated growth, Owen says, is on his mind when he recruits employees.

Owen's mother and grandmother, meanwhile, were especially concerned with reducing labor turnover "and getting enough help" on the rapidly growing farm. The family was overwhelmed with work. As Gail and Olivia tell it:

> GAIL: I mean, Wayne [Gail's husband] was just, the kids were little and he was working and he would work twenty-four hours a day sometimes— *thirty-six* hours a day [*laughing*]! So he'd be trying to sleep and we had four kids running around the house, it was hard to keep quiet. "Shh, daddy's sleeping, shhh, daddy's sleeping!" That was hard, and they wanted to play with him and he was just too tired.

ALISA: How long did that go on?

GAIL: I probably don't have an objective answer. It seemed like a *long* time.

OLIVIA [Wayne's mother and Owen's grandmother]: It probably felt like it was forever.

ALISA: When did it change?

GAIL: Well, even after we moved up here [onto the farm] in 1999, there was times when we wouldn't have enough help and he'd milk nights.

OLIVIA: Yeah, it'd have to be until we got adequate help to do what we are doing, so we had to ride the bus for a while.

GAIL: Even like when [Nelson] [Owen's brother] was a senior in high school, I remember calling him into school sick because he had worked all night and we were short on help. So he'd work all night, so then he'd—honestly he wasn't *sick, sick*, but he was so tired that he wasn't any good in school and then there were even times he would go to school and he was really tired, because I remember people talking about yeah, he knew which classes he could sleep through [*smiles ruefully*].

Work on the Bauer farm was growing so rapidly and becoming so all-consuming that it was difficult for the Bauer children to study or play, or for the parents to get much sleep. Work was also becoming more complex, and it occurred around the clock, every day of the year. The Bauers needed people who could "reliably" fill shifts and perform difficult work.

Remedying Unreliable Recruitment Practices

The Bauers initially recruited single men to work on the farms, but as Gail and her mother-in-law, Olivia, explained, single men got lonely in Dairy City and left. Loneliness often led to depression, and several people skipped shifts or disappeared. Gail told me, "We had a kid here from Vermont that worked here for a while, I don't remember how long exactly. Some of them [the first employees we recruited] were just here limited times or, you know, maybe a year and then change over. And he was another single guy [the 'kid from Vermont'], you know, kind of, as we were finding out, families were more apt to stay and work." Olivia and Gail elaborated on changes they began to make after "finding out that families were more apt to stay and work." Olivia goes from referring to employees as "hired help" to "your [her] people." Her comments reflect tensions in the Bauer business philosophy, as well as a shift from blaming employees to recognizing that her business practices were to blame for problems at work. The shift in emphasis—ultimately—may reveal the seeds of their efforts to increase profit by crafting dignity.

OLIVIA: And the transition [bringing in employees] at that time probably was the hardest.

GAIL: Yeah, [Eric] [a local employee] got hurt that time.

OLIVIA: Or people wouldn't show up. Yeah, that's what happened with hired help. They wouldn't call, they just plain wouldn't show up and they never came back. So, there you are. Nobody to work that shift and there were things like that.

GAIL: It was the South Africans that did that to us . . . We got involved with a program, when there were the [temporary] visas, and of course that is kind of the short-term fix.

OLIVIA: Yeah, but things like that happen. That hasn't happened for a long time, has it?

GAIL: No, it's been *much* better.

ALISA: How did that work [with the temporary visas]?

OLIVIA: He [the South African employee who had a temporary visa] was here two months, three months? Not very long.

GAIL: I'd say closer to a month but maybe it was longer than that.

OLIVIA: I remember him, and I think he got terrible homesick, and he just picked up and left. He said, "I am going home," and I don't know where he went.

GAIL: 'Cause we finally got the keys and went in the house to make sure he was okay, you know, you think, "what if the guy passed out and hit his head on the tub or something?," but anyway, he was gone. And then we finally contacted the program people and they somehow checked his plane ticket or something [to verify that he had left].

ALISA: Did the program find you or did you find them?

GAIL: We contacted the program. And we had, I can't remember if we had friends in on that or somebody we knew was using that kind of help first. Well, the one guy came from [Hoffman's Dairy]. He had been working down at [Hoffman's] and it was like a nine-month thing and then you had to go to a different place. You could only stay somewhere for nine months.

OLIVIA: That [turnover] was tough in this situation, any farming situation. Anyway, when they don't know anything about it [farming] . . .

GAIL: [Interrupts] I mean, we tried lots of things.

OLIVIA: If you take care of your people and your herd, they will take care of you. If you treat them well, they will perform well, they will do well. In return you will get more income off of them than if you don't, you know, if you neglect to take care, that type of thing.

Olivia explicitly references "getting more income off of them," but she emphasizes that increasing profits requires treating employees well. For her part, Gail at first blames employees for absenteeism when she says that they "did that to us," meaning they skipped shifts and disappeared, as if they "owed" her, but in almost the same breath she acknowledges that the employees she blames were lone men on temporary work visas, as if realizing that it wasn't people trying to harm her but the exploitation—exacerbated by family separation—that made them unable or unwilling to stay. Olivia noted that the men Gail blamed for absenteeism were "terrible homesick" and must have been anxious to get home, and that Dairy City wasn't a home to them. Their comments highlight awareness of links between managerial practices and labor turnover. Once they began remedying their practices, both Gail and Olivia noted that absenteeism and turnover got "much better" and "hasn't happened for a long time."

Olivia's and Gail's conversation suggests they saw employee "reliability" as stemming from people immigrating with their families, and the farm's success as rooted in "treating employees well." This contrasts with how farmers in New York conceived of "reliability" as they recruited people to work on their farms. Dairy employers in Sexsmith's (2019) study said they preferred to hire lone men because they believed single men would work harder than men who were "distracted" by their families. One New York farmer said, "The Hispanics are here to work, that's all they want is to work. They want 65, 70 hours. The local [white] guys need to spend some time with their family and other activities or it doesn't work for them" (Sexsmith 2019, 726; see also Harrison and Lloyd 2013). These New York farmers think that "because immigrant workers are separated from their families and communities, they see any time not spent working as a waste of time that prolongs their separation from family members at home" (Sexsmith 2019, 726). Another farmer told Sexsmith (2019, 720), "When you're a single guy living on the farm and your nearest relative is 2,000 miles away, I suppose you can text them or call them on the phone, but it doesn't matter to you whether it's 4 in the afternoon or 6 in the evening." Farmers claimed that lone men are therefore most "reliable" (Sexsmith 2019).

Many full-time dairy employees at PVD and Bauer have requested time off or schedules that enable them to spend more time with their families, as well as to attend doctors' appointments and run errands. Instead of treating people as if they are "unreliable" for requesting time off, PVD managers decided to hire part-time workers to fill in, though it took them a few years to systematize these practices. PVD initially implemented "emergency scheduling" protocols before the lead manager realized that was inadequate, so he designed a system for full-time employees to arrange for additional time off. Peter hired a team of part-time workers who want only a few hours occasionally and are willing to jump in at a moment's notice. Peter told me that his main criterion for hiring part-time employees is "they need to say yes when we call and ask them to fill in." When I expressed surprise at this—I had interpreted it as employees being on call, he reiterated that he had a roster. Pablo told me that "employees don't even have to tell the managers when something happens because they [the managers] have a plan in place to deal with absences and substitutions in a way that doesn't over-burden the other workers." The Bauers later followed suit, gradually hiring more people to fill in as needed.[8] Both farms also upgraded their "common areas" and installed showers and lockers so that employees could quickly change clothes and get from work to school or social events faster, without having to cut their hours or take detours to stop at home when they are in a hurry. This was a popular move. Previously, people either rushed to school and other events in dairy attire, or they arrived late.

Immigrant employees on farms in New York and Wisconsin, by contrast, find themselves isolated and trapped on farms, unable to participate in community events. This is because many farmers have attempted to create "reliable" workers by isolating and entrapping them (Keller 2019; Gray 2014; Zúñiga and Hernández-León 2005).[9] In New York, Sexsmith (2019) found that most immigrant employees lived on the farms where they worked and had few opportunities to leave (see also Gray 2014). "The primary reason for workers' reliability is that they hardly leave the farm, because they also reside there . . . If they do not show up for a shift, they can easily be found and asked to return to work" (Sexsmith 2019, 726; see also Hondagneu-Sotelo 2007). An employee in Wisconsin said of his job, "From my job to my room, nothing else . . . I was enclosed every day" (Keller 2019, 2). When Keller (2019, 2) asked him why he didn't leave, he emphasized that he didn't have a car and *couldn't* leave.[10] Many employees Keller (2019) interviewed lived in trailers on remote dairy farms. One worker "lived on the farm in an old house with no stove and without any transportation to buy food" (Keller 2019, 2).

Many farmers across the country have also entrapped people under the "reliability" guise through debt peonage (Gray 2014; Martin 2009; Barrick, Lattimore, Pitts, and Zhang 2014).[11] On a farm in Kansas that raises heifers for dairies in several states, for example, Hegeman (2018) found that the employer recruited lone workers by asking existing employees from Mexico if they knew anyone in Mexico seeking work in Kansas. He then paid cash for a smuggler to bring the lone prospective employees to the farm (see also Barrick et al. 2014). Employees were housed in trailers on or adjacent to the farm, but away from town. The employees had to work off the smuggling debt, averaging $7,000 (see also Keller 2019). Once the employees had worked off the debt, the farmers would try to sell them used cars or other expensive items on credit to keep the employees in debt and on the farm. The farm owner did not pay overtime, sick leave, or any health (or other) benefits that would enable employees to pay off the loans. Immigration and Customs Enforcement (ICE) investigated the farm, fined the owner $10,000 for hiring people who have been denied authorization to work in the United States, and sentenced him to home probation and community service. One of the employees was deported (Hegeman 2018).

While most of the Bauer and PVD recruitment practices diverged from those found on other farms, one of my research assistants and I encountered an instance of possible surveillance and another of peonage. In the first case, a former Bauer employee, Máximo, thought that Owen was checking up on him when he called in sick to work several times. Máximo told me that Owen drove by his house, as if checking to see if he was home. One of Máximo's relatives, however, who is a Bauer employee, overheard Máximo (he told me this story in public) and later told me that Máximo frequently called in sick. Máximo disliked dairy work, so he quit, took a manufacturing job in a nearby town, and moved. In the instance of possible debt peonage, a PVD manager who sometimes lends money to employees when they want to buy a house or a car threatened to take loan repayments from the wages of a worker who had borrowed money and then began skipping loan payments and shifts. This employee told me and my research assistant that he had asked the manager for the money, and they had worked out the terms ahead of time, including what would happen if he neglected to repay the loan, so he said he "understood" why the manager threatened to garnish his wages, but he was frustrated. He lived alone in Dairy City (unlike most of his co-workers) and he was eyeing opportunities to live and work in a larger city. He was eager to leave. He didn't want to work at the dairy, but he put in overtime, with increased pay, for several weeks to pay off the loan. This is still a debt peonage situation, but he was able to pay the loan quickly and leave. In neither case were dairy managers able to offset the adversity of dairy work for these employees.

Not unlike some industrial employers of the early to mid-twentieth century, Bauer and PVD have attempted to secure employee "loyalty" using benefits (Davis 2009, 63). That's not to say they have never taken advantage. The act of lending money to people with limited credit positions owner-managers as paternalist or maternalist, even if the loans are low (or no) interest and are designed to help people buy homes and settle down (which several people have—some people have even sold the original home at a profit and bought others for themselves and their extended families—see below). The same was true of twentieth-century corporations that acted in ways that were at once benevolent and controlling—if the corporations were the only meaningful game in town and made people "overly dependent" on them (Davis 2009).

Over time, both Bauer and PVD have raised compensation. Olivia told me that when the family started hiring people from abroad, white residents accused her of wanting to hire people she could exploit. "Yeah, people were saying [when we first recruited people from abroad] that 'you just want that cheap help.' I says, 'well, we pay them just as much as we would pay you if you were going to get a job at our dairy!' You know, because they're worth it! That [treating them as cheap labor] was *not* our idea." Bauer and PVD recently added health insurance for full-time employees. Employer-provided insurance in agriculture is rare (Gray 2014; Rosenbaum and Shin 2007), but it is critically necessary and it was overdue. Several employees had already gotten hurt. Prior to providing health insurance, managers had in some cases paid directly to cover variable degrees of treatment, but coverage and care were inconsistent, and many employees had to shoulder costs (see Chapter 4). Another difficulty that employees have faced is lack of childcare. Neither farm assists with childcare. Both farms, however, provide housing assistance for employees and their families.

Housing Assistance

Bauer and PVD housing assistance is a recruitment and community development tool. Employees who live in Bauer-owned single-family homes within the town of Dairy City, or neighboring towns, pay $150 per month in rent for the first year and then no rent thereafter, though they usually pay utilities. Tomás and Lydia told Zaira that their rent began to fall faster—after just three months working at Bauer. Tomás said, "They [the Bauers] give all their employees a house. When you start working there, you pay a bit less than $150 per month [for the house] . . . Then at three months, it's less than $100 . . . When you reach six months, it's about

$48 for the whole month. Then you pay only the utilities . . . If you don't want a house, . . . I think they help you with gas, but it's more likely for rent . . . For that reason we really liked it here." The decrease in rent is meant to encourage people to stay. Many people told me that they live "rent-free" in Dairy City, though that disregards low rent in the first year and utilities thereafter. The Bauers pay for house repairs and upkeep, and they remodeled several homes a second time following severe storms that caused damage in 2018. The Bauers have written rental agreements that employees who want housing sign when they are hired. Rental contracts in farmer-supplied housing are almost unheard of (Keller 2019, 86). Dairy employees in other towns/states have reported not knowing how much their employers deduct for rent, and housing is often substandard, over-crowded, pest-infected, and unsafe (Keller 2019, 85; Gray 2014). In New York, anywhere from one-third to nearly two-thirds of eighty-eight im-migrant dairy employees surveyed by Fox et al. (2017) in 2014 reported holes in doors and floors, broken locks, insects, and air problems (Fox et al. 2017 in Keller 2019, 88).[12]

Bauer employee housing in Dairy City consists of single-family homes in the heart of town, within walking distance of the school and most area businesses. The distinctiveness of this situation may partially stem from farm owners' decisions to expand and recruit following a period of pre-cipitous economic and population decline. As the Bauers and PVD began recruiting people, there were many houses in town that had been vacant for years. Other farmers who went out of business, retired, or passed away had been unable to convince younger generations to stay or return to a depressed Dairy City. Anticipating that newly arriving employees would need homes, the Bauers began buying the vacant houses and fixing them up. The housing market is now saturated, as reflected in Gail's initial statement, but when she began buying houses in the late 1990s, the situ-ation was different:

GAIL: Housing is not easy to find around here.

ALISA: How did it go? How did you find housing?

GAIL: Well, we started buying houses when they came out on sale.

ALISA: So you must have started that in the late nineties, mid-nineties?

GAIL: In the late nineties. Yeah, 'cause if [Rubén] came in 1999, that was one of the first or second houses that we bought.

ALISA: How were houses available? . . .

GAIL: . . . Most of them were, [Dairy City] has an elderly population. It's, well, probably still is about the same, but it was, yeah, the first house that we bought was a guy that—or a woman that passed away, so her house came for sale. That [Tom Smith] house, he was a younger guy and he sold it to somebody that was working for a hog farm and he was, it was like a one-year job he had, so he wanted out of here and we bought his house and little by little. It has just been one at a time.

OLIVIA: And you have fixed up a lot of the homes you bought and you made them better homes, like [Ingrid Fritz's] house. You know, it was an elderly lady too and she passed away and when her property came up for sale and that is where you bought the majority of them, you know.

GAIL: You just have to keep your eyes open.

In the following passage, elaborating on how they fixed up the homes they bought, Olivia and Gail fumble over an exploitative remark about housing standards, as well as an inaccuracy, which they both seemed to catch and amend. Many of their employees had lower-middle- or middle-class life-styles abroad. Despite that, Gail and Olivia emphasized a small subset of employees who had substandard housing abroad. To correct themselves, they both said, "Well, some of them."

OLIVIA: You try to make a nice home out of them. And they [employees] were really appreciative because they weren't used to very many nice amenities in their homes. Well, some of them weren't, but it didn't take much to please them, in other words, I mean [*halts*].

GAIL: Well, some of them have never lived somewhere with running water before, they were straight from Mexico and this gal was telling me, and, well she's got little kids, she is more like my kids' age, she was talking about, yeah, going down to the river and washing your clothes and . . . yes, carrying water. So, you know, it doesn't, some of them, it doesn't take much to make them happy at all, but, you know, they [employees] want nice clean homes, and we've done some fixing up on some of them. Things that needed to be done, like new floors maybe, or we would re-do the bathroom, make it a little nicer, etcetera. 'Cause, you know, sometimes, when you go into older folks' homes, they're outdated.

Olivia's comments about employees being "really appreciative" read as patronizing or proud, and they mask the Bauer's dependence on employees, but Olivia seemed to catch herself; e.g., she said, "in other words, I mean," before halting. Her point seemed to have been, "you try to make nice homes out of them," as in, employers should try to make nice homes, and that is what they are trying to do. Gail stuttered in speaking about some employees having had limited amenities abroad, even as she tells the story about an employee who came straight to Dairy City without having had any amenities elsewhere in the US. She hastened to add that all employees "want nice homes," and she emphasized the need to make improvements to "outdated" homes. Gail knows from spending time with employees and their families that many people had very nice homes abroad, as I explain in Chapter 5, and everyone wants a nice home. Gail and Olivia seemed to recognize this, as reflected in their housing practices.

Invited by employees and their families, I spent time in four of the sixteen houses the Bauers bought for employees. Research assistants spent time in two additional houses, and we drove by nearly all of them. All but one had updated floors and fixtures. They were in good repair. The condition of the home that was an exception was tired and in need of repair. The employee who was living there with her family has since moved to an updated home in town. All of houses that we spent time in were two-story homes with single-family occupants.

Between the Bauers' home purchases and PVD managers' decisions to back mortgage loans for employees, the Dairy City housing market became completely saturated. There is not a single house for sale or rent. Gail, in fact, has struggled a couple of times when employees want to buy their homes from her. She says that she would be willing to sell to them if she could somehow ensure that they would keep working at her farm "forever." Since that is impossible, and she always wants to have houses available for employees, she has declined offers. This perhaps hints at a sort of "bondage" through work, but not through debt.

ALISA: How many of the families you hired have tried to buy homes in [Dairy City] or around here?

GAIL: A few are starting to, like [Julio] owns a home in [Dairy City] now, a few have asked about it now and we are kind of between "okay, if we sell it to you will you keep working for us and or will we be out of home and then if we need a home for somebody to live in we would be short a home then?" And you can't make them sign a contract that they will continue working for you.

ALISA: Are the homes nearby, where it doesn't end up being a long commute?

GAIL: We have two homes in [Fairview], everything else is in [Dairy City]. You know, we had a couple that wanted to live in [Greendale] for a while and so we helped them buy a place and they ended up wanting to live in [Dairy City]. They decided it was too far to drive. And so they own that home, but they live in [Dairy City]. So, yeah, it was interesting how that worked out. It was their choice, but they found out that that really is far away to drive full-time.

OLIVIA: And the couple that lives in [Fairview], maybe I have told you this, but [Jennifer] [Olivia's friend] just loved that family that lived there, you knew that?

GAIL: Yeah, I did.

OLIVIA: And that was always so helpful because [Natalie] has gone to assisted living in [a city] now, but anyway, they sold her home, but they were neighbors to one of the [immigrant employee] families and she just loved them she said he was always concerned about her and he could come over and take care of her yard and "can I do anything to help you?"

Olivia was smiling and animated as she spoke about the closeness between neighbors. It seemed meaningful to her, as did the opportunity for Olivia to speak about it with Gail—as though Olivia was praising Gail.

The family Gail referred to lives in a Bauer house, and they can rent out their second home or save it for extended family visits from Mexico. Many people who work at Bauer and PVD have helped their parents either come to Dairy City for visits or move to town permanently. This adds pressure on the local real estate market while simultaneously creating new opportunities for growth. At the same time, and as Olivia's comments indicate, face-to-face interactions key for building social capital emerge.

Due to a tight real estate market, most PVD employees and former Hoffman employees must find housing in nearby communities, many of them smaller than Dairy City. PVD managers subsidize rent for their employees, provide low-interest home loans, and/or help employees get bank accounts and lines of credit at one of the local banks. Many PVD employees have bought homes in neighboring communities. One of the PVD managers also likes to help families make repairs. The Hoffmans, who initially used a temporary visa program to employ immigrants from South Africa and Eastern Europe, and later hired people from Mexico and Central America, also subsidized housing in nearby towns. The Hoffmans, however, ultimately laid off most of their workforce.

Another point of divergence between the Dairy City farmers and those interviewed in other parts of the country (Sexsmith 2019; Harrison and Lloyd 2013) is that Dairy City farmers wanted to grow their farms in order to stay on the farm as a family. It's unclear whether it was this desire, rooted in what scholars call a "patrimony," or endeavoring to make conditions better for the next generation (Salamon 1995) that informed family-friendly labor strategies, including recognizing employees as whole people, not just employees. Work by Harrison and Lloyd (2013) suggests otherwise. Multigenerational famers typically try to hire immigrant employees to fill the most menial positions and take the worst shifts, while the owners' family members pursue more profit for themselves and "middle-class" lifestyles (Harrison and Lloyd 2013). They do not seek to extend their own experiences of family-friendly work to immigrant employees, nor do they typically work alongside their employees (Harrison and Lloyd 2013). What is clear in Dairy City is that farmers wanted to create stable farm growth capable of supporting additional members of the family, and they began to realize that the better they treat employees, the more their farms grow (see especially Chapter 3).

The Bauers say that bringing more of the family into the business was a key motivating factor in expanding. Olivia said,

> One of our biggest highs, I have to say, while [Gail's] here, is when they [Gail and Wayne] went into partnership with us, that they cared enough to come out and do what we did. That's why I say that's one of the highs is when our son [Wayne] decided to go into partnership with us and continue our dairy, you know, what we started, and try to improve, and then when their sons came in and said we want to be part of the dairy, makes you proud.

Olivia's comment about Gail and Wayne caring enough to come into the business and attempt to improve it underscored times when Olivia seemed to be trying to praise Gail for her business practices, noting how Gail tries to make employees happy. Wayne and Gail's sons, Owen and Nelson, also wanted to buy into the business. As Nelson put it, "My vision was, down the line, to make the business big enough to bring in one day my boys if that opportunity arised, and it has, it did. Because you know, if I guess, if we were the same size we were twenty or thirty years ago, the operation wouldn't be large enough to support my kids." By contrast, Sexsmith (2019) found that most farmers she interviewed wanted to hire employees so they could spend "more time...with family *off* the farm" (Sexsmith 2019, 708, emphasis in original).

Based on my interviews with others and local news stories (see the methods section in the introduction), the Hoffmans also wanted to farm with their children, but they went about it differently than the Bauers and the PVD managers. Hans and Sandy Hoffman, the oldest of two generations on the farm, bought the farm from Hans's father. Hans's family has owned a local farm since the late 1800s. Four of five of Hans and Sandy's children currently work on the farm. The children moved back to the farm after Hans and Sandy laid off their employees and replaced them with robots. Prior to that, the Hoffmans had relied primary on H-2 visas that provided only short-term employment.[13] The Hoffmans' labor practices hindered immigrant employees' local incorporation.

Conclusion

The Bauers and PVD decided to expand their farms on the heels of demographic and economic decline in Dairy City that threatened their extensive business interests. After making several mistakes, they gradually devised plans to grow their farms in ways that would also grow other local businesses and institutions, partially laying the foundation for crafting dignity. With an eye to simultaneously reducing harmful labor turnover on their farms and rebuilding a clientele for local businesses, the Bauers and PVD managers developed recruitment practices that differed from those of other dairy owners across the country. Instead of recruiting and isolating lone workers, subjecting them to low wages and trapping them in debt peonage, the Bauers and PVD managers recruited whole families, helped provide housing in single-family homes in the heart of town, and began using benefits and incentives to attract workers. Their notion of what makes workers "reliable" differs from what Sexsmith (2019) and Keller (2019) found on the East Coast and Midwest, where farmers exploit immigrant employees' isolation and family separation to force them to work at all hours (see also Harrison and Lloyd 2013). On these farms, it is just a matter of time before highly exploited employees leave to reunite with their families. They have every incentive to escape their isolation, exploitation, and deplorable living conditions.

Pursuing "growth with people" creates conditions that facilitate the face-to-face interactions that are crucial for building social capital and crafting dignity. The Bauers' and PVD owner-managers' farm consolidation coinciding with their interests in stably repopulating the town created a model of territorialized growth with people. This model contrasts with deterritorialized growth models and farming with few-to-no people and more technology (e.g., Gibson and Gray 2019). In the next chapter, I focus on how those interests interact with recent immigrants' experiences of moving to a remote rural dairy town.

RISKY BUSINESS

2

In the early months of 2020, the novel coronavirus, COVID-19, hit the United States. It quickly became clear that US dairy farmers were in for a roller-coaster business cycle. In February 2020, new export restrictions on milk suppressed global trade (Laca 2020). By March, however, US consumers were panic buying bleach, toilet paper, eggs, and *milk*. For the first time in years, milk flew off the shelves. Processors ordered more milk to make goods like cheese and yogurt that people hoarded during the pandemic (Wakayama 2020). Farmers initially thought they could ramp up production. Then schools closed. A major milk market, the National School Lunch Program, evaporated (Schneider 2020). Scores of restaurants shuttered and canceled orders for dairy products (Schneider 2020). Milk prices plummeted (Schneider 2020). Some large US dairy farmers faced the prospect of dumping their milk to prevent spoilage (Schneider 2020).

As the pandemic spread, I anxiously awaited word of what was happening in Dairy City. When news began pouring in, I was surprised. People were upbeat. Instead of discussing the pandemic, two immigrant families asked me to weigh in on college decisions for their children. Another family called me from the car while running back and forth between their house and the Bauer farm, telling me that things were "hopping" at the dairy. Humberto, who has worked as lead mechanic on the farm for over a decade, said, "We're great, everything is great!" In fact, he said, he and many of his co-workers felt bad for people across the country who were being laid off, infected with COVID, and/or evicted from their homes.[1] He said the Bauers and Pleasant Valley Dairy (PVD) managers were paying $600 bonuses to people who agreed to avoid nearby towns with high infection rates. Months later, both farms gave employees paid time off to get vaccinated. People's jobs and houses were secure. The Bauers were also building a new milking parlor, which they hired Mateo's eldest son to help design (Mateo, who provides veterinary care and serves as the farm safety officer, was among the first people the Bauers recruited). The Bauers had also bought a ranch for raising more calves and heifers. Their expansion trajectory was still on course. This was good news for them—the more high-quality milk farmers produce, the more revenue they generate, even when they face oversupply and price drops (see the appendix).

In the previous chapter I explored how the Bauers' and PVD owners' interests in growing their farms and stably repopulating the town interacted with their recruitment strategies. In this chapter I build on those connections while simultaneously shifting the focus to people's experiences of immigrating to Dairy City. Many people sought stability and household or family cohesion in a "tranquil" rural community. While these patterns have some features in common with previously documented cases of "new destinations immigration," in that many people immigrating to rural communities seek greater stability than what they have found in "traditional gateway cities," the difference is that rather than exploiting waning alternatives, the Bauers and PVD managers try to offset risks in dairy farming by increasing security for employees.

Many rural US producers, by contrast, try to compete with global producers by cutting wages, benefits, and labor protections (Hirschman and Massey 2008; Zúñiga and Hernández-León 2005; Donato, Stainback, and Bankston III 2005). As non-union production moved to rural areas and firms sought people to take short-term, "low-status" jobs, the US labor market further bifurcated into low-end service jobs and capital-intensive jobs with long-term stable employment (Hirschman and Massey 2008). Most jobs available to people immigrating to rural areas were of the low-end type with "no promising future" (Hirschman and

Massey 2008; Zúñiga and Hernández-León 2005; Donato et al. 2005). Many recent immigrants, scholars found, were still "willing" to "accept" such jobs because they sought to exit cities with saturated labor and housing markets, and they had few alternatives (Hirschman and Massey 2008; Zúñiga and Hernández-León 2005; Donato et al. 2005). Employers attempt to heighten profits by perpetually replacing them with new workers possessing even fewer rights and opportunities (Ribas 2016; Martin 2009; McWilliams 1939 [1979]).[2] These processes create a downward spiral of worker suppression and job and community degradation (Hirschman and Massey 2008; Zúñiga and Hernández-León 2005; Bonanno and Constance 2001).[3]

Unlike many of their counterparts, the Bauers and PVD managers sought to recruit people in a positive-sum manner. Nonetheless, there are still contradictions built into their efforts. In a place like Dairy City, where jobs are permanent instead of unstable, and where there is relatively more intact household/family immigration than in other cases, "quality" of life is still characterized by its relationship to the destabilization of work and living conditions more broadly. People who moved to Dairy City in the past twenty-five years have been concerned about job losses—including middle-class job losses—in other parts of the US and abroad, rising rates of violence and instability in large cities, and the high cost of living, declining quality of education, and the decline of good job prospects for their children. These experiences underscore people's common emphases of "peace of mind" in Dairy City, despite the onerousness of dairy work and the shock of moving from urban areas to such a small rural town. This may help to explain how Bauer and PVD managers were able to "entice" people with a broad range of backgrounds to a remote rural community with limited amenities. Here and throughout the book, I explore heterogeneity in people's backgrounds, which is often mentioned but more rarely described in studies on twenty-first-century rural "new destinations" immigration (see also Zúñiga and Hernández-León 2005), to learn more about how differently situated people came together in their struggles with globalized social changes, as well as what dynamics emerged in Dairy City.[4]

"Estamos a Gusto Aquí"/"We Are Comfortable Here"

Tomás told Zaira, my research assistant, that when he first traveled to Dairy City, he saw "rolling hill after rolling hill, with no towns in sight." He laughed and said it reminded him of "that horror film, *Jeepers Creepers*." He was unnerved by how remote and rural Dairy City is. People drive dozens of miles to reach a city of 10,000 or more people. Although many people who recently immigrated to Dairy City from cities struggle with the town's remoteness, they also said they like Dairy City precisely because it is so "calm" and "tranquil." This is particularly true for people who immigrated to Dairy City with their children (rather than alone, which is rarely the case in Dairy City) as well as for people who said they were tired of the traffic, expense, need to work multiple jobs, problems with schools, and experiences of crime in the cities where they had lived. Arturo and Julieta said their daughter was bullied at a school in Chicago but was thriving in Dairy City, including by becoming a local "basketball star." Mateo said about Dairy City, "It's small but very comfortable to live here." He noted that children have less freedom to get in trouble in Dairy City than they would in a big city. "If they drink [*disapproving look*], at least they just hang out in a field or in the trees [*laughs*] . . . That's a better thing for us [the parents]." Mateo said his kids "were always happy" growing up in Dairy City. "They never wanted to be in the house. They always wanted to be at school. They loved it." Mateo's children are starting families of their own. Even Tomás and his wife, Lydia, have come to enjoy Dairy City, largely because their young son, Sebastián, is thriving. Tomás's sister and brother-in-law, and their two children, also live in Dairy City and work at Bauer, and they enjoy being close.

By contrast, people who are single say they want to live in a bigger town where they can meet more people who are also single. In one case, Andrés, a man in his early twenties, said he was dating a woman in a much larger town nearly two hours away. When he visited her, and especially when they went out at night, he dreaded having to drive through the extremely dark and remote countryside to get back to Dairy City. Andrés decided to get a job in construction in the town where his girlfriend works, and he left his job at Bauer. Although Andrés enjoyed some work-life balance through the dairy, he didn't much enjoy his time off. People raising children, however, typically enjoy attending school events.

Themes of people seeking better schools, less crime, and more affordable housing are notable in other studies of recent rural immigration, but people in these studies tend to experience high turnover and geographic displacement (Gouiveia, Carranza, and Cogua 2005; Zúñiga and Hernández-León 2005; Keller 2019).[5] For example, Keller (2019, 9) found that while some newly arrived employees in other dairying towns "put down roots and raise children who attended the local schools," most people stayed for only three to four years. Far fewer employees in Keller's (2019, 13) study had children with them in the United States and approximately 40 percent were childless. By contrast, in Dairy City, many employees have accumulated well over a decade of tenure on the Bauer dairy and/or PVD, and their children attend school through graduation. Many people are also having more children who are growing up entirely in Dairy City. This means that people are having extended interactions with local social institutions. These distinctive patterns (except see Valentine 2005) first became apparent in an early interview I conducted with Olivia and Gail Bauer in 2016. After Gail told me a story about how she and her husband Wayne had asked a friend in another part of the state to publicly advertise jobs at the Bauer farm, I asked Olivia and Gail to walk me through how the first people they recruited arrived. In their narrative, it's notable that two of the people they mention, José and Mateo, still work at the farm and live in Dairy City, giving them farm employment tenures running on eighteen to twenty years as of late 2024, though Mateo worked for a few years in another state. In Olivia's and Gail's telling, José's and Mateo's tenure appears to be at least partly connected to their children's experiences in the local school. To the extent that the Bauers used the school as a recruitment tool, connected with their in-town housing offerings, their recruitment strategies affect employee incorporation in a positive sense, in contrast with temporary labor arrangements that reduce people's interactions.

GAIL: [Fidel and Pablo] came up and they spoke no English and we tried to meet at the Quick Shop [in Dairy City] . . . We went to the Quick Shop and they [Fidel and Pablo] didn't show up. It was December. It was cold and snowy and they had car trouble. Finally, I got this phone call, "we're at the Quick" [*miming holding a phone receiver to her ear*]. I said, "stay there." I was not going to try to give anybody any directions— I didn't speak their language . . . I sent Wayne to town . . . [Wayne] brought [Fidel and Pablo] to the dairy and showed them the cows so that they knew that, you know, . . . that they really were going to a dairy, and not that they had just met some random guy at the Quick Shop! [*laughs*] . . . We had a house for them to stay in, so we took them to the house for the night and then they started working the next day and after a month, [Fidel] left and [Pablo] brought his family.

ALISA: [Pablo] and [Fidel] were not the first to arrive?

GAIL: No, they were the second two, I think. I'm pretty sure. Yeah, and then after we got [Aurelio], then he knew [Mateo], you know, from when they were in Mexico, and that was his brother who was wanting to get to a better life . . . Then [José] came, too, because they knew [José].

OLIVIA: [José] and [Mateo] are best friends.

GAIL: They are good friends. And [José], I don't know just what year he came, he has been here for ten years, yeah, I would say at least ten, or twelve, and he is still here with his family.

OLIVIA: 'Cause his boy wasn't in school yet, and he is now a freshman in high school, so he has been here ten years, and they have had three little ones since they have moved here. And [Silvia] was in grade school when they came.

GAIL: She was in eighth grade.

OLIVIA: And she could speak English.

GAIL: Not when she came here.

OLIVIA: Not at the very first but they picked it up quick, she learned it fast. Yeah, real quick . . .

GAIL [*interrupts*]: But that was a few years apart [they came a few years apart], 'cause [Mateo] wanted to come for a long time and [Celia] did not.

ALISA: Where were they?

GAIL: Mexico.

ALISA: And why didn't [Celia] want to come?

GAIL: It's cold up here. I think that was part of it. They came, but I think that she had friends and family down there and . . .

OLIVIA [*interrupts*]: That had been her home probably, for her whole life. She grew up there. I couldn't imagine. I wouldn't want to pick up and go to Mexico, either.

GAIL: And their boys weren't that old at the time. [Antonio] was just four. I remember that the little one, [Carlos], I can't remember how old he was, but I remember [Antonio] being only four. He was just a little guy and now he's an eighth-grader, or maybe a freshman now or a sophomore. The boys are four or five years apart, so [Carlos] must have been around nine-ish.

Unlike what Olivia and Gail describe, most of the people Keller (2019) met in other dairying communities were lone men who did not put down roots. This raises questions about employers' respect for family integration and work-life balance. Managerial practices and work experiences affect people's perceptions of the town (and vice versa), as well as their incorporation (see also Gouiveia et al. 2005; Zúñiga and Hernández-León 2005). For example, Ramiro recounted to Zaira how he initially convinced a manager at PVD to hire him, and then the manager worked to convince Ramiro to take the job. The manager's efforts took Ramiro's family into account, and Ramiro's perceptions of PVD affected his feelings about Dairy City.

We [my cousin and I] didn't know the area at all. All I knew was that my brother was working at a dairy. So one day we decided to drive around and see where the work was. We set out into the countryside. It was snowing. We spent hours looking for the farm. We slid off the road and got the truck stuck in the snow. We had to leave the truck and we walked for like five hours. It looked like the car was close! [But it wasn't—distances are deceiving on the plains.] We finally walked into a town and asked for help. When we got back to the house, my wife was *so* mad. "Where were you? " . . . So the next day I asked my brother, "where on earth is the farm?" This time we managed to stay on pavement [there are a lot of dirt roads surrounding Dairy City].

We arrived at [PVD]. The first thing I saw was this little old guy and he offered me work! He didn't give it to me just then, I still had to go back to Nebraska where I was working at the time . . . My family was here with my brother. But I didn't feel good being there with my family here. My wife told me the old man [from PVD] had called, and there and then I decided to come. And thank God. It has gone well here financially for us. I already have more, financially, for the family.

When Zaira asked Ramiro to say more about "the little old guy," Ramiro's nickname for the PVD manager, Ramiro said:

The person who gave me a job was a really good person. I really liked working with him.[6] They treat you really well there [at PVD]. And not having to go find other work, that is really great. Firstly for the work, we have liked it here . . . It was difficult for me to enter that dairy [PVD], [though], because when I arrived to ask for a job, he [the manager] told me that he had never hired anyone from Mexico . . . And I told him, "I have a need, give me the opportunity to work." I had a letter of recommendation from my other job. And yet he told me that he had never hired a Mexican and didn't know if I would be a good person or a good worker. I told him, "give me two weeks and if in two weeks you don't like my work, fire me and don't pay me a single dollar." We agreed on that deal, that if he didn't like how I worked, . . . [trails off]. But I have always liked to be responsible with my work. He watched me after that. He got there at six in the morning to watch how I was working. He came back at ten, and I got nervous because he watched me from the office upstairs, and I was working down below. He said, "[Ramiro], I'm not going to wait the two weeks. You have work here with me for many years. I want you to meet people." I had two kids, a four-year-old girl and my month-old son. He [the manager] put us in his truck. He took us to the local grocery store. He said, "this is [Ramiro], he works for me. His wife, [Nidia], his daughter [Alejandra], and his son, [Miguel]. Help them in whatever they need." [We went] to the bank, the post office, the mechanic, to the town's businesses so they would know me. Then I went back to work. I finished around eleven in the morning. [The manager said], "the day is over, you can go home." I thought, "I'm going to starve to death working six hours a day!" I told him, "is that all I have to do?" I was used to being forced to work twelve to fourteen hours a day, but I went home. Then I started working every day [at PVD]. I have had many employers in many states, both in the United States and in Mexico. And I have never had a boss like him.

The PVD manager's enthusiasm in hiring Ramiro and wanting him and his family to meet people made an impression on Ramiro, as did their ongoing working relationship. The manager's efforts, while friendly, were also strategic. Recognizing people for their work and forging links between newly arrived employees and local businesses not only enables farmers to recruit people who are more apt to stay because they feel welcome and appreciated, but it provides new clientele for local businesses and institutions.

Ramiro initially worried about being able to survive on income from six hours of work, but he "did well financially" at PVD, and without having to get another job.[7] Saraí, Jorge, Maura, and Antonia say they also work six- to eight-hour shifts. Maura said she still struggled with daycare, so Peter let her bring her daughter to the dairy to study or watch TV on her iPad in the breakroom. Most people we interviewed at Bauer worked six- to eight-hour shifts, though at both farms, people who took promotions with added responsibilities tended to work more hours.

When I met Owen Bauer in 2015, he told me that he and his brother Nelson had been recruiting people from Chicago in the aftermath of the financial crisis. Peter and the Bauers recruited several people who had been working multiple jobs and living in what they described as "rough neighborhoods." They had also endured long subway commutes. Several additional people came from California. Paloma's sisters, nieces, nephew, and their children moved from Los Angeles when a crowded housing situation put unbearable stress on the family. One of Paloma's nieces said she and her husband moved to Dairy City because "rent is so expensive in California and most people won't rent to families with kids, saying kids are too loud. There was also a crime against a kid in California and that was it. We decided to move to Kansas for the kids." Paloma's sisters, niece, and several of their relatives had been working in service in California and "spent all the money they had just on food and rent." Paloma said work was so hard to find that she wound up collecting and selling recycling until one of her sisters met a military man from Kansas and they all moved. Tomás emphasized, "Where we were [in California], the cheapest apartment was like $800, for a small apartment, on the low end $800 or $900." In recent years, this situation has worsened for millions of people across the United States (Dougherty and Barbaro 2024).

US housing costs have increased by at least 40 percent and rents by 50 percent since about 2020 (Dougherty and Barbaro 2024; Wamsley 2024). Humberto's expression of concern for people outside of Dairy City reflects recognition of these patterns, as well as the fact that many people lost their jobs during the pandemic and were ultimately evicted. The roots of the US housing crisis date to the financial crisis and a temporary glut in housing as many people lost homes to foreclosures (Dougherty and Barbaro 2024). Subsequently, many home builders went out of business, older homes deteriorated, and far fewer new homes were built than before the crisis (Dougherty and Barbaro 2024). A growing population of smaller households seeking more housing units then increased demand (Dougherty and Barbaro 2024). That increased demand, combined with the pandemic and rising interest rates, placed upward pressure on housing costs and rents. Owners of older units decided to sell at high prices, removing "naturally occurring affordable housing" from the market and forcing people into higher-rent units (Dougherty and Barbaro 2024).[8] The pandemic increased the prices of building materials and the demand for more homes from which people could work remotely (Dougherty and Barbaro 2024). The costs of building new homes became unaffordable for all but the wealthiest home builders (Dougherty and Barbaro 2024). People moving to areas with lower housing costs drove expenses up in those areas such that by 2024, there were few places left in the US with affordable housing (Dougherty and Barbaro 2024). More people are relying on mobile/manufactured homes that are vulnerable to climate disasters, fewer people can afford first homes, and more people are spending larger shares of their incomes—one-third on average and sometimes one-half of their salaries—on mortgages or rents (Dougherty and Barbaro 2024; Howard and Flavelle 2024).

In Dairy City, however, families have largely felt they can relax. Several people told me they live "rent free" in Dairy City—this is how they describe Bauer's housing practices—and say they like the houses. They have more space and privacy while also living close to one another within town. As an example, Paloma's nephew, a DJ, liked to use his professional DJ equipment to play music videos loudly in the living room where he, his wife, and three sons regularly held dance parties (once when Jill and I visited, he played Michael Jackson's "Thriller" so loudly their three young boys ran around the house shrieking and covering their ears—none of the neighbors complained, even as the walls vibrated). Paloma's niece said that she and her husband often put the DJ/dance/party lights on in the house to dance with the kids. The couple also liked walking their children to and from school until they were old enough to walk alone.

Paloma was among the people who mentioned that she liked living in the countryside generally. She especially liked "the tranquility." In what follows, I focus on Paloma's accounting of "tranquility" because it powerfully illustrates the tensions at play. Paloma emphasized relief from exposure to physical violence paired with work that is arduous but still provides "peace of mind." There are few places to go out, she said, but Dairy City has at least given her "peace of mind."

> We have met very good people, very good people. And here in these little towns, I have nothing bad to say. The people are very good. People are very kind . . . I told my children that I would like them to be here with me, right? Because there are no dangers here. Here it is tranquility. Well, I know the work is hard. Yes, it is heavy, but you are calm. There are no—you go out into the street and there aren't shots being fired, no one is being assaulted. And I tell them [my adult children], if they could see, it is very beautiful, in the form of tranquility . . . There is no Disneyland, we don't even have Kentucky [Fried] Chicken here. Nothing, I tell you. We have a gas station, a restaurant, that's all. And

a bar where all the families enter . . . There aren't many places to go to but there is a field. And the main thing is the tranquility here, right? Yes, I like it. It's how I describe it to them. There is not much to tell you, but I believe that peace of mind is everything.

Paloma is one of the few people whose children are abroad, which is difficult for her and her husband. (One of Paloma's children came to Dairy City briefly and Owen hired him to drive a tractor on the farm, but he was trying to finish school in Mexico, so he returned.) Paloma has been tempted to return to Mexico to be with her children, but she says she and her husband have built so many years of tenure at the Bauer dairy that have come with raises and promotions that she "doesn't want to start all over again at the bottom" somewhere else. Paloma told me she "knows *a lot* of people in Dairy City" (her emphasis). Her networks may also be keeping her local.

Paloma's comment about dairy work being "hard" and "heavy" juxtaposed with her statements that she is "calm" and has "peace of mind" is notable. It speaks to crafting dignity in the sense that employers must make extra efforts to make difficult work as good as it can be for people, through fair compensation, respect for work-life balance, demonstrated compensation, and dependable employment—all of what Ramiro recounted about his experiences at PVD (Bolton 2007; Lucas 2015; Roscgigno et al. 2021).[9] There is tension in this, though, because "comfort" is still informed by the struggles associated with confronting multiple intersecting violences, including declining work and housing options as well as relocating under a hostile immigration regime and trying to keep households intact (Durand and Massey 2003; Massey 2020). For example, while Paloma was one of the few people to be living apart from her adult children, many people were living apart from their elderly parents, who remained in Mexico and Central America. Some people have been able to bring their parents to Dairy City either for weeks or months at a time, or even permanently, but not everyone has. Regular face-to-face interaction in Dairy City thus sometimes comes at the cost of frequent face-to-face interaction across international borders. Further, no one we spoke with had imagined working on a dairy farm in a remote, rural US community.

Overview of Recent Immigration Patterns

In the past twenty-five years, Bauer and PVD have recruited people from a broad range of places and backgrounds. Across the rural US, immigrant employees are often from Mexico (between 60 and 80 percent), between the ages of twenty-five and forty-four (67 percent), and male (90 to 95 percent) (Fox, Fuentes, Valdez, Purser and Sexsmith 2017; Keller Gray, and Harrison 2017; Sexsmith 2019).[10] Approximately 45 percent of immigrant employees in Dairy City are women. Data on women immigrant employees on US dairies is limited, but per available data (Keller 2019; Sexsmith 2019; Harrison and Lloyd 2012), this is unusual. It may in part be due to Bauer and PVD managers' efforts to recruit whole families, rather than single individuals—typically men—as is common on other farms (Keller 2019; Sexsmith 2019; Harrison and Lloyd 2012). Most people who immigrated to Dairy City are from Mexico, but a preponderance came from urban areas, not rural ones as is typically the case (Sexsmith 2019, 717; Baker et al. 2021; Fox et al. 2017).[11] This shouldn't be too surprising given that urbanites comprise the majority of Mexico's population (Instituto Nacional de Estadística y Geografía (INEGI) [National Institute of Statistics and Geography] 2024; Bada and Fox 2022).[12] Although a much greater proportion of people in Mexico work in agriculture than in the United States (13 percent versus 2 percent) (International Labor Organization and World Bank 2024), people who immigrated to Dairy City are from at least eight Mexican states with "majority urban municipalities," per Bada and Fox's (2022) adjusted measures, where they worked in non-agricultural jobs. Since even the most rural states in Mexico also have a significant urban population (i.e., at least 33% of people living in urban municipalities within the state) and only 4 are in fact majority "rural," "rural livelihoods [are] becoming increasingly articulated with urban areas" (Bada and Fox 2022, 39-40).[13] Further, fewer people from rural Mexico are seeking jobs in US agriculture (Zahniser, Taylor, Hertz, and Charlton 2018). Dairy City may reflect some of these changes.

In what follows, I introduce several people who immigrated to Dairy City to show the range of people's backgrounds and experiences.[14] Following analyses in the next two chapters of how managerial practices affected people's work experiences and institutional growth in Dairy City vis-á-vis recent immigration, I return to these stories in Chapter 5 to analyze how economic restructuring abroad interacts with people's experiences in Dairy City and affects their decisions about whether to stay.

From the Big City to Dairy City

In 2001, Mateo drove twenty hours from Chihuahua, Mexico, to visit his brother, Aurelio, in Dairy City. Aurelio worked at the Bauer dairy. In Mateo's account, Aurelio introduced Mateo to Wayne Bauer, who immediately tried to recruit Mateo. Mateo recalls Wayne telling him, "If you ever want a job, one is waiting for you here." It made an impression on Mateo. Mateo was working as an accountant for Chrysler in Mexico at the time. "I studied to be an accountant and went to work for large companies, first in mining and then in fabric, then batteries, and then for ten years for car companies. I was always in administration, not operations." Mateo handled warranties for Chrysler: "If a customer came in complaining about a faulty radio, the dealership would say, 'no problem,' and they replaced it. But then I had to call the plant and get the money back. We had lots of fights with the plant [*smiles*]." As much as Mateo enjoyed getting great deals for customers, what Mateo liked best about his job in Mexico was that he got to travel. The company often flew him to Mexico City and Monterrey, as well as a few other states across the country. But Mateo and his wife began to worry about how much it would cost in Mexico to educate their son in English, which they felt was necessary for him to have a great future—in wind energy or electrical engineering, they hoped. Things were changing in Mexico (see Chapter 5), so Mateo accepted Wayne's offer, and the family moved to Dairy City. He said that he liked the countryside and knew he would have stable employment at Bauer. And when Wayne learned of Mateo's love of travel, he sent Mateo to dairy conferences in Minnesota, Wisconsin, and across the Midwest. Mateo then shared what he learned with Wayne and his sons. Mateo, along with Paloma and Agustín, also from Mexico, now provides veterinary care on the Bauer farm. Mateo recently also took over as safety officer. Mateo says that when he is completely fluent in English (he *is* completely fluent, but his standards are sky-high), he wants to do accounting for the farm. Mateo's wife, Ana, is a personnel/shift manager at Bauer and she milks and raises calves. She started working at Bauer in early 2005 and has worked there ever since. Laughing, Mateo said that Ana "has too many friends here and is always out visiting."

Paloma was a travel agent in Mexico before she moved to Dairy City in 2011. After she learned how to milk and care for cows, she took a job overseeing veterinary and calf care at the Bauer dairy. She said it was a major transition from the kind of work she did in Mexico, but she is relieved to have a stable job and income. She has put three children through college in Mexico and is building houses for each. Her husband, Xavier, worked for a municipal government in Mexico. When Paloma first arrived in Dairy City, she cleaned schools, houses, and hotels with her sister's cleaning company. Paloma tired of the work and joined her husband, Xavier, at the Bauer dairy. Xavier worked as a herdsman and then did office work after he was injured. In the office, Xavier was able to heal. When I asked Xavier if the cows are dangerous, noting his injuries, he looked at me and said, in his soft-spoken manner, "No, they are very noble creatures. Very noble." Paloma says that she loves the veterinary side of her dairy job because she once dreamed of being a doctor, but she would also like to drive the Bauer's combine. Paloma says she has watched Gail Bauer driving the combine several times and wants to learn. Paloma has many ideas for other kinds of businesses she would like to launch locally, including gold merchandising, one of her passions. Her ultimate dream, however, is to be a television news reporter.

Xiomara and Víctor, a couple in their mid-forties who have worked for over fifteen years at PVD, say they moved to the United States primarily for their eldest child, who was struggling at school in Mexico. His teachers often called Xiomara into the principal's office and told her that her son "didn't pay attention, didn't do his work, and just drew during class time." Xiomara said that there was a lot of violence in their neighborhood and at the school. She suspected that other kids were bullying her son. In Dairy City, though, her son really likes school, and "he is doing great." Xiomara says that life is all around easier in Dairy City than where they lived in Mexico. Xiomara grew up in a *ranchito* (a very small rural community) without lights or water. She and her husband, Víctor, then moved to a "tiny house" in a large city in Mexico where Víctor was a cab driver for many years before coming to Dairy City in the early 2000s. Víctor got a job at the Hoffman farm, but he "hated it" and moved to PVD. At PVD, Xiomara is training to be a shift manager—she wanted to do insemination but thinks she isn't tall enough, though she's also interested in vaccinating. Víctor is learning the software that the managers use to monitor cow health and productivity so that he can become a herdsman, though he and Xiomara have spent many years milking or pushing cows. Víctor says that the managers at PVD work with him and Xiomara to create schedules that allow them to spend time with their children when they are not at school.

Víctor says that by the time he got to the Hoffman farm in the early 2000s, most of the employees were from Mexico and Guatemala, not Romania or South Africa, as they had been in the previous couple of years (Romanian and South African employees had worked on nine-month H-2 visa contracts and then left). On the Hoffman farm, Víctor's boss was "really mean" to him and his co-workers, Xiomara said, and Víctor had to work "*all* the time." Xiomara said there was no way to swap shifts and Mr. Hoffman didn't always pay his workers. She said Mr. Hoffman "yelled at the workers a lot." After Mr. Hoffman laid off his employees and installed robots to milk and feed the cows, Xiomara said she really wanted to go see the robots. She and Víctor drove to the farm to see them but feared that Mr. Hoffman would get mad and run them off, so they turned around. Xiomara's youngest child, however, went to the Hoffman farm with her kindergarten class. She told Xiomara that there are around "twenty huge robots" (there were about half that many—their large size likely made it seem like there were more).

Humberto worked as a managing mechanic for the Tecate parent company in Mexico before taking over as lead mechanic on the Bauer farm. Humberto was shocked when the company downsized in 2009 and laid off much of its workforce, including him. Unemployment in Mexico was on the rise, and he and his wife had accumulated debts—two houses, several cars, and an investment in a local restaurant. They were also paying for their daughter to pursue a degree in accounting. Humberto and his wife decided to fly to the United States to investigate job opportunities. In a moment of desperation to pay his mortgage in Mexico, Humberto took a job cleaning a football stadium in a town about an hour away from Dairy City. He knew someone working in a poultry plant nearby, but he didn't want to work there. "Imagine," he told me, "working as lead mechanic, flying all over the country [Mexico], and then . . ." Tears suddenly welled up in his eyes. He grabbed a cup of soda and started sipping it rapidly, looking up toward the ceiling, unable to speak for several moments. He took a breath and resumed his story, saying that a friend told him about the large dairies in Dairy City, and Humberto asked to meet with the Bauers. He presented his training certificates to the family, and the Bauers hired him to manage their machine shop. He now maintains and repairs large farm equipment. His friend, I later learned, works as a carpenter for the Bauers, maintaining and sometimes remodeling the single-family homes in downtown Dairy City that the Bauers bought for employees.

Humberto's wife, Hilda, worked for a bank in Mexico. She flew back to the US several months after Humberto took the job at the Bauer farm. She dreaded living in a small rural town and working on a dairy farm. For several months after arriving, Hilda said she sat at home, feeling depressed, but Humberto urged her to go out. When she did, she ran into the lead manager of PVD, who encouraged Hilda to take a job on his farm. Hilda has scoliosis and she said she was surprised to find that the physical labor of her farm job—mostly milking—alleviated her symptoms, which had been contributing to her depression. The more she worked, she said, the better she felt, but she still wanted to have flexibility in her schedule. She negotiated with the manager and largely makes her own hours. She says she is partly able to do this because she actually likes night shifts, and she convinced the manager to pay more for night shifts because staying up all night is taxing. Hilda favors the pay structure at PVD over Bauer, and since she and her family already live in a Bauer house "rent-free" (Humberto works at Bauer), she gets all the benefits she wants from the two farms. Humberto and Hilda's eldest daughter, who became an accountant in Mexico, moved to Dairy City to work at PVD and raise a family. She had been unable to find a job in Mexico. The couple's next eldest children are both in college in Kansas—one of them on a prestigious four-year scholarship.

Agustín followed his wife, Elena, and her family to California to find a job in the 1990s. He had only been able to study through the third grade in Mexico, and he struggled to find enough work. Although he found odd jobs in California, the cost of living was expensive, and he was sick of having to share space with his wife's extended family. He wanted to have a home where he and Elena could start a family. Agustín's brother found work in a furniture factory outside of Wichita and recruited Agustín. Agustín loved the work and became a trusted employee. His plan was to save money and rent a house in Kansas so his wife could move out from California, but before Agustín met his goal, the factory went out of business. Agustín went to work for a road construction crew, laying new pavement during the brutally hot Kansas summers. On one of those jobs, he found himself near Dairy City. People in the area told him about jobs at the dairy, and that the dairy provided housing. Agustín went to speak with the Bauers. They hired him and provided a single-family home about three blocks from the school. Elena joined Agustín shortly after. They have two children.

Agustín worked his way up from night shifts milking to day shifts, and then into insemination, hoof trimming, and veterinary work. The Bauers told me and my research assistants that they can't believe that Agustín, who is doing some of the most advanced work on the farm, had access to so little formal education in Mexico. Agustín makes his own hours, though he has a lot of responsibility. He is training other workers to do some of the work he specializes in so he can take more time off. He works from around seven in the morning until his oldest child gets home from school, around 3:45 in the afternoon. He takes weekends off to be with his family.

Lydia and Tomás came to Dairy City because they felt unsafe raising their son in Michoacán, Mexico (Paloma also fears for her three children, who are in Veracruz, calling them every evening to make sure they are okay). Lydia and Tomás told Zaira:

Tomás: We love our country, and we love this town [Dairy City]. We couldn't live as we liked there [in Michoacán]. The situation was really ugly. I should say, in nearly all of Mexico, the situation is really bad. In Michoacán, though, it is much worse. We couldn't even safely walk outside, and no one wanted to leave their houses. People left [home] because they had to, but they always looked over their shoulder because you never knew when the bullets would fly. The shooters don't care who they hit, it's just one less person to get in their way. One time, while she [Lydia] was pregnant, we went to a store in Mexico that's called Ahorra Más [Save More], which is like a Wal-Mart, but with fewer options. Anyway, we stopped to get a popsicle before going to the store . . .

Lydia: I was craving a popsicle.

Tomás: So we stopped to get a popsicle before going to the store . . .

Lydia: And when we got to the store, there had just been a huge shoot-out. There were all of these soldiers. They had captured two or three *narcos* who they had face down on the cement near a car that was totaled, with water and glass smashed all around it . . .

Tomás: And that little popsicle, the popsicle saved us . . .

Lydia: People say it's gotten even worse . . .

Tomás: It used to be that even at midnight or one in the morning, people would still be out on the street. In the plaza, women with their children or seated out in front of their houses, taking in the fresh air in the evenings. Before it was really tranquil. Not anymore. It has gotten really bad.

For Lydia and Tomás, it took moving to rural Kansas to find tranquility again. Several people moved from other large cities in the United States to Dairy City. Gabriel, for example, moved from Denver, which he said is "full of gangs." He was robbed two or three times, he says, and once, his car was stolen. It was a freezing cold morning. He started the engine and then stepped inside his front door to grab something. In the time that it took him to run from his car to the front door, someone hopped in the driver's seat and sped away. Gabriel called the police and eventually got the car back, but it was "all trashed." He said that rent in Denver was "super expensive" and life was stressful. His son wasn't doing well in school and he and his wife were worried. A friend in Dairy City invited him and his family to visit. They toured the town and the local school, and his son got to spend several hours in classes and playing sports. Gabriel said that his son loved the school, so he and his wife decided to move immediately. They went back to Denver, packed up their belongings, and moved to Dairy City.

Gabriel and his cousin, Luis, were the first people I met in Dairy City, but I didn't get to spend much time with them over the years. They migrated from a town in Guatemala near the border with El Salvador, close to where I had conducted research for my dissertation about ten years earlier. They were the youngest immigrant employees I met in Dairy City (they appeared to be in their twenties). Although we excitedly discussed familiar places in Guatemala and El Salvador, Gabriel and Luis told me that they had been chronically un- or under-employed and life was difficult for them in Guatemala. They felt "hopeless" about their prospects there. Luis told me that in Dairy City, he and his relatives all have stable work at the local dairies. I asked where they live, and Luis told me, "in a dairy house." His other cousin lives with his wife and son in a nearby town about fifteen miles away. They own their own home. I asked how many people from the dairies live in the neighboring town, and he said, "Four families. It's small but nice." When Luis jumped in and said, "You can't beat the rent here in Dairy City, it's free!," it meant that he had been working for the Bauers for more than a year (at which point employees receive free housing).

Conclusion

Whereas many rural employers use a lack of viable alternatives available to people who immigrate under hostile immigration regimes to heighten exploitation (Hirschman and Massey 2008; Zúñiga and Hernández-León 2005; Donato et al. 2005),[15] the Bauers and PVD managers enhanced the relative attractiveness of dairy jobs and remote rural residence in the context of broader crises. This represents an unfair advantage, which positioned the farmers to recruit people who otherwise would likely not have considered doing dairy work. Nonetheless, their efforts reveal the seeds of labor strategies involving dignity at work—at and beyond the worksite. In treating people who immigrated to take dairy jobs as whole human beings desirous of work-life balance, they created conditions that appealed to people seeking stable working and living conditions. Such appeal was still rooted in broader hardships across the US economy and society. Employer efforts to make work as good as possible for people would thus become increasingly important for crafting dignity. In the next chapter, I turn to managerial practices on the three farms to analyze these dynamics.

3

Contemporary US dairy farmers typically have the power to manage work as they wish. They are unlikely to be subject to shareholder dictates. Whereas most food production in the United States today is controlled by large corporations, at least 97 percent of US dairy farms are family owned and operated (Lobao and Meyer 2001; USDA 2024). Of the few dairy farms that are corporate owned, "nearly 90% are closely held by the operators' families rather than external shareholders" (Sommer, Hoppe, Greene, and Korbe 1998 qtd. in Lobao and Meyer 2001, 106; USDA 2024). Agri-businesses avoid investing in milk production because it is regarded as being too risky. Cattle diseases, natural disasters, and climate change can interrupt production while international trade wars and variable milk markets can destabilize prices (Kardashian 2012; USDA 2024). This means that while farmers retain managerial autonomy, they are also personally liable for their large capital investments. If their farms fail, they are on the hook.

The Bauer, Pleasant Valley Dairy (PVD), and Hoffman farms in Dairy City have used their managerial autonomy to implement a range of labor practices. Owner-managers on the Bauer farm, a multigenerational operation, opted for sociable forms of craft-like managerial practices. PVD is the incorporated farm owned and managed by a variety of local farmers. PVD adopted bureaucratic forms of labor management before incorporating aspects of craft-style management to open career paths and foster collaboration between employees. Bureaucratic management is designed to "guarantee" minimum levels of work effort nominally through a "fixed division of labor," "hierarchy of offices," and "rules that guide activity" (Hodson 2001, 27).[1] It is supposed to raise profit through the achievement-based "allocation of rewards and power," though it tends to promote prioritize individualism over collaborative problem solving and innovation potentially hindering production (Hodson 2001, 27–35).[2] The Hoffman farm, also a multigenerational farm, opted for more common "lean flexibility." Lean flexibility generally involves hiring temporary workers who are ineligible for benefits, imposing circumscribed or "strict task regimens," and/or accelerating work instead of increasing efficiency or allowing employees to focus on product quality (Crowley and Hodson 2014; Davis 2009; Hodson 1999).[3] After experiencing labor conflicts and production problems, the Hoffmans replaced nearly all of their employees with robots that feed and milk cows. In this chapter, I explore these variations and their implications for employees and farms.[4]

The Bauer Farm: Sociable Forms of Craft-Style Management

Of the three dairies, the Bauers have employed the greatest degree of sociable forms of craft-style management, which is crucial for the broader concept of crafting dignity. Crafting dignity refers to the application of "managerial citizenship behaviors" to craftwork (Crowley 2016; Crowley and Hodson 2014). Craftwork involves "working precisely to high standards," which is facilitated or impeded by how an operation (in this case, a farm) is organized (Sennett 2008, 20, 28, 30, 241). Managerial citizenship behaviors mean managers communicating clearly and in a timely manner with employees, providing needed resources, working closely with employees, "getting their hands dirty," and inviting workers to "speak frankly" and engage in "sharp mutual exchanges" (Sennett 2008, 31; Crowley 2016; Crowley and Hodson 2014).[5] Such exchanges enable employees and managers to identify and solve problems, and to innovate. In the process, they develop tacit knowledge—a "repertoire of procedures"—and "self-conscious awareness" (Sennett 2008, 50). "At its higher reaches, technique is no longer a mechanical activity; people can feel fully and think deeply what they are doing once they do it well" (Sennett 2008, 20).[6] However, if community in work is lacking (the sociable aspect), "effective critique, awareness," and craft-like work are unlikely to develop (Sennett 2008, 50, 30).

Wayne Bauer began organizing work on his multigenerational farm in a craft-like style from the moment he took over in the 1980s. Two of his sons, Owen and Nelson, bought into the farm in the aughts. In the past several years, Owen and Nelson have taken primary responsibility for managing work. The two sons face industry pressures to bureaucratize the farm. Unlike their father, who was trained in a craft-like manner, Owen and Nelson received a mix of craft-style instruction from their parents and grandparents and bureaucratic-style training through college. This blend of experiences is evident in their management style, especially when compared with Wayne, who, along with Gail, is the most popular Bauer among employees. Wayne consistently worked side-by-side with his employees, sought and provided advice, and sent employees (instead of his sons) to regional conferences. Several employees have told me that if Wayne remained in charge, they would "stay at the dairy forever."

Since Wayne's sons took over, however, many employees think relations have been turbulent. People who work in the milking parlor and spend the least amount of time with Nelson and Owen regularly misperceive their ages, thinking they are younger than they actually are, implying their youth is equated with inexperience and mismanagement. On several occasions, employees told me, "They are in their twenties, they are learning, but there are problems." While they have made mistakes, like paying workers by the shift instead of by the hour, they also endeavor to retain elements of their father's craft-like style. To demonstrate, I review the overall organization of work on the farm and then focus on three employees—Paloma, Mateo, and Humberto—who exemplify common variations in the connections between craft-style management and dignity at work.

Positions at the Bauer farm for non-kin employees currently include: milking; "pushing" (moving groups of cows into and out of the milking parlors and barns); maternity; medical; feeding and feed science (program development, feed maintenance and delivery); mechanics and equipment maintenance; machine operation; welding; pen and structure mainte-nance; hauling; personnel or shift management; and the development and oversight of farmworker safety. Immigrant employees at Bauer are thus not confined to milking and pushing positions, as they have been on many dairies (e.g., see Harrison and Lloyd 2013). Although the system for pro-motion is fluid rather than fixed, most employees start milking cows, then push, and finally pursue maternity, medical, and/or mechanics, depend-ing on their interests and the Bauers' needs. The most turnover occurs in milking positions. That has been a source of concern for the Bauers.

The Bauer farm has grown steadily, meaning that opportunities for promotion have been growing. Promotions come with raises,[7] though there have been delays, as in Paloma's case, which she complained about and eventually had remedied. Employees sometimes move back and forth between positions, and employees with the most experience know a great deal about the work associated with each kind of position on the farm. They also have significant autonomy. Employees will often "run" to the farm in "off" hours to check on cows or equipment, and they freely invite me and my assistants to visit, even though the Bauers (like most dairy owners) have strict policies about allowing visitors to tour the farm. The confidence with which Paloma and others have invited me has, on several occasions, given me the sense that in certain ways, they feel like the farm is theirs. This is exactly what the Bauers claim they want; unfortunately, non-kin employees have yet to buy shares. Nonetheless, the more invested employees become through their craftwork over the years, the more likely they may be to seek ownership shares (see Chapter 5) (Sennett 2008).

Paloma does not currently anticipate buying shares in the Bauer farm, but she knows she has made a lasting mark on it, and she is proud of her work. Paloma plans to keep working on the Bauer farm until she eventu-ally retires with her husband, Xavier. One day she said to me, "If [Xavier] and I return to Mexico, they are *really* going to miss me [*laughing*]." She elaborated:

I've always said to my boss, "if I am doing anything poorly, you tell me. I'm not going to get mad." . . . And he says, "no, it's all good, I need two of you!" So the truth is, they are happy with the work we accomplish . . . I am leaving my mark. From the month of October until this month [January], I have not lost a single calf. And that is a kind of satisfaction that one can take with her. Sometimes my co-workers say to me, "why do you work so much?" I tell them that I can't sit still, I feel good doing my work.

Paloma regularly expresses pride in her work.[8] "I take care of them [all of the calves and most of the heifers], I give them penicillin, everything they need—treating a hoof, a navel, because you have to crack it [the navel], practically operate on it—everything having to do with the calves is my work, and now he [Owen] says 'all of this is possible [healthy calves and no deaths] because of you, [Paloma]!' And I feel good, you know?" Paloma has a craft mentality—her work is more than a job. She goes above and beyond organizational requirements to do it well and she takes pride in it. She is also recognized for her work, both on the farm and in the community. The Bauers have regularly honored her at public events.

While Wayne consistently fostered the kind of workplace dignity that Paloma demonstrates, the younger Bauers' more bureaucratic managerial practices somewhat circumscribe Paloma's experiences, as she herself notes. Paloma contrasts her own employee dignity with a lack thereof among some of her newer co-workers, and she blames the latter on recently implemented, poor work organization. In one conversation, she told me that during one of her annual ten-day paid summer vacations, many calves died. By contrast, when she is on the farm, and especially when she works double shifts (because cows do not go into labor "on schedule," she said, explaining her double shifts), "there are no deaths." I asked why and she said some employees feed calves "colostrum that is too hot and it burns the calves' stomachs. They get diarrhea, malnutrition, and die." Owen, she says, couldn't figure out what was going wrong while she was on vacation. Paloma says that some of her co-workers "notice a problem but their shift is over and they want to go home." Paloma, by contrast, will stay late and clean all of the hoses, equipment, and "the floor where they bring the big machinery in and out." Clean spaces, she says, are healthier for the cows. "When cows are sick, it takes me three times as long to feed and care for them. When they're well, I can do it in an hour, so [my co-workers] are losing time."

Paloma wants everyone to work this well, and she complains when new hires "slack off." Paloma says that Owen hasn't installed any video cameras outside of the parlors where some "people just wander around, not doing any work. And Owen doesn't notice." I asked if people quit at the end of their shifts (without resolving any problems that arose when they "just wandered around during their shift, not doing any work") because they don't get paid overtime, which several workers mentioned, and she said, "Yes. I get paid well, but not as well as I hoped. I hoped that when I started taking on more responsibility, they would pay me more." Paloma then launched into a story about an incident earlier in the afternoon—Owen brought in two veterinarians and another "outside expert" to talk with workers about cow health.

> Everything they told us, we already knew. The real problem is that [Owen] breaks his own rules. If the rule is to check on the calves at 6:30, and then he says that it can happen later, it doesn't happen. He doesn't need to be harsh or demanding, just specific about what the rules are and that he expects people to follow them. If people do what he has already asked, it will go better.

She says that Owen has improved as a manager, but he still makes mistakes. "Then he brings in expensive outside people when he doesn't need to. It's a waste. I should run the meetings." I asked Paloma if Owen takes her advice for improving performance, and she said, "Yes, and mostly he just says, 'what would I do without you?!'" "Yeah," she tells me, laughing, "imagine how much they save on vet bills alone having me around!"

Paloma's exhortation for rule enforcement could either be read as a call for more rigid organization, which could diminish employee dignity, or as a means for developing a "repertoire of procedures" that promotes craftwork by enabling workers to more easily complete some tasks while finding better ways to accomplish other, more complex ones (Sennett 2008). For the latter, a clearer system of training and oversight at Bauer could enhance employee dignity while fostering tighter bonds between workers and with the animals. In contrast, as I explain below, PVD managers opted for more rigid work organization, which creates transparency but also interferes with employee dignity.

When Owen first took over for his father, employees complained that he was authoritarian—demanding degrees of cleanliness and precision that no one else ever had, and in a harsh manner that shocked and discouraged many workers. This is contrary to Rubin and Brody's (2011) concepts of "relational and operational competency," in which managers set reasonable expectations and assist employees in attaining them.[9] Fortunately, several employees felt comfortable enough to confront Owen about his attitude and practices, and they were able to convince him to change. This reflects a degree of rapport and mutual respect that had developed in previous years when Wayne still managed the farm, and which gave long-term employees the confidence to speak up, in a sociably craft-like manner. This restored relational and operational competency. Ignacio, Iris, Tomás, Augustín, Mateo, and Paloma told me they had spoken to Owen, and, they felt, Owen had listened. Paloma described in detail an instance in which she complained to Owen. As she described it, Paloma turned a meeting in which Owen had planned to review her performance into one in which she reviewed *his* performance:

> During the meeting, I said to him, "You want to run things here, but I need to tell you something." I told him that he didn't know how to manage people, and I asked him if he wanted to be a good manager. He said, "yes, [Paloma], I want to be a good manager." He told me that! "I want to become the best manager I can be." So I said, "*change.*" I told him that I had been a manager in my previous work . . . I told him, "when people are talking to you, *listen.*" I said, "because if I come to you and tell you to please come examine a calf carefully because she's going through such and such, just say "okay" and do it. If you don't take me seriously you are going to miss what's happening. If I have to repeat the same thing to you again a little while later, you're going to say, 'you already told me,' but I have to say to you, 'yeah but you didn't examine her!'" Lots of things like this. "You tell me to go

check on someone, but I already told you she wasn't doing her work well and you never said anything to her, but you are demanding more from people who do their jobs well. That is bad. Do you see? Leave the people who are doing their jobs well in peace . . ." I told him all of that directly. And we went on talking like this for like three hours! He told me he wanted to be a good manager. And you know, the other day, . . . my husband [who also works at the dairy] was sick and I was vacillating about what to do and talking [with Owen] about all of the work I had to do, and he said, "don't worry about it, don't worry. We will help you with [Xavier], arm in arm, we'll be by your side. We're going to help you with the doctor, pay all the bills." Thank God! So things have changed a lot. They have really changed. All of the managers have changed for the better. All for the better.

By encouraging "frank speech," "sharp mutual exchanges," and listening, the younger Bauers are gradually developing more of Wayne's relational and operational competency, both of which are crucial for crafting dignity (Sennet 2008; Rubin and Brody 2011).

Mateo, who has been at Bauer for about twenty years, also exhibits the value of "sharp mutual exchanges" and how these reflect his sense of personal ownership and pride in his work (Sennet 2008). Mateo vaccinates and monitors cows' health, and he serves as the farm's safety officer. Mateo is particular about his work. He gets frustrated with co-workers who "rush their diagnoses of the cows," and often, he argues, get them wrong. For example, one co-worker recently thought a cow had pneumonia, but he thought she had indigestion. They both entered their respective notes into the computer and had to decide how to treat her. If the heifer failed to improve because they misdiagnosed and mistreated her, it would hurt Mateo because he cares greatly for the animals. If she failed to improve, they would have to try to sell her with medicine in her system, which would cost the farm because "they cannot slaughter cows with medicine." Sick cows are unable to produce healthy milk, and they are expensive to maintain, so dairy farmers sell them through auction or slaughterhouses that will only buy unmedicated cows.

Mateo, who has a quiet demeanor, says he often argues with his co-worker and Owen to make the case for his diagnoses. Together, the three of them formulate hypotheses they then test. This process helps them develop their skills in observing symptoms, making diagnoses, and successfully treating cows. Rather than just speeding through a task and making costly (and painful) mistakes, Mateo and his colleagues build knowledge together. This increases efficiency and makes the work more interesting and rewarding. Mateo and his co-workers express sympathy for the cows. They take heart in their well-being. Mateo thus gets upset with the few employees who "feel no sense of ownership, so they treat their work just as a job, but it involves animals, not inanimate objects. You can't be rough with them because they get hurt." This demonstrates Mateo's craftwork and employee dignity. As with Paloma, it is much more than a job to him.

By allowing workers to express and pursue their interests, the Bauers have established positive relationships with several immigrant employees who have greatly honed their skills, benefiting the farm. For example, Humberto took a job maintaining and repairing large equipment on the farm. After many years working at Bauer, each time I saw Humberto, I asked him about his day at work. He often burst into a huge smile, telling me about a tractor he repaired, a fuel pump he replaced on a four-wheeler, a part he is waiting for, or a diagnosis of a skid-loader problem that was particularly difficult. "I love my job, it's my *passion*!" he said one day. Another day, Humberto came to ESL class and asked me what a "stud" is. I asked where he had heard the term. He told me that Nelson had called him a "stud" because he fixed some equipment and "saved them a ton of money." He seemed really proud. Whenever I visited Humberto and his family at home in Dairy City, I always saw tools in the living room or by the front door. When I asked Humberto about them, he said he likes to think through difficult repairs and research new tools that would enable him and his co-workers to accomplish more in the shop. On at least one occasion of which I am aware, Humberto talked the Bauers into buying an expensive piece of equipment. After Humberto got the equipment, he sent the Bauers videos of himself using it to quickly change enormous tractor tires. The Bauers showered him, via text, with dancing emojis and enthusiastic verbal praise. Humberto had whipped out his phone to show me the whole sequence of interactions and smiled as I studied the screen.

A problem at Bauer is that while employees enjoy a fair degree of autonomy and perform a broad range of tasks (reducing boredom and repetitive stress), they have no clear paths for promotion, other than seniority, which all three dairies reward with rising wages (Edwards 1979). At Bauer, opportunities to perform different tasks materialize when people put themselves forward, like Humberto has, or when Owen perceives that workers are "enthusiastic and ready." Such "readiness," to borrow Owen's term, depends on workers training one another, and their appearing enthusiastic to Owen requires being observed by him. If employees work night shifts, when Owen is away, or if they quietly but nonetheless expertly perform their work, they may go unnoticed. When I raised these points with Owen, he agreed and told me that he and Nelson had been discussing how to make evaluations, and thus promotions, more systematic and "objective." He currently keeps few written records of job performance. The only records he regularly keeps are forms that he asks employees to sign pledging that they will not hurt the animals—he takes those pledges very seriously. But work performance is recorded "subjectively," he says, and workers receive occasional oral feedback during the day. Owen will also comment on the extent to which workers perform the tasks in their job descriptions in their first few weeks on the job.

Owen gives new hires a folder containing information in Spanish about compensation, farm/work safety, farm rules, and job descriptions. Owen acquired the template from a farm in Wisconsin and modified it. New employees are trained for up to six days, and then they ask co-workers and managers for additional training and help, which is common in craft-like settings. This provides more experienced employees opportunities to share their craft, and it saves the Bauers a lot of money—they don't have to hire people specifically to train new employees. In addition, several employees have indicated that the Bauers share their craft and training, with positive results for them and the animals, who they clearly care about. Although elements of bureaucracy have crept into Owen and Nelson's otherwise craft-like labor organizing, on balance, the craft style still dominates on the Bauer farm. This diverges from the initial PVD experience and is the opposite of what former employees told me about the Hoffman farm. At

PVD, bureaucratic management dominates, but elements of craftwork have recently begun to arise, largely in response to problems that bureaucracy created for employees and production.

Pleasant Valley Dairy (PVD): Bureaucracy

Some managers, like those at PVD, prefer bureaucratic modes of organizing work, which are designed to induce employee consent and guarantee minimum levels of work effort through a system of rules (Stinchcombe 1959). Bureaucratic organization typically involves maximizing monetary profit through the "rational allocation of rewards and power [usually achievement based]," constant employee surveillance, a rigid "division of labor, hierarchy of offices, set of general rules that guide activities," and "the differentiation of work roles from family life" (Hodson 2001, 22–27; Stinchcombe 1959; Crowley and Hodson 2014).[10] As dairy farms grow and industrialize, and farmers accustomed to working with kin suddenly manage employees who are strangers (at least initially), adopting bureaucratic management may seem logical. As Crowley and Hodson (2014, 92) find, however, these practices may cause "long-term impediments to organizational success, including loss of potential for human capital development, promotion of individualistic orientations that encourage workers to pass on rather than solve problems." Such "efforts to improve the bottom line might undermine not only the work experience but also the organizational functioning and success," and thus profit (Crowley and Hodson 2014, 92; Crowley 2016). Extreme forms of impersonal relations on the Hoffman farm created these kinds of problems.

PVD employees have clearly defined tasks and responsibilities, and scheduling is transparent—based on seniority. However, for a long time immigrant employees typically only milked or moved cows. Unlike Bauer employees, they rarely inseminated cows, delivered calves, vaccinated heifers, or maintained or repaired equipment. More recently, white managers have promoted immigrant employees to supervise other employees, and they are training a few people for other positions, but for years, and in Peter's (the lead manager's) words, "milkers milk and pullers pull." The managers, mostly all white, including one South African immigrant who formerly worked at Hoffman, serve as lead personnel, herd, and dairy managers (see also Harrison and Lloyd 2013). Immigrant employees provide most of the manual labor, much as they once did at Hoffman, as I explain below; however, whereas the Hoffmans hired immigrant employees temporarily, at PVD and Bauer, managers hire immigrant employees with the hope that they will stay *permanently*. To encourage permanence, PVD managers focus on providing a variety of financial benefits (see Chapter 1), including production-based bonus pay, which they refer to as the "employee incentive fund," to encourage employees to work as a team. When employees meet the production goals that the board of directors set each year, they receive cash bonuses. Bonuses are allocated per hours worked. Conversely, when problems arise, bonus pay for all employees declines, regardless of who is at fault, including when managers are at fault.

While PVD jobs are largely ethnically segregated, Peter promoted Ramiro to shift manager several years ago. Unfortunately, many employees mistrusted Ramiro and preferred to speak directly with Peter. Each time my research assistants and I visited the dairy, several employees asked us to interpret for them. They were worried that Ramiro had misrepresented them to Peter, jeopardizing their employment or preferred work schedules. On one occasion, Víctor told Peter how much he appreciates and likes his job, and then he expressed concern about Ramiro having more authority. He explained that Ramiro "gets into people's business at work and makes us do things his way or tries to get us into trouble." Víctor's comment suggests that he has his own way of doing things, resents being ordered around (especially by someone he doesn't respect), and feels that Peter will recognize that workers have a variety of valid ways to perform their work. Subsequent interviews and observations revealed that workers develop their own methods for best accomplishing tasks and meeting production goals, but only within their (fairly) tightly circumscribed positions. Xiomara, for example, has set a cleaning schedule and protocol for the pumps, which she guards carefully. When a new employee was recently hired to work on her shift, she anxiously asked me to confirm with Peter that she is still in charge of cleaning the pumps, and Peter responded, "Yes, please tell [Xiomara] that whatever she is doing, she is doing it perfectly." Companies in which "rigid organization—or where isolation, claims of superiority," and "badges of distinction" emerge (Sennett 2008, 245; 31) typically substitute craftwork with "received authority," which truncates employee experience, information exchange, critique, and dignity at work. PVD has struggled with this for years.

Ramiro left PVD to spend time in Mexico, and Peter promoted Beto and Ofelia to take his place. Three other employees told me that they are much happier now. They feel that Beto and Ofelia listen to them, respond well, and go above and beyond to make sure that everything runs smoothly. This not only makes work on a day-to-day basis more comfortable but also increases everyone's chances of getting year-end bonuses.

When I asked workers how they feel about their job at PVD, they overwhelmingly answered, "It's okay."[11] When they spoke with PVD managers, however, they consistently began by saying how much they appreciate and like their jobs. Roberta, when she asked me to interpret for her one day, leaned over and whispered that she couldn't sleep the night before because she was so nervous about telling Peter that she needed more time with her children, who were struggling, because she was "terrified" he would think she didn't appreciate her job and wouldn't let her come back full-time. Peter said he would temporarily reduce her hours and assured her that he knew what a good worker she is and that her full-time position and preferred schedule would be waiting for her when she wanted to come back full-time (he kept his word). She was visibly relieved. Roberta and several other employees have been deferential toward Peter in meetings. Peter spoke encouragingly with them, but several employees were tentative with him. Months later, at one ESL class, Beto and Ofelia told a new Bauer employee that Peter "will do anything for his employees." They gave an example of him going out and buying new tires for a woman who was having trouble finding the time and a good deal. My sense was that they were trying to recruit the woman to PVD.

It is clear that a "community of fate" (Stinchcombe 2005, 251; Plankey-Videla 2012) has emerged at PVD, in which everyone's well-being—in terms of status, salary, and job security—is interconnected. Even Peter's fate is linked with worker performance, because the success of the farm depends on it (and board members constantly evaluate him). However, the extent to which this community of fate is rooted in dignity at work is circumscribed, as Peter himself has seemed to notice over time. PVD's reliance on bureaucratic management created "fear, uncertainty, and tenuous relationships, thereby discouraging proactive effort and mutual support" (Crowley and Hodson 2014, 92). For example, after reading a long list of "dos and don'ts" to employees at a staff meeting—including pleas to avoid hitting metal gates with canes (used to guide cows), and warning that additional cameras with audio-recording capabilities would be installed around the dairy (employees caught with cell phones while working would be given one warning, and if they violated the policy again, they'd be kicked out of the employee incentive fund for one year)—Peter told workers that "we are family, and we have to work together." Several employees averted their gazes, and when Peter asked if anyone had questions, four employees quickly raised their hands and started accusing co-workers of using their cell phones and sitting around in the break room "doing nothing." Another set of questions ensued about whether pullers had to help milkers with their work, and whether pullers who helped milkers had to help *all* of the milkers or just the people they prefer. Bureaucratic procedures are intended to clarify task regimens, but as Crowley and Hodson (2014) predict, at PVD they instead seem to induce "tenuousness in employee relations," as well as bureaucratic rigidity where some craft-like flexibility is needed. The fact that employees had been confined to one job on the farm, rather than getting to work at a variety of tasks, may exacerbate this. It creates boredom while diminishing the sense that people are building careers at the farm.

In the absence of craft-like relations, employees often become demoralized and "grow physically angry in the presence of those whom they must nonetheless obey" (Sennett 2008, 54). In this kind of environment, "authority" may trump rationality, suppressing the vitality and growth of the enterprise (Sennett 2008, 30–31, 102). PVD employees who are resentful of one another, arguing over who has to help whom and with what, are much less likely to share insider knowledge (Crowley and Hodson 2014; Crowley 2016). They often strategize to help promote their friends, putting disfavored co-workers at a disadvantage. If they need more hours, a day off, or help with a task, they often circumvent managerial mechanisms for placing requests. Furthermore, whereas managers would normally negotiate schedule changes based on impersonal criteria, workers who dislike but need their jobs make personal arrangements. Such competition between employees and with managers undermines "implied norms of mutual obligation (i.e., respect for workers' rights and maintenance of production viability)" (Crowley and Hodson 2014, 94).

Although PVD's incentive fund is meant to encourage employee cooperation, it has, according to several workers, at best allowed them to "tolerate each other." Peter maintains that the fund enables "you as an employee [to] do things above and beyond and receive payment," but while employees (like Paloma at Bauer) like being paid more for doing more, the incentive fund itself is inadequate for promoting dignity at work (Crowley 2016). In a recent conversation about structural changes in the US economy, Peter admitted that immigrant employees at PVD are "stuck in milking and pulling jobs." I suggested teaching employees more about the veterinary, engineering, and personnel jobs on the farm, as well as mentoring and promoting them. He said he is looking into it, and several employees have expressed interest. It would be a powerful complement to the efforts Peter makes to assist employees in obtaining mortgages and loans. It would help employees to build careers and employee dignity at the farm.

In the years since my conversations with Peter about creating more career-like trajectories for immigrant employees, he has promoted several people to managerial positions, though of the lower/middle range. He has also begun training several employees to operate the farm's management software. I supplied Peter with a few used laptop computers that he gave to employees. Peter loaded the software onto the computers, taught interested employees how to use it, and then let them practice at their leisure. Once they can show Peter that they are comfortable with the program, he lines them up for promotions. I have also noticed that Peter has gradually become even closer with his employees, taking an ever-greater interest in their lives, families, and work. Although he always cared about and enjoyed spending time with his employees, Peter often lamented that he wasn't seeing them often enough because he stayed in his office most of the time and never interacted with people working the night shifts. He has since made an effort to spend more time outside his office, and he has begun learning Spanish. It has made a significant difference for his relationships with his employees. They tell me that he comes to the dairy and happily greets them in Spanish, which makes everyone feel good (he apparently belts out greetings earnestly and enthusiastically, which tickles people). To the extent that Peter is working alongside his employees, soliciting their advice and communicating more regularly (and directly) with them, he is taking a more craft-like approach. As people get to try new tasks, and depend on one another to do them well, they may develop a greater sense of community in the process. He has recently been more successful in establishing relational and operational competency and honoring employees' desires for work-life balance, and several people have told me they are now happier in their jobs than they were before. Peter hired more part-time workers to fill in for full-time employees who want time off, and he does the scheduling with employees' input. If managers like Peter can create more operational competency at work, improving communication and cooperation between employees, they will craft even more dignity at work (Rubin and Brody 2011; Bolton 2007).

The Hoffman Farm: Lean Flexibility

For many years, the Hoffmans relied on temporary employees to help them care for their herd. Based on what former personnel and other people familiar with the farm told me, most immigrant employees worked six ten-hour shifts per week, for under a year at a time. Their responsibilities were typically limited to milking cows and moving them in and out of the parlor, though some workers performed fence maintenance and cleaned cow bunks as well. Former employees said they generally liked the opportunity to earn money quickly (see also Schwartzman 2013) while having little time to spend it (they had savings goals), but the intensity of the work took a toll on them. When they became ill or needed a break, there was no mechanism to call in sick or swap shifts. They had to skip work. The Hoffmans struggled to cover shifts. Rather than improving their managerial practices, the owners reduced milking from three times a day to twice a day, and milk production declined. A dairy expert familiar with all three farms told me the Hoffman cows were producing around 16 percent less milk than the Bauer and PVD cows.

As the farm struggled, Hans Hoffman reportedly fretted over the decision about whether to adopt robots. A manager at another dairy offered to manage work for Hans, but Hans declined. He decided to replace workers with robots. After doing so, Hans commented publicly that now that he wasn't telling workers what to do, he had more time to train his children to run the farm. Hans's comment suggested management by "fiat" rather than cooperation (Sennett 2008). As Sennett (2008) argues, workers are often demoralized by commands from managers who don't take the time to share their skills. Had Hans taken time to help employees develop their own mastery and autonomy, employees might have been better able to commit to the work. Former employees told us they did not feel cared for, and that work was often disorganized. This undermined dignity and atomized workers. Atomization of workers through impersonal management (Crowley 2016; Crowley and Hodson 2014) not only undermines productivity, but it also makes settling in remote rural communities with few services unappealing and difficult.

Hans told an industry expert that milk production on his farm has increased since he replaced workers with robots and that he has "very low labor costs" (he still hires people to repair fences and service the robots). Some industry experts, however, are skeptical. They say that producing milk with robots is more expensive than doing so with a stable, skilled workforce. "The lowest-cost milking parlor systems equate to 25 cents to $1 per hundredweight in milking costs, compared to $2 to $3 per hundredweight with robots" (Mark Brown qtd. in Perkowski 2015). Some scholars find that robots are best suited to small rather than large farms like the Hoffman dairy (Rotz et al. 2003). The sheer expense of robots may be an obstacle to rapid growth. One robot costs approximately $200,000 and milks and feeds about seventy-two cows (Shulte and Tranel n.d.; Rotz et al. 2003; Perkowski 2015). Cows with "imperfect teat and udder conformation" are "unsuitable" for robots (Jacobs and Siegford 2012, 1583). The arms of the robots cannot reach or connect with all cows' teats, so cows whose teats and udders don't align with the robots must be removed.

Several scholars studying dairy farmers' use of robots in Europe, Australia, and other parts of the United States have found that robots are so expensive that cows must be extremely productive to compensate for their cost, especially on large farms that require multiple robots (Holloway, Bear, and Wilkinson 2014, 1350; Driessen and Heutinck 2015; Rotz et al. 2003). Cows may be unable or unwilling to "cooperate" with robots' demand for efficiency or productivity (Holloway et al. 2014, 1350; Driessen and Heutinck 2015; Rotz et al. 2003). However, cows typically adapt to robots within a couple of weeks, becoming calmer and more productive over time (Jacobs and Siegford 2012). Some agricultural extension agents in Kansas predict that a growing number of farmers, even those with very large herds, will soon adopt robots for milking and feeding cows, leaving more complex work than milking, feeding, and pushing open to employees (the Bauers are currently experimenting with this). They argue that managers who anticipate such changes early and begin training employees for the remaining technical, veterinary, mechanical, and human resources jobs will be in the best position to expand their operations. The Bauers and PVD managers are very well-positioned.

The Hoffmans' initial steps in implementing robots after laying off most of their employees reveal the organizational changes that automating labor entails. Upon adopting the robots, the Hoffmans told a reporter that cows like getting to decide when to be milked. He said the cows are happier and less stressed. Holloway et al. (2014) studied the sales and implementation of automatic milking machines (robots) in the UK and recorded similar observations among farmers there. Holloway et al. (2014) argue that such claims are rooted in the notion that herds are hierarchical and, by allowing cows to be milked individually rather than in groups, the robots interrupt intra-herd bullying. Individual cows are perceived as being more relaxed, happy, and healthy. However, "the implicit suggestion is that the cow might be expected to care for herself or to foster the productivity of her own body life in pursuit of the higher yields of milk." (Holloway et al. 2014, 1350; Driessen and Heutinck 2015; Rotz et al. 2003). This "liberatory discourse" conceals the ways in which cows continue to be highly controlled while downplaying the importance of other essential tasks (Halloway et al. 2014). Cows cannot vaccinate themselves, provide their own veterinary care, create or maintain safe and sanitary conditions, or calm their own anxieties. Robots only feed and milk cows, leaving much of their care undone. Holloway et al. (2014, 135) find that while robots create the illusion of freedom for cows, new kinds of "micro-management" are produced by the mass of data robots generate. Farmers receive data on 140 different measures for each cow, every minute of the day, and they use it to optimize their feeding and milking. Farmers can construct barns to encourage certain cows to eat and be milked more often while discouraging others (Halloway et al. 2014). The data may also suggest making changes to feed, sleep, breeding, and the like, actually leading to *more* human intervention in a cow's life (Halloway et al. 2014). Cows that fail to meet production quotas can be "corralled, fetched, tricked, or culled," and they may be labeled as "bad" or "lazy" for failing to comply with expectations that they, too, want to produce as much milk as possible for farmers (Holloway et al. 2014, 139, 138; Driessen and Heutinck 2015). Only cows who conform to expectations are actually "left alone" (though they are still monitored, bred, housed, and confined). "Far from simply granting animals their freedom, then, cows are re-enclosed by a set of power relations and corporeal and behavioural interventions associated with this particular technology" (Holloway et al. 2014, 139).

Some scholars also worry about the effect of machines on craftwork more generally (e.g., Zuboff 1998; Sennet 2008). According to Sennett (2008, 99), machines can help humans to overcome limits, and thus to innovate, *if* technology "enable[s] human judgment and coordination to come to the fore." Under these circumstances, machines can serve to "propose new possibilities, rather than to command workers" (Sennett 2008, 103). The robot that feeds and milks cows frees up the Hoffman family to focus on breeding, business development, and cow nutrition. The extent to which the robot encourages human judgment and coordination, however, may be variable. The Hoffman family may be able to spend more time making decisions about genetics, breeding, and marketing, but they may do so with less coordination than if they had a more hands-on approach with their cows and more contact with other craftspeople with direct knowledge. The robot generates ample and detailed data about the cows, but it also changes the nature of work. Hoffman kin will likely specialize more in computer software and technology, nutritional and behavioral sciences, and genetics and animal husbandry. They may also rely on a different set of outside experts to maintain and repair the robots, unless they learn to do so themselves. At Bauer, long-term employees will move into a variety of positions as robots are incorporated to aid rather than replace them.

Managerial Practices in Comparative Perspective

The nexus of managerial and employee dignity on the Bauer farm—and increasingly PVD—contrasts with broader economic trends in which more is expected of workers who have less stable employment (Hodson 1999, 2001; Crowley 2016; Kalleberg 2011). In the broader economy, rather than developing insider knowledge among employees to increase efficiency, quality, and employee pride, many employers "relate to workers as atomized individuals," firing them when they "fail to achieve" (Crowley and Hodson 2014, 92; Crowley 2016). They implement "strict task regimens," electronic surveillance, and temporary work arrangements that generate fear and alienation among workers, who are then more likely to "pass on versus solve problems" (Crowley and Hodson 2014; Sennett 2008). This frequently occurs in companies with "rigid organization," in which managers substitute employee participation with "supervisory fiat," limiting employees' hands-on training and communication, and suppressing employees' ability and "drive to do better" (Sennett 2008, 50, 102, 241, 243, 245; Crowley and Hodson 2014). These patterns were evident in what former employees described on the Hoffman farm. The result was employee attrition and declining productivity. Though mixed, and though managers at PVD clearly care for employees, evidence of these broader trends was also visible at PVD. PVD managers, however, gradually learned to incorporate more craft-style managerial practices to retain employees.

Manager-employee relations on the Bauer farm demonstrate how sociable forms of craft-style management and dignity at work largely foster the accumulation and communication of insider knowledge, camaraderie, and pride in work. It also equips and motivates employees to prevail in the face of multiple adversities. Though there were periods of poor administration at Bauer, overall craft-style management prepared employees to confront those lapses and encouraged managers to listen. The impact of variable degrees of craft-style management can be seen in different sets of responses to problems on the two farms. When problems arise at PVD, it is typically white managers who respond. At Bauer, managers and immigrant employees alike attend to unexpected problems, often cooperating. As a case in point, for over a year PVD managers have struggled with employees regarding cows who regularly get lost on their way to or from the parlor, while Bauer employees fret over cow-sorting mix-ups and will often double-check that whoever takes the next shift encounters properly grouped heifers. Bauer employees call or text one another to check whether cows are properly sorted. Mixing cows—those that have been milked or treated with those that haven't—can have serious consequences, and employees at Bauer know this and try to avoid it. Employees care about the cows, and they wish to avoid creating more work for themselves and their co-workers by mixing them up. When cooperation breaks down, cows that need to be milked may get skipped, while those that have been milked may get over-milked, or sick cows may get milked, thus contaminating the milk supply. Since producers receive premiums from cooperatives based on volume and quality of milk, such mistakes cost farms. When dignity at work is cultivated, such mistakes are less likely because employees work together to avoid them, making their jobs safer and a bit less onerous (see also Sennett 2008, 245).

Conclusion

Producing ever-greater volumes of healthy milk requires stable care for large herds on highly mechanized farms. Dairy farm managers have great incentives to create dignity at work to induce high-quality, highly efficient production at the lowest possible cost under often volatile conditions (Crowley 2016; Stinchcombe 1959). Managers who provide on-the-job training, clear avenues for promotion, and grant workers autonomy and opportunities to participate in decision-making enhance employee dignity and tenure (Crowley 2016; Hodson 1999, 2001; Crowley and Hodson 2014; Sennet 2008). The relationships that develop when there is dignity at work further encourage employees to share "insider knowledge" (Crowley and Hodson 2014), saving farm owners money on outside experts while providing immigrant employees with informal social networks that provide critical resources otherwise unavailable to them in remote rural communities. Such employee dignity may in turn promote permanent settlement among immigrant employees and their families, strong social ties between newly arrived immigrants and long-term residents in rural communities, and population growth capable of supporting additional business expansion. These processes are crucial for rural community development, which I examine in the next chapter.

4

Just about everyone in Dairy City knows Humberto. With a
shock of gray hair and a smile that lights up his whole face,
Humberto often enters rooms saying, "heeeeey!," stretch-
ing his arms out as if greeting long-lost friends. Humberto
relishes bringing people together. He frequently invites his
bosses, the Bauers, to his house. He likes to host dinner parties. He also likes to invite people to parties that the Bauers
host. At one Bauer holiday party, Gail Bauer joked to me
that she and her husband "don't know half the people here!"
Laughing, she told me that Humberto "invites practically
everyone he meets" (he had, in fact, invited me and my husband). Last year, Humberto made a guest appearance as the
chef at a restaurant the Bauers used to own but recently sold
to a family from Mexico. Humberto packed the restaurant.
Reflecting on the experience afterward, he told me, "I think
more people know me than I know!" He was elated. The
Bauers were also elated. They asked Humberto if he would
consider a one-evening-per-week chef gig, in addition to
his work as mechanic on the Bauer farm, and he agreed.
The local newspaper picked up the story. For weeks, people
from surrounding communities came for Humberto's cook-
ing, until he decided to give it up in favor of more time with
his family.

   In this chapter, I explore how on-farm relationships have
affected off-farm relationships. This relates to a central concern for crafting dignity. Social links forged through dignity

at work are important for building community beyond the farms. As Le Guin (1974) and others have argued, working together meaningfully enables people to develop trust networks, which help people to access resources and engage in meaningful activities beyond the workplace (Sennet 2008; Hodson 1999; Manglos-Weber 2018). Trust "sometimes connects larger numbers of people who are carrying on some weighty, high-risk, long-term collective enterprise . . . [Members] can typically call on each other for aid on the simple basis of shared membership" (Tilly 2010, 271 in Manglos-Weber 2018, 23). This is especially true when mutual risk is involved, as is the case for independent dairy farmers and people relocating from abroad to remote rural communities in the United States.

Whereas people have largely been able to build networks via the Bauer farm and Pleasant Valley Dairy (PVD), former Hoffman employees say they were unable to do so on the Hoffman farm. For them, the Hoffmans failed to create dignity at work, shrinking the circle of shared membership, sources of aid, and productivity. Contrasting his experiences at PVD with knowledge of the Bauer and Hoffman farms, Ramiro said:

> My boss [at PVD], he does value what [people] do, that is [Peter] [at PVD], and [Bauer]. I do see that they [the PVD manager and the Bauers] appreciate the workers. Although there are others that are not like that. [Hoffman] looks at his people as if they were animals. He installed robots because he didn't want people there. He ran everyone off. My cousin worked there. I brought him [my cousin] from Arizona. My cousin was a hard worker, very responsible. But when [Hoffman] put in robots, he fired everyone. I talked to my boss [at PVD] and I told him if I could give him [my cousin] a job or tell [Hoffman] to keep him [my cousin] because he [Hoffman] would need someone. [Hoffman] said, "I don't need anyone, what with the robots." And I told my boss [at PVD] that this man is ... ignorant because he thinks that robots are going to do all his work. After three months he [Hoffman] was going backwards. The robot is not going to do everything for you. Robots are computers, but robots are not going to clean your pens, they are not going to take care of sick cows, all that. He [Hoffman] now has like two

or three workers. He lost a good worker [my cousin] . . . He [Hoffman] never did anything for them [employees]. It's as if they [the Hoffmans] don't value it [their employees]. On Christmas, they [the Hoffmans] don't even make them [employees] a grilled hamburger. Here with us [at PVD] . . . they make you your meal. They give you a bonus. They care about you to keep you happy.

Ramiro highlights the importance of managers showing appreciation for what employees do and caring enough to keep them happy. The absence of sociable forms of craft-style management and dignity at work on the Hoffman farm impeded the development of social networks that are key to household and community growth.

Isolation from social networks that convey information and provide resources is a key cause of poverty and instability, particularly with the decline of social services since the late 1990s (Small 2006; Hondagneu-Sotelo 2007, 13). Social networks may play an even more significant role in regulating access to resources in remote rural communities with limited services and highly circumscribed networks. Acknowledging the deleterious effects of social isolation and mistrust between people who recently arrived and long-time residents, Owen Bauer said, "We [the dairy owners] have to make things happen, we can't just sit around and talk." Peter, Owen's counterpart at PVD, said, "I want people to think about being here forever. I don't know if they feel it's possible, but I want to do all I can so they feel that way."

The Bauers and PVD managers are well-positioned to "make things happen." The Bauer family has held several consecutive mayorships, including the current one. One of the Bauers represents regional dairy farmers in the Kansas Legislature. The Bauers and the lead PVD manager, Peter, own other interconnected businesses in and around town. Peter and the Bauers serve on the city council. Bauer and PVD owner-managers are further interconnected through business dealings, as former classmates, and through holding local government office together. They also have family members serving as local health-care providers, police officers, the sheriff, EMT responders, court officials, bank managers, and school staff and administrators. Among the most important connections, the local public school principal was a classmate of the owner-managers of both farms. The school principal and the school more generally are key links in networks that grew from the farms to the broader community. School support for recent immigrant families also fed back into the farms by clinching several immigrant employees' decisions to stay in the community.

Resembling what Small (2006) refers to as "resource brokers," the Bauers and PVD owner-managers used their local ties to connect recently arrived employees to information and resources related to schools, retirement, housing, banking, material goods, and health care. Resource brokers "[possess] ties to businesses, nonprofits, and government agencies rich in resources, which then provide the neighborhood institutions' patrons with access to these resources" (Small 2006, 274). As connections are made, some organizations may become community-based organizations (CBOs). CBOs help create a growing network of interlinked institutions that help convey additional information and resources. One example: community-based daycare centers "offering parents a surprisingly wide variety of resources, including those provided by businesses, nonprofits, and government agencies" (Small 2006, 276, also cited in Manglos-Weber 2018). These other agencies may also act as CBOs (Small 2006).[1] The Dairy City case highlights interactions between social networks and institutional or organizational networks, and how these interact to affect the information and resources available to people.

The Bauer farm and PVD began building connections with other local institutions, organizations, and businesses. Networks of trust extended from the farms to these entities. The school emerged as a key CBO. In the end, a broader ecology of institutions/organizations developed in relation to immigrants, driven by interorganizational connections. This ecology provides a more positive settlement context for recent immigrants, a stronger local economy, and a more inclusive community. It also shows how people who have not recently immigrated depend on those who have. In what follows, I explore these connections, how they work in practice, and what they mean to individuals and the broader community.

"The School Is More Influential than the Church"

At the outset of rapidly increasing, renewed immigration to Dairy City in 2000, the local public school principal at the time, a lifelong Dairy City resident, said that he "trusted" the local dairy farmers were engaged in what Poppo, Zhou, and Li (2015, 1) refer to as "good faith efforts" to "grow their farms and the community." While he was unfamiliar with immigration, he said that the immigrant families who came to work on the farms and who were enrolling their children in school were trying to support both their families and the community. His trust initially stemmed from his close relationships with the Bauers and PVD managers. The principal knew the farmers well. "The guys who run the dairies were my classmates. We had a big class and we were one of the few groups that either stayed or we left and came back home. And we're still a pretty close-knit group." As immigration picked up, the principal applied for federal migrant program funding to support recently arrived students and families. "When our migrant program grant kicked in, we had a very large amount of money that we could use, and we were able to buy supplies and we were able to hire people . . . We have an afterschool program for migrant kids. We have an ESL [English as a Second Language] program. We have two full-time ESL paras [paraprofessionals] and we are fortunate that they are bilingual." Both paraprofessionals had recently immigrated from Mexico. They moved between classrooms, providing support to teachers and students. They also promoted multilingual and intercultural learning at and outside of school. In the principal's words, the migrant program is

> for the migrant students. We have our two ESL teachers and our paras go in and they work primarily with the elementary grades . . . We offer transportation home . . . And then twice a year we have their afterschool programs—we have the parents to come in and, when we first started, we might have the local owner of the store come in and, you know, "what are some things we can provide for you?" Different speakers come in. Right now, we just sent a letter out with the

[Presidential] Administration's new rules [about the Deferred Action for Child Arrivals, or DACA program]. We didn't send it out as a school thing, but we . . . want to have a meeting and [Veronica's] going to talk to them [migrant families] about, "hey, be careful who you're talking to . . . there are people out there that are going to take advantage of you, they're going to charge you money to do something that you might not even have to pay for." So, she wants to visit with all of them [migrant families] and say, "hey, you know, be patient, let's see what's happening." So that's another way we open up our [school] buildings for them [to have community meetings and workshops].

It was at one of these meetings, with an attorney from Kansas City who provided a "know your rights" workshop in 2015, that I first met most local families who had recently come from abroad to Dairy City. Veronica, the school's main paraprofessional, had posted flyers in Spanish all over town announcing the event. The meeting was held on a Saturday at the school. It lasted all day, with people coming to hear a talk and then having individual consultations with the attorney. People brought food and drinks into the library and talked to each other while they waited for their consultations with the attorney. Children ran up and down the school hallways, shrieking gleefully as Veronica called to them to "do something productive!" (i.e., get their homework done). Since I began doing research in Dairy City, three successive principals have hosted special workshops for immigrant families, including meetings with officials from the Mexican consulate in Kansas City, a bilingual recruiter from a nearby university, bilingual health-care providers, local 4-H clubs interested in getting to work with "migrant families," and the sheriff's office, which sponsors traffic-safety workshops with recently arrived families. The school secretary also recruited several recently immigrated families to a nearby Catholic church, where the children participate in youth programs.

People who immigrated from Mexico and Central America have since stayed in Dairy City for so long that the school is now ineligible for the migrant program. "Our Hispanic or migrant population grows but the amount of enrollment money or the amount of assistance we get has actually decreased," the principal told us. He explained that the proportion of permanently settled immigrant families outweighs recently arrived immigrant families, which decreases federal funding for the school. As a result, the school was only able to retain one paraprofessional. Nonetheless, years of support through the migrant program helped families settle in. It also helped to structure relationships in the classroom and beyond, which created ongoing avenues for more recent arrivals to make connections with other local residents and a variety of organizations and agencies. The program enabled the paraprofessionals to translate school documents into Spanish, encouraged recently arrived families to attend school events (which occur every night except Wednesday and Saturday), and helped teachers learn how to help new immigrant students. These practices have had lasting effects. Several recently immigrated parents told me that the Dairy City school itself was what convinced them to stay. For example, Gabriel, who is originally from Guatemala and moved to Dairy City from Denver to get away from gangs after his car was stolen right in front of his apartment, said that his son hated school in Denver. "He was miserable! He never wanted to go and got really upset and depressed. But here in [Dairy City], he loves the school. So that was it. We knew we were going to stay." Several parents told me similar stories about children "hating" school in other towns in both the US and abroad but loving it in Dairy City.

As a result of twenty-first-century immigration, the school, which was on the brink of closing following massive attrition and depopulation during the previous two decades, has found itself on solid ground. According to the principal,

> You know when all the other schools here in Kansas have been seeing their enrollment decline, ours has progressively grown over the last three or four years ... Without that input, that student enrollment, we easily could be talking about the future of [Dairy City] schools, because if you take [away enrollment stemming from immigration], ...that's probably not a very good number if you want to keep your building open. So, and they [immigrant students and their families] are very involved ... They have been on homecoming royalty. They play on our athletic teams, they are part of our cheer squad, they are

always willing to donate, they always bring stuff for classroom events or fundraisers. Actually, the joke is when we have classroom parties and stuff, that's the classroom you want to go to because that's where you get the tamales. Kids are lined up and so are the staff!

When I asked if there were any events that immigrant families did not attend or participate in, the principal said,

They tend to shy away when we, like, if we are doing a classroom fund-raiser, maybe working in the concession stands or something like that. And I understand, I think that's probably a little bit of the language barrier. I think they feel like they might not be able to do that. They are always willing to donate, they always bring stuff for fundraisers and class events . . . We have a . . . boosters club and they don't join that, but they come to all the scrimmages and stuff and they're part of it. They attend their kid's games and they're always here.

The language barrier the principal mentioned may be one reason the paraprofessional volunteered to host ESL classes for adults. She told me that children have access to language resources at school, but adults don't. She wanted to ensure adults had access as well.

According to the longtime pastor of the local Lutheran church, which historically was the heart of rural communities in the area, the school has become the most important "unifying agency" in town. In his words,

The school now is the controlling agent within the community, or at least it seems to me and some of my other brothers. It seems the school makes a lot of things happen. There are not many nights that families spend at home anymore because of things happening at the school— basketball tonight, tomorrow a speech or tournament, then junior high night . . . I think the school is more influential [than the church].

Several school staff actively broker resources, and they also create opportunities for parents and students to network and create their own ties throughout the community.

Speaking with students who immigrated to Dairy City, matriculated to the school, and were about to graduate from high school (several of them having started their education in Dairy City in kindergarten), it becomes evident that, despite some significant missteps early on, like holding some students from the first cohort back a grade when they were struggling to understand English (which the administration soon stopped doing),[2] the school facilitates bonding between recently arrived and longtime students. To highlight how this works, I'll provide a lengthy excerpt from interviews Jill, my research assistant, conducted with Rafael and Enrique:

ENRIQUE: [When I first arrived, in sixth grade] I didn't speak any English. Um, a little bit, maybe a couple of colors and stuff like that, but not really . . . But it was made easier by the people who helped me. [Daniel, a classmate] was there to help me the first three months. He got me through it and I got used to the things, like how it worked and stuff, and lining up at 9:15 and stuff like that, . . . going out to the gym. I got used to all of that. So, he really did help me by telling me . . . And [Veronica] [the paraprofessional]. She helps a lot of kids who don't understand. She helped me for the first year and then she thought I was smart enough to figure it out . . . And [Daniel] would not translate everything for me 'cause that would force me to learn, 'cause if everything is translated for you, you're not going to learn anything. But [Veronica] would take me out like an hour and I would have all my assignments with me. So, she would go through them and tell me what to do. And, actually, there was this thing we did after school where we would stay an hour and actually work on the assignments if you didn't speak English . . . It wasn't a requirement, but she pretty much made you. Yeah, she [Veronica] would get mad at you if you didn't come [*laughs*].

JILL: How do you feel about the fact that the school had a resource like that for you?

Enrique: It was great, 'cause I could actually do sports and stuff like that during sixth grade. Like, I did track and basketball during that year.

JILL: What do you see the benefits being of playing sports in middle school?

ENRIQUE: Knowing people, that was a big one. Definitely. I met a lot of people from other schools, too.

RAFAEL: Yeah, and like [when I was coming to Dairy City from Mexico] I was just imagining going to school here and stuff. Like I was really excited, 'cause my cousin used to go here so I was like, oh yeah, "we're going to be in the same class and . . ." so . . . I was really excited. I don't know . . . Yeah, I just walked in and seeing everyone, and I didn't know what to do. Like, everyone talking, and me not understanding anything. And, just like, I didn't do anything 'cause I couldn't speak, I just . . . Like, [Carly] she was in my class at the time. I used to tell her everything, like if I needed to go to the bathroom like, "Oh can you tell her [the teacher] I need to go to the bathroom?" I thought it was going to be really hard. But it just happened, like you just learn without even knowing and stuff. I think sports really did, like, help.

JILL: . . . How would you describe [Dairy City] to someone who just arrived [from abroad]?

RAFAEL: It's a small town, everyone's friendly, everyone knows each other. And yeah, everyone's friendly, everyone will help you, not only me, 'cause everyone's going to try to help and everyone's going to be your friend and stuff. So I feel comfortable, I like living in a small town, 'cause everyone's, like, friendly, everyone knows each other.

JILL: How would you tell them it's different than Mexico?

RAFAEL: It's different 'cause there's no violence here almost. Like Mexico is like . . . I used to get like in fights and stuff. And here there's like nothing. Everyone, yeah, there's no need to, 'cause no one's bothering you and stuff.

JILL: What's it like growing up in [Dairy City]?

RAFAEL: Uh, growing up in [Dairy City], I like it 'cause you know everyone so you're really confident about everything, going to work, asking questions to people and stuff, and just learning a new language too. And that's it, I think just knowing everything in the small town, not having to worry about big ol' cities and going everywhere.

On the other hand, many young people in Dairy City complain about how "boring" it can be to live in a small, remote rural community. Fortunately, and again thanks to the school, there are activities most nights of the week, and sports practice during the summer.[3] Many youth also work part-time on local farms or at the grocery store, gas station convenience store, or the restaurant.[4] They get together to play video games like *Fortnite* or a kid-friendly version of *The Sims*, or just hang out. Kids who live in town (the majority) usually walk to one another's houses, while those who live in neighboring communities drive (if they're old enough) or hitch rides from their parents or older siblings. This differs from other communities where few people have cars, family members are often separated across long distances, and immigrant employees live in trailers on farms they rarely leave (Gray 2014; Keller 2019; Sexsmith 2019).

When we asked the principal what impact the dairies have had on the school, he said,

> From an enrollment standpoint, tremendous, because of the Hispanic population, which is the majority of those workers, we have currently about twenty percent of our student body is Hispanic. Our first Hispanic student showed up I'd say probably fifteen, sixteen years ago [in 1999] and he currently, him and his wife and child live here in [Dairy City]. He works, he is on our EMT staff. So he was able to go and do all of the studies and that is not an easy test to pass. And he also works, he is a geriatric aide. He works at the local nursing home. Real nice guy. Once he came and then we saw a couple more families show up and a couple more families show up so we had to adjust our whole teaching and looking at different things . . . And we have learned, I have learned as much as they probably have, as, well, you know, about the Hispanic culture, and in fact now at this point when a family moves in and they can't find housing here [because the housing market is saturated] the first people they call is us . . . So that's kind of nice.

He also referred to the parents of the first Hispanic student to graduate from the school: "They are still here and they still actually work part-time at the dairy. Yep, they were the first Hispanic family to buy a house here in Dairy City." In fact, three generations of that family are currently living in Dairy City, which is becoming increasingly common (in some cases, there are four generations).

When I asked the principal if there is as much immigration to surrounding communities as there is to Dairy City, he said, "Not to brag, but they [neighboring communities] know we have programs in place and they, so they [new immigrants] kind of, you know, they come here." The school has become a CBO, and immigrant families have saved the school. The principal, in turn, contends the school is the largest employer in town. Had the school closed in the early 2000s, dozens of teachers and administrators would have lost their jobs. If faculty and staff had also sold their homes and moved away, they would have taken business with them.

In serving as a CBO, the school has also helped recruit employees for the dairies. Families like the school and the programs it offers so much that it influences their decisions to stay and work. As the principal said, "Without the workforce, they [the dairies] can't do what they need to do, and then that's a business that's going to go belly up pretty quick. Yeah, they have the workforce, you know, when they're working 24/7, they've got to have workers that are willing to go out there and do that." Increasingly, people are also going to work for other local businesses and, in some cases, buying and starting their own small businesses.

"A Very Small Town, but Very Calm"

The city council, in collaboration with one of the school's paraprofessionals, has worked to build trust between recent immigrants and local law enforcement officers. According to Veronica,

> Most of the police here are pretty nice, but when you have a new policeman, I mean, they [newly hired officers] do stop them [newly arrived immigrants] . . . So you know, normally the sheriff knows me, so he calls me and I go there. You know they [people who have just arrived] have the kids in the car and everything, well, they don't have car seats, they just got here. So, you know he [the sheriff] always laughs 'cause he says, "I don't even know why I call you anymore" [he doesn't need Veronica's help anymore]. Then they [the sheriff's office] provide booster seats and car seats for the kids, for free! So, he [the sheriff] is great because once a year we bring them [the sheriff and his officers] here [to the school] to, you know, teach them how to get the

seat belts, I mean the car seats in the cars and everything and then they bring new car seats for all of them [newly arrived immigrants]. So it's awesome because, you know, so and then they get to meet everybody.

Many people arrived in the United States mistrusting the police. News about hostility toward immigrants and racial profiling against Black and Latinx/e people generates fear. "Even legal permanent residents and naturalized citizens saw their rights and privileges diminish, as campaigns against illegal immigration metastasized into more generalized xenophobic attacks on all immigrants, including those here with legal authorization" (Hondagneu Sotelo 2007, 13). Xenophobic attacks have exacerbated police profiling across the US (Armenta 2018). Lalo told us he thought it would be even worse in Dairy City because it is such a small town in a politically conservative state, where political conservatism typically equates with anti-immigrant sentiment: "I thought that I wouldn't ever even be able to drive here. Because you hear lots of stories in Mexico and I thought that I wouldn't even be able to leave the house . . . I thought it would be a town of persecution. And when I arrived, I realized that this is a very small town, but very calm."[5] When Zaira (my research assistant) asked Lalo what he meant by "calm," he said,

To this day, [the police] have never bothered me or my family, for any reason. We have not had a single problem. Even when my wife had an accident and we were beside ourselves, the sheriff came and knocked on my door at eleven at night, and believe me, I thought something bad was going to happen. And they behaved really well! They were really nice. My wife had crashed in a wind and dust storm. And I have to tell you that the police here, in [Dairy City], I have a lot of respect for them. Because they won't bother you. They have never stopped me to ask me about my [immigration] status. Yes, I want to make this very clear, it's important for me to say because we live peacefully here. They respect the community. Maybe you've heard that in other places it isn't like this, and maybe elsewhere I've encountered a racist or bad cop, but . . . I don't know how to explain this . . . My daughter, [Marta], had a drug [education/prevention] class over the course of two or three weeks, and we felt like a united community. It doesn't matter what your traits are, it doesn't matter if your ancestry is from Mexico or from wherever, that doesn't matter. That class was for everyone.

When Antonio accidentally backed into a car at the local store and the police came, he said the police just asked him and his wife, "'Where do you work? Who are you? Where do you live?' I told him where we live [in Dairy City], I gave him our names and information about where we work [the Bauer farm] and nothing more happened. So, the police in this zone have been really respectful in their manner toward people. Toward me."

Provine, Varsanyi, Lewis, and Decker (2016) found that greater local diversity, positive narratives about immigration, liberal-leaning political framing of immigration, and a city council or county governing board that favors immigration result in more positive police comportment toward immigrants (Provine et al. 2016). Dairy City is rediversifying. Dairy owners and managers, as well as the school principal, all serve on the city council. They favor immigration and promote positive narratives about it, but there is little to no liberal political framing of immigration among white residents. In fact, many of Dairy City's white residents seem to oppose immigration nationally but support it locally. They seem to think of recent immigration to Dairy City with a kind of exceptionalism. This may have initially been rooted in their knowledge of and trust in the local dairy farmers. White people in town often said things like, "They [the farm owners who recruited people from abroad] are very above board, very above board." But trust among people who did not recently immigrate has likely also grown since then through social interaction. Dairy City is a small town. People live, work, and go to school in close proximity.

In contrast to politically conservative white residents, many recent immigrants are politically liberal. This contrast became evident on several occasions, particularly during the 2016 presidential election. For example, at a joint Bauer/PVD staff meeting (held occasionally when cows are culled from the two farms at the same time to save on transportation costs), people started debating Donald Trump's and Hillary Clinton's immigration policies. At the end of the meeting, I casually asked one of the white Bauer managers if he knew which presidential candidate employees favored, and he said, "[Humberto] said he would vote for Trump." I asked, "Really? [Humberto] said that?" He said, "Yes, [Humberto] said so himself." The manager told me this with apparent seriousness, so when I saw Humberto later that afternoon, I asked him about it. Humberto laughed out loud, nearly guffawing. He said, "I was being totally sarcastic! I can't believe he believed me!"

Paloma later told me that she got into a debate with a white truck driver (who was collecting milk) when she directly challenged Trump's candidacy. The debate wound up being about Pelosi's House leadership, but Paloma said the truck driver had seemed surprised she opposed Trump. While most people seemed comfortable debating politics, Hank, a white dairy employee, said he feels intimidated speaking about US politics with his Latinx/e colleagues. Hank told us he did "not like to talk about politics at work," but his co-workers would ask him who he was voting for. Hank told his co-workers he did not like either candidate, but that he was going to vote for Trump. And then, he said, his co-workers immediately started "shunning" him. After that happened a couple of times, Hank said, he would just tell people he was not voting at all so he would not have "issues" with his co-workers. Hank said that he did not want to "appear racist or a bad guy," and he was worried his colleagues would perceive him as such.

An Emergency Medical Technician (EMT) told us a story suggesting that Dairy City has a pro-immigration reputation in the surrounding areas. The officer said he was dispatched to drive an ambulance for a woman who was in labor and whose car had broken down on a remote stretch of highway in the middle of the night. When he and his colleague reached her, she told them she was from Mexico and was living in a city about an hour away from Dairy City. She was trying to get to Dairy City or the adjacent town because she wanted to give birth there—she had heard that the nearby hospital gave out free car seats to natal patients. This was likely a misplaced reference to the sheriff's office providing booster and car seats to recently arrived immigrant families. The EMT said he had to "turn on the sirens and floor it to the closest hospital," which wasn't the one the woman wanted, because he didn't think she would make it much farther before giving birth. He was struck by the woman's efforts to get to the Dairy City area.

Miscommunication and Conflict

While people tended to emphasize good communication between those who had recently immigrated from abroad and those who hadn't, there were public misunderstandings and conflicts. The first misunderstanding I observed related to confusion about parking rules at a public building, and the second related to attendance at formal religious services. Regarding the latter, after members of a local congregation finally invited recent immigrant families to attend a formal service (after years of only contemplating doing so), the lead organizer expressed disappointment that "only" fifteen people had attended. When I pointed out to her that the dairies operate twenty-four hours a day, every day of the year, preventing most people from attending, and that fifteen people is a great turnout, she was startled. She visibly softened, but she had spent weeks mistrusting the immigrant community. She said, "Well, we tried, and they did nothing, so it's on them now." Such misunderstandings can affect trust in both directions—currently, most immigrant residents attend other area churches.

A more public misunderstanding in 2017 involved a few recent immigrant families overlooking a parking sign indicating that drivers should stay clear of two garage doors where Dairy City's fire trucks are kept. According to a councilperson, the superintendent complained that "immigrants were 'flouting' public safety rules." Several people pushed back and asked the superintendent to post the signs in English and Spanish, which he did. People who had previously misunderstood the parking signage were able to keep clear of the doors. The superintendent had failed to update all signage, however, and an old and faded "handicap parking" sign that was hard to read led to more confusion at a city building. The superintendent disrupted an ESL class to rudely rebuke me for not providing instruction on the parking signs after he observed someone parked there without the required plates. I told Peter about it and he and Owen called and met with the superintendent. They told him the problem, once again, was that the signs had not been translated into Spanish, and they raised the translation issue with the city council. When I asked one family how they felt about the superintendent after he scolded me, Rosaura shrugged her shoulders and said, "He's always like that—really cranky." My research assistants and I were angry.

The councilperson who spoke with me danced around the issue, saying, "The city council . . . is 'small town USA,' but, you know, it's things like that. And we send our bills out, the city, we send them out and we translate them into Spanish so they [Spanish speakers] can get the water bills and trash bills. So, it's taken a while, but I think we are coming along, coming around, you know." When I pressed, he said, "I pointed it out several times that, you know, we aren't exactly the original settlers of the area. We got to think about this a little, but you know, we are talking about guys that are in their seventies and eighties [who complained] and they just, I don't know if it is distrust or what. I think that it's probably their upbringing and background." I understood the councilperson to be saying that the people he mentioned held racist attitudes against people who recently immigrated. Disputes over the signage language were the most blatant instance of racism that my research assistants and I observed, and the city council and other local institutions have a significant role to play in eliminating it.

Language

Many local descendants of German immigrants reference their own polyglot history when discussing recent immigration. Several people mentioned their children study second or third languages in college, implying that multilingualism is a good goal. Local reporters have published stories about local language classes for adults that have been offered over the years. Mauricio, however, told one reporter that some people in town give him a hard time when he is struggling to say something in English. The reporter, Julie, responded by saying that "California was Mexico one hundred years ago and many people in the United States speak Spanish." She added, "Most people around here used to speak German and Swedish, but sometimes they forget." Julie then asked a question that put everyone on the defensive. After inquiring about how long the language classes have been happening, how they're going, how many people moved from other states in the United States, how long they've been in the United

States, and how long they plan to stay in Dairy City, she asked, "Why now? Why learn English now, after so long in the United States?" Maura said, "Because there was never an opportunity!" Maura and Paloma went on to explain to Julie that in most US places where they've lived, "we were always working," and the people around them only spoke Spanish. "Here [in Dairy City] there are fewer people who speak Spanish, and more people who speak English," which gives them more opportunities to practice English, but they needed a class to help with questions, they said. Viviana nodded and added that in Mexico they had classes in English, but that was a long time ago.

People's reaction to Julie's comment seemed to reflect perceived stigmatization (Mizrachi, Drori, and Anspach 2007; Fleming, Lamont, and Welburn 2012). Their responses suggest they may have been "managing the self" by emphasizing strong work ethics and professional and educational competence (Mizrachi et al. 2007). This may have helped to protect them from a feeling of being "othered" by Julie's question. Julie reacted by telling a joke, which could be interpreted as a "marker." Markers indicate intense emotion, and possibly emotional conflict or turmoil (Pugh 2017). The joke did not go well. Julie said, "What do you call someone who speaks three languages? Trilingual! What do you call someone who speaks two languages? Bilingual! What do you call someone who speaks one language? American!" People politely chuckled, but Maura and Paloma exchanged a quick glance. Julie's version of "American" excluded many people who are American and multilingual.

Julie has since attended several parties that recent immigrant families have thrown in and around town—not with a notebook or camera in hand, but to spend time with families she is getting to know. She has developed friendships with several families. Julie is among a growing number of white residents who regularly attend religious confirmations, birthday parties, weddings, and quinceañeras hosted by recent immigrant families. The Bauers and a few of the white neighbors who live adjacent to the families hosting the event are also regulars. Peter also started attending more events, along with other local business owners and service providers, many of whom requested Spanish classes, which Zaira taught for about a year. They often asked Zaira questions about how best to greet people respectfully in Spanish, what time to arrive at events, what the best gifts to bring for different occasions are, and much more.

La Posada

The Bauers and PVD managers regularly host and attend community parties to help foster sociality. The Bauers throw an annual Christmas party, and usually public Mother's Day and Father's Day celebrations, which are very well attended. The Christmas party has become the town's official Posada, a celebration of the Holy Family gaining entrance to the inn where Jesus was born, which is celebrated across the Americas. This Posada proved to be an important opportunity for building communication and trust.

The first year that a Posada happened in Dairy City was 2015. It took place in a huge machine shop on the Bauer farm (picture a warehouse emptied of combines, forklifts, huge tractors, and other heavy machinery). Paloma was in charge, though she had lots of help from her family and friends. She distributed candles to dozens of people, as well as leaflets with lyrics in English and Spanish. Paloma then gathered more than a dozen mostly Spanish-speaking revelers and instructed them to stand outside. She asked everyone else to gather inside near the door and made sure everyone's candles were lit. Paloma then directed the people outside to begin singing. They sang in Spanish, asking for admittance to the inn, represented by the interior of the dairy machine shop. Those of us inside sang back, in Spanish, denying entry. Nelson Bauer, who at first didn't understand what was happening, read the translated lyrics and began shifting his weight from one foot to the other. He tried his best to sing the words in Spanish. Finally, people acting as the innkeepers sang an invitation for the Holy Family to enter, and the door opened. Eleven-year-old Maricela, dressed as Mary and carrying an infant doll, stepped into the room. She was followed by dozens of singers, most of them crying as they entered.

The emotion and symbolism of the event were stunning. After the song was finished, people greeted each other tearfully. Many of the white people in attendance asked Latinx/e people more about the Posada. Some people hugged. The many layers of symbolism are not to be overlooked. On one level, it is a tradition that many immigrant families in Dairy City have taken part in throughout their lifetimes. For people who immigrated to Dairy City after several other stays in US cities where they faced hostility, the Posada may also symbolize their own journeys in a narrative parallel: In Dairy City, they are finally (mostly) welcomed. In many cases, it is the message that, as Paloma often says, "we are all God's children, and equal in His eyes," even as we, unfortunately, treat each other differently, she said. For people who have been treated poorly in and around Dairy City, as well as elsewhere, this kind of event is a powerful opportunity for them to publicly express values of inclusion to people in the broader community, particularly those with the most power and greatest tendency to exclude. It is an opportunity to sing out their desire for inclusion and equal treatment—and to be heard. That this ceremony is conducted in the machine shop on a dairy farm gives the event both a sacred and secular feel, and that intersection is important. The sacred helps people to publicly address secular discrimination. Monolingual English speakers' willingness to sing in Spanish, and to learn Spanish, means a lot to the people who make extra efforts to learn English during very busy and exhausting days working on dairy farms.

As monolingual English speakers attempt to learn Spanish, making themselves vulnerable by venturing to say phrases and listening closely, Spanish speakers feel more empowered and seen. There is a kind of communion that happens. Language is key to self-expression and identity, and many people do not feel fully known when they lack opportunities to express themselves in the language that they feel most comfortable using. However, rather than only expecting Spanish speakers to learn English, and criticizing them when they struggle, the efforts of English speakers to learn—and the earnestness and eagerness with which several people did so—signal respect for the collaboration that is required in building a multicultural community. It also lays the groundwork for compassion, as more people acknowledge how difficult it is to learn a new language, especially as an adult, and, by extension, how difficult that can make life for people who are not initially fluent.

The following year, Zaira attended the Bauer holiday party with me. It included a Secret Santa exchange and Posada. In reflecting on the event, Zaira mentioned feeling "honestly very happy with the Posada" (a tradition she shares). She observed,

All the employees and employers got in a huge circle and one by one revealed their gifts to one another. It was so sweet to see very personal gifts and hear "ooooh and awwws." For me, the best part was when a non-English speaker gave a gift to a non-Spanish speaker, or vice versa. It was so sweet to see them hugging and thanking in their own languages, then having everyone translating what they said as a collective. They gave gifts to everyone and their families. Even I got a bag of candy with the [Bauer] Family Dairy logo. Another fun part was when everyone participated in the Posada singing. Everyone got a little votive candle and a script—in Spanish. A small group stayed outside the doors, acting as the Holy Family, and the majority of us stayed inside, acting as the inn keepers. We sang back and forth for about fifteen minutes and to my surprise, the white English speakers actually tried to at least hum, if not pronounce, the lyrics. But they all looked happy to participate, nonetheless. For the most part, [Paloma] and [her sister] [Gloria] ran the show with [Humberto] introducing us to everyone and talking to everyone.

Something that personally made me very happy was seeing all the owners' kids playing with the workers' kids. Or seeing some of the Hispanic teenagers taking their white dates. Seeing interracial friendships and relationships is something very dear to my heart, as I see what good it does to not only the community and work relations, but to individuals.

Zaira went on to note that several people had mentioned not interacting much with their neighbors on a daily basis, and she reflected on whether the festivities were an exception or just a way for people to carve out time to get together. With this in mind, we asked people about their relationships with their neighbors.

Neighbors and Trust

Most recent immigrant families we interviewed either knew and liked their white neighbors or described them as minding their own business. Everyone lived in integrated neighborhoods. Humberto told us,

My neighbor on the right-hand side is the only one I don't know anything about. He's a bit strange . . . He's a nice enough guy, about my age. He lives alone. I have no idea where he works. On the left-hand side, my neighbor is a super hard worker. He's an American. He's really nice and I get along really well with him—as a neighbor, though, nothing more. And across from me, we just call out to one another, "good morning, good evening!" And the other one in front, his father owns [a farm] . . . And the last one in front of me is a firefighter.

Several people from the Hispanic community told me that they get along better with their "Americano" neighbors than their "Hispano" neighbors, and that their Americano neighbors have offered them help.[6] Nubia told me that once she learned some greetings in English and spoke with her next-door neighbor, her neighbor came rushing over to apologize for not having said "hello" previously and welcomed her to the neighborhood with food and an invitation to visit. Within the next week, Nubia's car broke down and her neighbor drove her to work every day until Nubia's car was repaired. Ramiro said that when he told his neighbors that he and his wife and children were moving back to Mexico because his parents are aging and he is afraid of not seeing them again,

> People [who are white] around town told me, "We heard you were leaving, don't leave!" I told them I was going to see my family and they said, "*We're* your family! We've watched your children grow up!" Even the owners of [a local business] told me, "We don't want you or any of your family to leave." If I didn't have family in Mexico, I wouldn't leave. But to see my mother's smile once more, that's also important.

Paloma said,

> So the Americans, they are all really good people. They are really nice. Really, my husband hurt himself—first a knee, then he hurt his arm. It's the Americans who offer to help! They've asked me, "Do you need help covering bills? Do you need any help covering rent?" And my answer is always, "Thank God, I have work." Right?! So, I answer, "No, thank you very much. Where I work [the Bauer dairy], they don't charge me rent and I can pay my bills," because thank God, I have work. And since I have arrived here [in Dairy City], I have always had work. And by God, I am not going to take money from another person

who probably needs it much more than I do. So I tell them, "Thank you, I've got it covered."

When we asked people about their comments of getting along better with "American" neighbors than Hispanic neighbors, Mateo explained, "It's been great living with American neighbors. They have really adapted to Hispanics. I don't see any problems with the Americans. I see problems more with Hispanics. It's more common, just because sometimes there's envy. Yeah, sometimes there's envy, that's the only thing." Diminished trust within immigrant networks could indicate that recent immigrants have fewer resources to distribute through these networks, or that they fear too much will be asked of them. White people who are more privileged may seem more "trustworthy" because they have more security, stability, and resources to draw on (Manglos-Weber 2018), though Paloma's comment about "not taking money from another person who probably needs it much more than she does" suggests that she sees her white neighbor as having fewer financial resources. It may also be the case that Hispanic residents expect less from their white neighbors than they do from their Hispanic neighbors and are more casual and relational with "the Americans." Hispanic residents may also better acknowledge offers of help from white neighbors because they expect it less from them than from Hispanic neighbors. They may be more surprised and attentive when "Americans" are forthcoming.

Health, Communications, and Financial Organizations

The Bauers and PVD managers have tried to connect recent immigrant employees with local financial, communications, and health-care providers—the only ones around for miles. One local bank, which had long done business with the dairy farms, decided to open accounts for recent immigrants fairly quickly, and gained most of their business as a result. Humberto told me he received a loan from this bank for a 2007 car with an account he'd had open for less than a year because he works for the Bauers: "I told the bank I work for the Bauers and they asked me how much money I wanted!" Humberto was pleased, and he referred other people to the bank, assuring them that they would be treated equally well. Another bank, however, was slow to open accounts, and the telecommunications company has yet to do so, leaving most immigrant households without internet (Dairy City is so remote that there is no competition—the local rural provider is the only game in town). The internet provider told several immigrant families that without established credit in the United States, they were ineligible for accounts. When I asked an executive about the company's rejection of recent immigrant customers, he listened to me and then told me that he realized the company is "leaving a lot of money on the table." He seemed less interested in serving immigrant families than opening accounts. He began acknowledging that new clients could simply pre-pay for services and forego credit checks. Immigrant families, however, do not trust the provider, and they overwhelmingly rely on cellular data (or school Wi-Fi) for their online needs. It will take a lot of work on the part of the telecommunications company to build trust and attract new clients.

Health care is another critical resource that the Bauer and PVD farms have brokered, ultimately by purchasing insurance for their full-time employees. Employees at Bauer and PVD now have health, dental, and vision insurance. Unfortunately, the Bauers and PVD managers began providing insurance only after many years of employees having to shoulder most of the financial burden. In US agriculture, farmers are not required to provide health care to farmworkers, and few do (Gray 2014; Rosenbaum and Shin 2007).[7] Prior to insuring their employees, the Bauer and PVD farms sometimes paid out of pocket for treatment for long-term employees who were injured at work; alternatively, workers would use vouchers from federal programs and doctors would be reimbursed at low Medicaid rates, which doctors disliked. This resulted in poor medical treatment. For example, when Xavier broke his arm on the Bauer farm, the doctor missed the break. Xavier remained in terrible pain, so he consulted another doctor, who took an X-ray and immediately found the break, as well as several torn or stretched tendons. Xavier decided to have surgery to repair the tendons, though he was upset with the doctors and had little faith in his care. Furthermore, while the Bauers paid for treatment and surgery, they didn't pay Xavier wages while he was off work, though they did try to find light office work for him when he was well enough to be in the office. Xavier was frustrated, and he made it known. Mateo was also frustrated, saying that he once broke several ribs and suffered a torn meniscus, and he had to pay for treatment. The Bauers have since added disability insurance to help employees who are unable to work while injured, and Xavier says he feels more confident in the follow-up care he receives for his injuries.

Between 2015 and 2019, I spent time with two regional health-care providers, Sandra and Nancy, who at the time each had about fifteen years of experience working in and around Dairy City. When Sandra first started working in the county where Dairy City is located, she said she encountered a lot of hostility by health-care providers toward people who had recently immigrated. Now, she says, "people [doctors, nurses, and hospital administrators] have really come around." I asked if it was new people or the same people at the rural clinics and hospital who had come around. She said, "The same people except for one hospital administrator who has since retired." The hospital's new administrative director is "much better." One of the primary care doctors who, she said, was "grumpy with patients who don't speak English—taking the attitude that 'if they make an appointment, they should be able to communicate,'" and who refused to hire an interpreter, has also retired. His replacement hired an interpreter, and several people in Dairy City have told me that they like the new doctor.[8]

Since 2015, I have been called on twice to interpret for English-speaking doctors and Spanish-speaking patients from Dairy City. On the two occasions I was called in, the hospital either hadn't hired an interpreter or the interpreter was busy. Ironically, the hospital lacking the interpreter was in a nearby city of about 50,000 residents, while the latter (where the interpreter was busy) was the local hospital near Dairy City, which serves a significantly smaller population. In both cases, the doctors and nurses spent well over an hour providing information, answering questions, seeking further information, and making sure the families had everything they needed (and understood their medical instructions).

Several relatives of PVD board members and managers, as well as one current Bauer employee (he has two jobs), work for the local hospital.

They have helped rectify early miscommunications that arose between some recent immigrants and doctors. A nurse who is married to a PVD manager told me that she had had to explain to doctors who got angry about people missing appointments that people sometimes can't get off work (the dairies have since remedied this). Sandra said that she has also talked with recent immigrants about preventative care, which local doctors want immigrant families to have. But doctors don't understand, Sandra said, that many families "don't want to miss work only to be told that everything is fine—'breathe in, breathe out, all well, go home.'" This may change with insurance coverage and better managerial practices at PVD and Bauer.

Relationships between recent immigrants and local doctors have improved since the dairies bought insurance for their employees. Doctors can negotiate higher reimbursement rates from private insurers than they could with federal vouchers. With private insurance, many immigrant employees say they are now more willing to seek treatment when they feel they need it, or as a preventative, rather than having to wait for an emergency. This improves people's health. It reduces emergency fees and creates a stable clientele for local doctors who might otherwise be unable to sustain a local practice due to prior depopulation. Doctors receive higher rates of compensation from private insurance. They may be more willing to offer a greater range of services, and people who are well-insured are more likely to seek them. This dynamic creates new opportunities for additional interorganizational growth and community health.

Conclusion

The more that farmers include immigrant employees in social ties extending from farms to local organizations, the more mutually reinforcing those ties become. This strengthens farms and area institutions, and, ultimately, the local community as a whole. This happens largely through a process of farmers referring employees to local organizations, organizations responding to new immigrant clientele by expanding their services, and, in many cases, making additional referrals to other organizations. In the process, interorganizational ties develop, supporting a broader ecology of growth viz-à-vis immigrants.

Two important mechanisms in the organizational ecology of growth are trust networks and community-based organizations (CBOs) (Small 2006; Manglos-Weber 2018). Trust networks reinforce referrals. CBOs provide links between privately and publicly funded institutions that are information and resource rich (Small 2006). CBOs have become increasingly important since the 1990s because of the decline of social services (Small 2006). In Dairy City, the school may be the single most important CBO, acting like the hub of a wheel through which resources and opportunities are channeled. The dairies were instrumental in initiating the school as a CBO, demonstrating how social networks/ties interact with organizational growth. Farmers knew the principal, who trusted the farmers and built a support system for people who had just arrived. Paraprofessionals became direct and indirect advocates, creating new ties and facilitating people meeting each other and building connections through school events. The school directly conveyed resources and facilitated network building to offer more opportunities, resources, and information. The better the school, the more attractive the community, which also helps the farms—and other employers—to recruit people (see also Gibson and Gray 2019).

CBOs that are deeply rooted in the community, reinforced by trust networks, and connected with other service providers make referrals to yet more service providers. The better the reputation of the CBOs, the more weight their referrals carry (Small 2006). When people consume more services, they create new opportunities for business, service, and organizational growth. The more services are available to people, the better able they are to build wealth, maintain good health, access education, and create meaningful lives in their communities. In the next chapter, I explore prospects for additional growth moving forward.

5

In 2018, a Spanish-speaking recruiter from a four-year university came to Dairy City to talk with parents and students about opportunities to attend college. Clad in high heels and a sharp black suit, Daniela walked to the front of the room and cheerfully greeted the dozen or so families gathering around tables. She introduced herself by telling the audience her parents immigrated to a meatpacking town in Kansas when she was a child. Daniela said that in immigrating from Mexico to the United States and taking a job in a meatpacking plant, her father had "traded a coat and tie for an apron and gloves so his kids could have a future." She tilted her head and paused for a moment. A few people leaned forward, struck by Daniela's words. Mateo raised his hand and said, "We did, too." Daniela nodded. She acknowledged how important it is for parents to "see their children have opportunities, including graduating college in the United States."

Many people in Dairy City immigrated from Mexico to provide upward mobility for their children. Several of them traded suits, honorifics, and office jobs abroad for physically taxing work on large US dairy farms. Mateo said,

> I was not used to working physical jobs. When I lived in Mexico, I worked in an office, and when I arrived here [in Dairy City], I had to work in physical jobs, and I had

to work up to ten or eleven hours daily. I learned a lot, but it was very, very difficult. I would arrive home dead tired because I just wasn't used to it. That was a radical transition in my life, doing physical work.

Hilda told us, "In Mexico, the work was mental, not physical. I was always well put together, all made-up." Mateo, Hilda, Paloma, Xavier, and many others had attained higher education or even advanced degrees. However, several people realized they were unlikely to obtain jobs in their selected fields, and/or their jobs lacked adequate pay and benefits for them to continue studying while contending with rising costs of living—especially when emergencies or other life events suddenly plunged them into debt with no means for relief in sight. People were also concerned for their children. Edberto noted,

> I was studying at the university—civil engineering. I completed three years and three semesters. But my girlfriend became pregnant, so I dropped out and went to work [for a cosmetics company]. I needed money for the birth and hospital fees. And when my son was born, I waited like forty days and, because in my country there are no companies that pay benefits or even enough for subsistence. I decided, thinking of my son, to come here. I started in Long Beach, California at the bottom, for like six months. Then I came here and started getting ahead. I built a house for my family and provided the money for my girlfriend to start two businesses.

It wasn't until he reached Dairy City that he "started getting ahead" and meeting some of his goals, despite his civil engineering training and seeking other opportunities within Mexico and other parts of the United States. Edberto worked at the Bauer dairy and later took a welding job at a small local manufacturing company.

Although surveys of immigrant dairy employees in Vermont, New York, and Wisconsin found that most people had lived in "poor rural communities" in Mexico and Guatemala and had limited access to higher education (Sexsmith 2019, 717),[1] Perez (2020) found that several people working on dairy farms in Wisconsin and Minnesota had attained advanced educations in cities abroad and moved to rural areas only after leaving low-wage jobs in cities—a kind of reverse migration. In one case, "by the time [Maria] took the job [at the dairy], [she] already had earned a law degree in Mexico and had worked once before in the United States. The law degree didn't lead to a job, and the work—low-wage jobs for a cleaning company, airplane parts factory, and car wash in North Carolina—didn't allow her to save" (Perez 2020, 8). Maria's experiences align with what several people in Dairy City experienced, though these patterns are seldom noted. Most studies find that "the work available in rural [US] labor markets typically comprises low-wage, low-skill jobs"[2] that are typically filled by "recent Hispanic immigrants" who have faced the greatest barriers to education and mobility (Lichter 2012, 16; Donato, Tolbert, Nucci, and Kawano 2007; Farmer and Moon 2009).[3] Recent variations in these patterns suggest that the forces of precarity driving people across borders and from urban to rural spaces are expanding.

Economic restructuring in Mexico and Central America is displacing people not only from poor rural areas, but also from urban industrial spaces. Intersecting violences—structural, legal, symbolic, and direct/physical (Alvarez 2019)—drive migrations across borders, as well as from US cities to rural communities. Low wages and high costs of living in US cities offer few footholds. Structural violence is violence that is "built into the structure and function of a system" and involves the "systematized reduction of life chances" through the decline of education, health care, housing, and employment opportunities (Alvarez 2019, 6–7). Symbolic violence involves the "normalization" of violence and suffering, while legal violence deprives people of rights and protections (Alvarez 2019). As poverty and inequality expand, direct violence rises along with these other types, threatening people's lives and livelihoods and driving them across borders in search of safety and security (Alvarez 2019; Menjívar and Walsh 2017). Intersecting violences affect people in both rural and urban spaces in Mexico and Central America, and they help to account for why people with a wide range of backgrounds are finding themselves on remote rural dairy farms in the United States. As Sennett (2008, 35) argued, "Job loss is no longer merely a working-class problem" in the "new economy."[4]

While the underlying collapse of stable jobs and "welfare and social protection systems" increasingly shifts "the risks and responsibility for many social insurance programs to individuals and families" (Kalleberg 2018, 3), the responsibility for redressing these problems remains with governments and employers. To this end, Dairy City farmers as employers have reached a turning point. Though the Bauers and PVD owner-managers offer stable jobs and seek to retain immigrant employees permanently by creating dignity at work, they need to do more. People who immigrated to secure their livelihoods and a future for their children are beginning to see their children attend and graduate from US colleges. Families' decisions about whether to remain in Dairy City will be affected by how integrated they are. If immigrant employees leave to follow their children as they pursue other careers, or elder employees decide to retire in Mexico or Central America, farmers will face immigrant employee turnover, as well as an increasingly hostile immigration regime. Dairy City farmers are concerned with preventing attrition, both of current employees and future generations. Rural exoduses of the 1980s and 1990s remain fresh in local memory.

In this chapter I explore farmers' prospects for building on the growth they helped generate through dignity at work. In so doing, I return to the question of why current immigrant employees relocated and what their aspirations are. I delve deeper into their stories of immigration to explore the extent to which insecure employment and uncertainty for workers is proliferating. Such insecurity and uncertainty affect people's long-term assessments of dairy work, as well as whether to stay in Dairy City, move to other parts of the US, or return to countries of origin. Second, I explore the tension between Dairy City farmers' desires to recruit the children of immigrants with parents' aspirations for their children. I consider how these tensions cohere in a refrain that is common among dairy owner-managers in Dairy City: "Imagine this is your farm." This refrain represents both possibility—pointing a way forward—as well as a core contradiction, in that the idea of immigrant employee ownership is currently only symbolic and, to that end, exploitative. Making employee farm ownership a reality may help build virtuous circles of dignity at work and community growth.

Restructuring

Like several of his friends, relatives, and colleagues, Edberto moved to Kansas from cities and states in Mexico that were hard-hit by economic restructuring in the 1990s. Companies ceased paying benefits or even a living wage—let alone enough to maintain a middle-class lifestyle and send children to school (Babb 2003; Hernández-León 2004). Edberto and many people had to move to the US and take dairy jobs, representing significant career deviations, to begin "getting ahead" and ensure robust opportunities for their children.

Edberto's and several people's misfortunes were caused by the collapse of "peripheral Fordism" and urban industrial restructuring in Mexico. Peripheral Fordism was a set of industrial labor relations that "developed and reproduced" a highly skilled industrial working class that enjoyed significant "job security and lifetime employment" (Hernández-León 2004, 430, 425). However, the system had historically been dominated by a "corporate paternalism" in which workers "ceded all effective authority to management" in exchange for "subsidized housing, health clinics, and savings and insurance schemes …, as well as vocational schools and an entire leisure and recreational infrastructure" (Hernández-León 2004, 429).

The implementation of the North American Free Trade Agreement (NAFTA) paired with aggressive privatization programs contributed to peripheral Fordism's demise and the rise of restructuring in the 1990s (Hernández-León 2004). "Because it forced many public and private companies to shut down, downsize, and modernize by adopting new technologies and methods of production, increasing unemployment in the short run and degrading the overall occupational structure of Mexico's urban-industrial centers in the long term, restructuring has entailed the uprooting of thousands of members of the formerly protected skilled and semiskilled working class…" (Hernández-León 2004, 425). At the same time, the "social welfare provisions of Mexico's post-revolutionary state" evaporated (Hernández-León 2004, 426). People lost their jobs, health care, retirement, and financial assistance with home ownership.

Many people were forced to "participate in the international labor market" (Hernández-León 2004, 425; Massey, Arango Hugo, Kouaouci, and Pellegrino 1999; De Haas, Castles, and Miller 2019).[5]

Humberto was among the people whose lives were suddenly uprooted by restructuring. "I had a good position [in Mexico]. I was in charge of 300 trucks and 5 towns, as well as a big city that served as the headquarters for the main workshop where we oversaw the other distribution centers." Like María in Perez's (2020) study, Humberto had begun studying law but began to doubt he would attain a legal career, so he switched to being a mechanic. He was hired along with engineers and made a good wage. Over the course of thirteen years, he was promoted from mechanic to shop supervisor to regional supervisor. He explained that even when his employer started laying people off, he survived two years of cuts and thought he was "safe." He and his wife, Hilda, who was working at a bank, took a large loan to buy a house for their family:

> Without knowing [that 2009 would be my last year working for the company], I took a loan to buy a house in a residential zone. It was a brand-new house. It cost nearly a million pesos. It was 750,000. I also bought a brand-new car. I never imagined that come July, I'd lose my job. So, with all those debts, and since I had already given a good amount of down payment for the car and the house, and I did not want to lose them, that was what moved me to come here. I needed to pay the bills . . . The only available jobs [in Mexico], they're all the same. You're never going to regain the position you formerly held. You have to start over at another company [from the bottom]. When the company I worked for liquidated, I tried to start my own business. A restaurant. But the rent ate me alive. It was so expensive, the rent. I had to close the business. I only lasted about three months. I knew I had to come [to the US] to work.

As Humberto noted, when people seek new positions at other companies following layoffs, they are often slotted into the most insecure and lowest-paying jobs. Hernández-León (2004, 441) found that many people in Monterrey, one of the areas hardest hit by restructuring, experienced downward occupational mobility and periods of employment instability as they probed the local labor market for jobs with pay and benefits similar to their previous ones. This process often involved stints in the service sector and in low-skill manufacturing, either as self-employed or as wage workers. Regaining access to manufacturing jobs was blocked by not only the glut of skilled operatives in the local labor market but also the labor control strategies of many Monterrey-based corporations, which discriminated against workers more than forty years old and those who had labored in so-called red-union shops . . . [6]

Humberto was nearly forty. So were several of his Dairy City colleagues. Mateo said that in Mexico, "it's really hard at that age . . . It means starting over. Starting in *maquila* jobs, or, well, if not in maquila jobs, at maquila wages. And speaking of age, that's why I decided to move to the US. It was that hard to start again [in Mexico]."[7] Whereas most immigrant dairy employees on US farms are between the ages of twenty-four and forty-four, people in Dairy City skew a bit toward the higher end of the age range. The skew may in part be due to people staying longer in Dairy City than they do in most dairying communities (Keller 2019; Sexsmith 2019; Harrison and Lloyd 2012). It may also be linked to dislocations from restructuring and the demise of peripheral Fordism in Mexico. Several people were displaced from urban industrial or administrative jobs and faced age discrimination as they sought new jobs. Age discrimination in Mexico may also influence people's decisions about whether to stay in Dairy City, as I discuss further below.

With their combined incomes from Bauer and PVD, Humberto and Hilda have paid nearly all their debts in Mexico. Unfortunately, Humberto says that the Mexican government recently raised interest rates on their home loan, adding to their costs. In the meantime, the couple's eldest daughter, Cecilia, who had been living in the home while she finished her accounting degree in Mexico, was unable to find work after two years on the job market. In 2020, she decided to follow her parents to Dairy City. Cecilia now works full-time at PVD. She recently married and has two children, both born in Dairy City. Cecilia says she plans to raise and educate her children in the United States to give them a more secure future than she thinks they can have in Mexico, based on her experiences. Cecilia's younger sister, Lilly, who has lived in Dairy City since she was about six, recently earned a four-year scholarship to a university in Kansas. Her family (her mother in particular) is elated.

Asking Humberto and Hilda how conditions in Dairy City compare with their previous middle-class, urban lifestyle in Mexico, Humberto responded by comparing his houses in Mexico and Dairy City. He said, "There isn't much difference. The house here is good, it's comfortable. In Mexico we had a two-car garage, and here we have a one-car garage. We just park our second car on the street or in the driveway and we don't miss the extra garage space much. The comfort is about the same." When we asked Hilda, she said, "What I like best about living here [in Dairy City] is that I have so much more time for family. The pay is better and the town is better, everything is so peaceful." Stable employment, relatively good pay, time with family, and a peaceful town are more attractive than the violent disruptions Humberto, Hilda, and Cecilia experienced prior to moving.

Several people who moved to Dairy City had experienced both structural and physical violence in cities in Mexico and Central America. Paloma came from a city in Mexico that was hard-hit both by restructuring and the rise of violent crime (Molzahn, Ríos, and Shirk 2012). Paloma explained,

There are many bad things in [Mexico] . . . Right now, they are starting to rob more than before. But it was in those years [early 2000s] that they began to rob me. [The last time they robbed me] in fact, where they robbed me, they had just killed a teacher, but I didn't know. They cut off her legs when they took her money. And when I was robbed, I had a lot of trouble. I had good work. I was a sales manager. But I was assaulted and I had a lot of trouble because I had to recover the [stolen] money and pay for the house and help my kids get ahead . . . That same year my husband had an operation and the next year my son had an operation, and then I had one, after they assaulted me. I had to pay all the hospital bills, which were accruing more and more interest. You won't believe it, but I owed a million pesos! It was pure chaos.

Paloma said that when she arrived in Dairy City, she got her first rural job. In Mexico, she "managed people—now I have to manage animals, so it was a drastic change. But, well, thank God, I've grown accustomed to it, and, thank God, we are getting there." Paloma's comment about the switch from managing people to managing animals is the opposite of what US dairy farmers say about expanding their operations—they struggled to go from managing animals to managing people. Paloma often advises Owen Bauer on his managerial practices, though she now specializes in calf care (she wanted to be a doctor when she was growing up, and the veterinary side of dairy work interests her). Paloma's colleague, Ana, by contrast, is a personnel manager, which is more in line with her professional work in Mexico, but she also raises calves and milks. While Ana says she likes her job at Bauer, she has less authority than Owen, as she has no ownership stake in the farm yet, though she still has leadership responsibility.

With her dairy salary, Paloma has put three of her children through college in Mexico and she is trying to build houses for each of them. She worries about their safety, though. She says she calls them every night to make sure they are in the house by 9 p.m. Even though Paloma's children are adults, violence is pervasive where they are living, so she checks in on them daily. Mateo and Ana have put, or are in the process of putting, their children through college in the US.

Restructuring in Mexico uprooted people living and working in rural areas as well. Rural dislocations have received more scholarly attention in studies of immigration to rural areas in the US. In Mexico, they entailed the dismantling of the ejido system (communal farmland) (Hernández-León 2004), and, in both Mexico and Central America, the opening of markets enabling the dumping of cheap grains and other US agricultural exports into local economies (Cornelius and Myre 1998; Madrid 2009; Equipo Maíz 2004).[8] NAFTA and the Central American Free Trade Agreement (CAFTA) accelerated these trends. In her study on immigration and dairy farming in Wisconsin, for example, Keller (2019) found that NAFTA caused overnight price drops for corn and coffee in Mexico, which imperiled small farmers in Veracruz, the same state Paloma and several of her colleagues are from, though they came from urban areas. Between 1992 and 2002, Veracruz went from being a minor "sending state" in Mexico-to-US migration to a top four sending state (Keller 2019, 55; Pérez Monterosas 2003). Underlying these patterns, violence in industrial states in Mexico has risen dramatically, "with drug-related homicides rising from an estimated 113 organized crime homicides from 2007 to 2010, to 888 such killings in 2011 alone. As a result, Veracruz moved from being the 16th most violent state in Mexico to the 6th place, in just one year." (Molzahn et al. 2012, 16).

As Lydia and Tomás explained, they moved to Dairy City from a rural town in Mexico "because many ugly things are happening there, and we didn't want our son to see all that. Also, there, one never knows if what one earns will be enough to pay the bills . . . We only made about 150 pesos a day. And for reference, a kilo of meat costs 130 pesos! It's not enough to eat. Here, with what one person earns in a single check, for one week of work, one can buy food and still have a lot left over. You don't spend everything you earn on food alone. There, you do." Physical and economic insecurity in Mexico combined to compel the family to move to the US. Though Lydia and Tomás lived in the countryside, they relied on the city, where they regularly encountered direct physical violence, for most of their needs (e.g., shopping, medical appointments). Bada and Fox (2022) find this is common, as rural communities are increasingly connected to urban economies.

Linthicum (2023) argues that the spread of gang and cartel violence in many parts of Mexico, including rural areas, is dissuading people from returning, as was their dream. By contrast, in the Kansas countryside the families say they feel safe. Lydia and Tomás's son is thriving in school, and they are able to keep saving for his future. This was a key theme for several families we spent time with over the years.

Education, Training, and Mobility

Not everyone who immigrated from abroad to Dairy City since 2000 had access to higher education. Paloma, Hilda, and Elena all told me that their fathers had discouraged them from studying further. Paloma said her father would say, "Why study just to get married?" Paloma's father was killed in a car crash when she was young. As she grew older, she worked at a pharmacy in Mexico to pay for school. However, she felt she had so many responsibilities in supporting the family that she was unable to graduate. Hilda was able to keep studying, but Elena was not. I also met two men in Dairy City who had been denied a full primary education in Mexico.

Regardless of their educational background, no one had previous experience on a dairy farm, let alone a large industrial dairy. As a result, even though many employees had attained some higher education (or more) abroad, on-the-job training at the dairies provided opportunities for some people to earn higher wages than they could have in many other occupations without pursuing additional formal education. That said, people who had already borne the costs of extended education abroad typically do not get credit for it in hiring—partly, they say, due to language barriers that favor dominant English speakers. Also, to my knowledge, no one receives degrees or certificates for the skills they acquire through on-the-job training on the dairy farms. If people had degrees or certificates in veterinary, animal, or feed sciences, they would likely receive higher wages for the advanced work they already do while having more opportunities for mobility between employers. Finally, everyone who moved to Dairy City had to undertake the costs of their relocations. On-the-job training thus facilitates some upward mobility at a lower cost than formal education, but it likely does not compensate for other costs immigrant employees bear. The benefits also depend on the degree to which existing employers reward employees for skill acquisition through raises, promotions, and interesting work.

Reflecting on her experiences of being denied access to a full education, Elena said that it was hard growing up with so many siblings because it meant that she only got to go to elementary school for three years in Mexico (resources were stretched thin between the siblings, limiting opportunities for all of them to pursue a full formal education, and compelling many of them to work from an early age). She taught herself how to read as an adult. She said that is why she limited herself to having two children, and why she brought them to the United States—to learn English and get more education than they could receive in Mexico. Frank, a white employee who has been in the US his whole life, noted that there is a man from Mexico working at the Bauer farm who "doesn't know how to read or write, but he is one of the smartest guys who works at the dairy. He can identify the cows just by looking at them, without even reading the tags. And if someone asks him where a certain cow is, he can tell them the location just by memory." The person Frank is referring to, Agustín, rapidly rose through the ranks at Bauer, first into hoof trimming from milking, and then into veterinary care and management. He has a lot of responsibility. Agustín's daughter told me one day, "Over there are the new ranches that the [Bauers] own [pointing off into the distance]. My dad got promoted to work at these ranches taking care of the cows." Her father had been promoted to a managerial position for the ranch, and he now outranks most of his colleagues.

People in Dairy City who traded professional careers in Mexico and Central America for dairy work in Kansas note that several of their colleagues lacked access to the same level of education and jobs that they received, and now, Mateo says, "those who do have some schooling belittle those who don't." This, Mateo thinks, and Paloma concurs, is because people who had little schooling in Mexico have ascended the ladder at the dairy, making on-the-job training more relevant to upward mobility in Dairy City than formal educational training, which was a marker of social status in Mexico and Central America. This is the opposite trajectory of the lead managers and older owners of the farms in Dairy City. The current generation of managers and owners accessed higher formal education that was out of reach for previous generations. For example, Wayne, one of the white farm elders, did not have the opportunity to complete a college education.

As previously mentioned, people who immigrated to work on the dairies want their children to attain advanced degrees in the United States. This has developed into a source of tension between immigrant employees and farm owners. Farm owners are concerned not only with retaining their talented labor force but also with preventing rural depopulation. The question then becomes whether work on the farms and life in the community are attractive enough to draw youth back after they graduate college. Farmers have had success recruiting young people who want to earn money for college—in one case, they recruited one of Mateo's sons to help design a milk parlor and a new ranch. Whether they will be able to recruit and retain the children of immigrants in the long run remains an open question.

Some parents also feel discouraged about the promises of education for their children. Mateo said that he has taken loans to help his two sons with college, but the loans are expensive and "doors are closing" to college graduates. His sentiments square with those of many people in the United States. According to Tough (2023, 1–2), while access to college in the United States is diminishing, in other countries, colleges are attracting growing numbers of people. Although a US college degree typically provides a 60 to 65 percent wage increase, the rising costs of college often eliminate those gains through debt (Tough 2023, 1–2). Measured as a wealth premium, instead of an income premium, the last generation to see a boost was born in the 1960s (Tough 2023, 3; Emmons, Kent, and Ricketts 2018).[9] People born after the 1980s saw the wealth premium decline, while it "disappeared altogether" for Black- and Hispanic-headed households (Tough 2023, 3). Many people in the United States report thinking that it is better to go into trades like plumbing or mechanics, which are lucrative and don't require a formal advanced degree, than to go to college and accrue debt for professions that are only modestly better paid (Tough 2023; Bureau of Labor Statistics 2023; Pew Research Center 2023). As economists point out, however, there are a limited number of jobs in plumbing or mechanics, so if people skip college and rely on such trades, they may be un- or under-employed. Further, a sudden drop in people studying for Bachelor of Arts degrees could imperil the US economy (Tough 2023), because well-paying, stable career jobs that do not require an advanced degree are scarce. The Bureau of Labor Statistics reports that people with a high school degree are most likely to wind up working as "health aides, food service workers, cooks, warehouse workers, and all of these jobs pay a median salary of less than $31,000 a year" (Tough 2023). For entering or staying in the middle class, people either need reduced college debts and/or jobs that don't require college degrees yet pay well enough to sustain a middle-class lifestyle.[10]

In writing about the resurgence of craftwork in urban areas, Ocejo (2017) finds that many people are returning to trades like microbrewing, butchering, bartending, distilling, and barbering. These tend to be lucrative, interesting, and "hip." As craftwork, they also promise dignity at work. Dairy work, by contrast, is not typically regarded as hip, though it is well-regarded in Dairy City. In general, however, dairy work is likely to be considered by immigrant employees as "honest, respectable, and necessary, but low-status, dirty, physically demanding, for people with few other work options, not jobs people would want their children to do if they want them to move up in the world, and certainly not culturally hip" (Ocejo 2017, xvii–xviii).

Mateo said that, at his age, he was discouraged by his prospects of working jobs with maquila-level wages in Mexico, so he sought a higher-wage job at the Bauer dairy. When he told a colleague in Mexico about his decision, the person said, "Don't go." Mateo said the person begged him to stay: "Here [in Mexico] you're Mister [Last Name]. Here you have your name. In the United States, you're no one. You'll be no one. You'll be just one more person. They're going to treat you badly. Don't go." Mateo smiled and said, "I didn't pay him any mind."

When Zaira asked Mateo what he thought of his decision now, he waffled. "There have been times I thought I made a mistake," he said. We asked for an example. He told us that after Owen Bauer first took over from his father, Wayne, for whom Mateo has great respect, Mateo struggled with Owen's initial managerial style, which he characterized as lacking in good communication. So, Mateo left to work in calf care on a farm in Minnesota. But Mateo's sons stayed in Kansas to finish college, and Mateo hated being separated, so he moved back. When he returned, Mateo's supervisory job was filled, and he had to take a lower-paying position at the farm. This experience made Mateo feel that his colleague in Mexico had been right. Mateo complained, and Owen promoted him to safety officer. This highlights the importance of dignity at work. While Owen was willing to correct his mistake, farm owners will need to do more if they wish to permanently retain employees and recruit the next generation.

Recruiting the Next Generation

Just as the Bauers want their children to farm with them in Dairy City, they and PVD managers also want employees' children to aspire to farm careers. Peter says he hopes that youth will find farmwork interesting, seek internships to learn every aspect of running a modern dairy farm, and then run the farm. Peter pays his employees $500 for every person they refer to the farm who stays at least a year, and some employees have begun referring their children, sixteen years and older, to seek after-school and summer work on the farms—largely to raise money for college.

While more youth are beginning to work on the farms, they have generally not expressed desires to pursue farm careers. Their motivations are more varied. Xiomara said that her eldest son had been working in a restaurant in a neighboring town, but that the restaurant didn't always have customers, and her son didn't always get paid. Peter hired her son to work at PVD on weekends and holidays during the school year and agreed to train him for positions he sought in the process. Saraí, Flor, and several others want their kids to get jobs at PVD as soon as they turn sixteen so they can start saving for college. Humberto's son, Joaquín, worked at the Bauer farm and restaurant (a family from Mexico now owns the restaurant) while he finished high school. He says it is a means to other ends. Jill asked Joaquín about his work and career aspirations (he has since completed two years of community college and transferred to a four-year university):

JILL: Did you ever think you would work there [at the dairy]?
JOAQUÍN: I knew I had to work there if I wanted to go to college or if I wanted to do something else.
JILL: Is that something your parents had told you?
JOAQUÍN: No, I just knew. I just knew because college is expensive, and you have to work for it.
JILL: So, how did you, how did you get your job? Like, who talked to you, who interviewed you?
JOAQUÍN: I mean, they're always looking for people . . .
JILL: So, you started out working night shifts milking. When did you start helping your dad in the [machine] shop [on the farm]?

JOAQUÍN: Um, after I realized that it was super hard to milk.

JILL: What did you do when the school year started?

JOAQUÍN: I just worked at the shop on Sundays.

JILL: And that's all you've done?

JOAQUÍN: That's all I did . . .

JILL: So, you don't milk anymore?

JOAQUÍN: I do milk now. I, you get paid more if you milk . . .

JILL: So, you work a lot!

JOAQUÍN: Yeah, I have enough money that I can say I am really proud of it. Like, yeah, it's not, like, a lot of money, but it's enough to get me started.

For Joaquín, working at the dairy was a means for raising money for college, not a step toward a career in dairy farming. When Jill asked Joaquín what he'd like to do for a career, he said, "I would say I have no idea, but because I'm going to be honest with you, probably nursing . . . I've always liked to help people who are hurt and stuff like that, and I like . . . [*trails off*]. I don't want to sound bad but I'm like apparently one of the better people in the school at art. But it's just not something that you can actually work on and make money at." Joaquín, like his parents, is concerned with earning a good salary.

Although the Bauers and PVD managers speak about immigrant employees and their children "learning every aspect of running a modern dairy" and then actually running it, they did not, to my knowledge, mention acquiring ownership shares. They do often ask employees to "imagine this is your dairy," which raises the specter that ownership rhetoric is used to "motivate" employees manipulatively instead of genuinely.

My Farm Is Your Farm?

At a staff meeting for PVD in 2017, Peter turned to his Spanish-speaking employees and said,

Congratulations! You have done an outstanding job this last year. You have met and exceeded most of the goals. I want to commend you on a job well done. There are a lot of working parts on a dairy. From the calving pen to getting heifers back and ready to calve, to calving a fresh heifer, milking her. Keeping colostrum that is tested good. Getting her bred back. Keeping her healthy. Getting the correct ration every day, feeding the correct feed daily. Keeping all parts of the dairy. Whether it is in the parlor equipment or a loader working properly.

Peter went on to explain that employees had been so productive that they had generated an *extra* $35,500 in profit that year, which PVD was giving back to employees via bonus checks. A few people asked about where any money had been lost—specifically if culling sick cows sooner would have generated even higher profits—and a conversation ensued about how to improve the practice moving forward. Several people were visibly excited about the bonuses, and Peter congratulated them again, but he quickly added that milk prices are dropping, and profits would likely be lower next year. Arguments about how to maintain profits ensued. At one point, Peter interrupted and said, "Imagine this is your dairy. Think to yourself, what would I do differently each day to make this the best place to work? To make my business the most profitable it can be?" As I listened, I was struck by how similar this speech was to phrases I heard Owen Bauer use on the Bauer farm. "I want you to think of this farm as your farm," or, "I often tell people to imagine this is their farm."

Peter's and Owen's statements about farm ownership raise several points of tension. As of yet, immigrant employees have not bought shares. They would need to be invited to do so. They would also need to remain locally resident to retain ownership. This would be a boon to the farms and the town, but it could have mixed results for employees (Kruse 2002). On the one hand, employees would have more say in farm operations and likely a greater share of the profits. On the other hand, they would become liable for some of the capital costs and risks of the farm. As experts, however, they would likely increase the farm's profitability and help manage risk.

The current absence of avenues toward farm ownership may lead to new waves of rural depopulation and decline (reminiscent of the 1980s–1990s). The first wave of immigrant youth to graduate from college remained fairly close to Dairy City, but those who are about to attend college dream of moving further afield. Recent college graduates have taken jobs as an EMT, ranch manager, and the owner of a car repair shop. One person is working on a postgraduate degree in psychology on the West Coast. Those who are about to graduate from high school in Dairy City are interested in pursuing advanced degrees in psychology, computer science, anthropology (archeology), engineering, graphic design, education, nursing, and English. If they pursue related careers in other regions, their parents may move with them.

Three ways to retain immigrant employees are to institutionalize maximum profit sharing, extend employee farm ownership (with appropriate risk management), and to ensure everyone has access to clear pathways for promotion all the way through to upper management. Perez (2020) gives an example of the second route on a farm in the Upper Midwest. "Omar Guerrero . . . started out . . . working as a milker, one of the toughest jobs on a dairy farm. At Drake Dairy, he learned more about the operation, took on new responsibilities and moved into management. Now he has a stake in the farm" (Perez 2020). The craft-like managerial style of the Bauer and PVD farms lends itself well to the replication of these pathways; the problem in Dairy City is the current ceiling on upward mobility, as none of the employees have yet to acquire a stake in either farm.

While the number of first-generation immigrant farmers in the United States appears to be growing, they still account for a minority of farm owners, despite providing a significant share of the nation's labor across the food industry (Rosenbloom 2022). Currently, most first-generation immigrant farm owners in the United States fill niches vacated by aging non-Hispanic white farmers whose children are uninterested in farming (Minkoff-Zern 2019, 4).[11] They tend to operate small and midsize farms. Seventy-eight percent of these farm operators "own all of the land they farm," while 6 percent rent all the land (Minkoff-Zern 2017; USDA 2022, 2). US Agricultural Census data suggest that "3 percent of the country's 3.4 million producers identify as being of Latino, Hispanic, or Spanish origin" (USDA 2022, 1). The number of "Latino, Hispanic, or Spanish origin" producers increased 16.9 percent between 2012 and 2022 (USDA 2022, 1). As of 2022, they operated 83,505 farms, covering thirty-seven million acres of US farmland (USDA 2022, 2). In 2022, they sold

$33 billion worth of agricultural products—41 percent were "livestock and livestock products" (USDA 2022: 2). However, only 34 percent of "Hispanic operated farms" specialize in cattle and dairy (USDA 2022, 2).

In her work with first-generation immigrant farm owners across the US, Minkoff-Zern (2017) found that people who left farms in Latin America often wish to "return to the land." US farm ownership enables them to do so. However, some people she interviewed were also motivated by desires to control their time and labor. Some people complained that as employees on other farms, they provided all the labor while earning little money (while non-Hispanic white farmers got rich off their labor) (Minkoff-Zern 2017). Most people also wanted to work alongside relatives—adopting an agrarian lifestyle of raising food sustainably on small farms. They hoped that farm ownership would provide a multigenerational "life and livelihood, not just a means of income" (Minkoff-Zern 2017, 16).

In Dairy City, few people have agrarian backgrounds or explicit desires to pursue an agrarian lifestyle. They do wish to maintain multigenerational lives and livelihoods. Few would be moving into niches vacated by the children of non-Hispanic white farmers, as one of the current owner's main motivations for expanding their farms is to farm with their children and grandchildren, most of whom *are* interested in working on the farms. For this to happen, farms need to be large enough for there to be work for everyone. And the larger the dairy farm gets, the more work that needs to be done, creating additional demand for employees. If farm owners were to go into business with immigrant employees, the situation could be one of more expanded multigenerational farm ownership. For that, true and meaningful opportunities for ownership are required.

Crossroads

Immigrant employees have raised productivity on the Bauer farm so much that the farmers have twice updated their parlors, and they recently acquired another dairy in the region. They have also expanded into calf raising (ranching), which they used to outsource. They are promoting several employees into new managerial, administrative, and technical positions. Owen Bauer told me that two other local firms, both farm equipment manufacturers, increasingly compete with the dairies for employees. He said the competition had driven county wages to $20 an hour by 2016, putting them ahead of the national curve. In 2014, the national median hourly wage for meat and dairy employees was $14.95. It rose to $20 in 2022 (compared with $20.11 and $21.51 for all US workers in 2019 and 2022, respectively) (American Immigration Council 2022, 1). Local firms in Dairy City—PVD and Bauer dairies included—also compete via benefits (see Chapter 1). Owen looked at me and said, "We can't raise the price of milk, but we have had to raise wages due to competition."[12] Demand for workers is fierce in agriculture (USDA 2023; Simnit and Martin 2022; Kane 2023),[13] but compensation alone is insufficient to compete effectively, especially if farmers hope to recruit the children of immigrant employees and avoid a repetition of historical patterns of rural depopulation and decline. "Fewer young immigrants are entering agriculture" (USDA 2023, 9).

US farmers increasingly complain of labor shortages while the costs and risks of immigrating to the United States multiply (Martin 2009; Bustillo and Hsu 2023). Creating prospects for US-born children of immigrants to remain on farms is now the issue, particularly as agricultural labor shortages rise. "For farmers across America, finding enough labor has become a top concern. Decades ago, whole families of migrant farmworkers, the majority of them from Mexico, would travel around the US in search of seasonal work. But over time, farmworkers began to settle. Now, many of them are aging out. And their children and grandchildren are finding opportunities in other sectors" (Bustillo and Hsu 2023; American Immigration Council 2022).[14] While dairy employment typically differs in that it is year-round and requires settlement, the same problem of fewer younger workers entering the dairy labor force holds.

At the same time, North American trade liberalization policies continue to suppress immigration. The free movement of capital, goods, and information has accelerated while opportunities for most people to move freely across borders and labor markets have further constricted (Durand and Massey 2003; Massey 2020). US immigration policy has become so repressive that even people who have access to pathways for regularizing their immigration statuses have fled nativist policies in places like

California in search of better wages and greater integration in the Midwest and Northeast (Durand and Massey 2003, 246–247). At the same time, many people in these situations have loved ones whose pathways to regular immigration status have been blocked or delayed, creating "mixed status" households. As a result, people who initially considered returning to Mexico or Central America to retire—or after a few years of working and saving in the United States—have decided to stay in the United States to keep their families intact (Durand and Massey 2003; Massey et al. 2016; Massey 2020).

The road to the middle class in the United States, and the means for staying within it, are changing. Stable jobs on the Bauer and PVD farms look better when examined against a context of growing precarity. Today, most people are employed in low-wage, precarious jobs in service (namely, retail and food service) that are "increasingly brutal" (Davis 2009, 90, 204). Tenure within these jobs is short (Davis 2009; Sennett 2008; Bureau of Labor Statistics 2022).[15] Employers often show little to no commitment to workers. People who seek to escape these jobs by studying to become a "symbolic analyst—computer programmer, securities analyst, engineer, or other cognitively oriented job . . . increasingly [find] themselves competing with equally qualified offshore providers available for a much lower wage" (Davis 2009, 194; Sennett 2008; Tough 2023).[16] In some cases, as in the Hollywood writers' and actors' strike of 2023, people are being threatened with replacement by "artificial intelligence" (Chmielewski 2024). Even autoworkers have had to fight to avoid being replaced by robots, as in the case of Nio electric cars coming out of China (Bradsher 2023). At the same time, with the US "housing market in free-fall and career employment an anachronism," community ties are loosening, and people often find themselves adrift (Davis 2009, 194).

The Hoffman farm laid off employees and replaced them with robots, but Bauer and PVD employees are at no risk of losing their jobs or their homes. Bauer and PVD owner-managers are still invested in their employees. As I discuss in the conclusion, however, their commitments need to go further to fully surpass paternalism (socially constructed "unhealthy dependence on the employer") (Davis 2009; Gray 2014). They need to be paired with full workers' and citizenship rights for people immigrating to the United States.

Conclusion

Regardless of whether people moved from rural or urban areas or had access to less or more formal education abroad, employers are responsible for providing a range of skilled jobs, with on-the-job training, just rewards, respect, well-being, and opportunities for promotion and career advancement (Bolton 2007; Lucas 2015; Rocigno et al. 2021; Casanova 2019). Doing so is not only good for people, but also for the firms/farms and the communities they serve (and in which they do business). Dignity at work (Bolton 2007) is important for generating larger groundswells—meaning networks of deep social connections that challenge hostile immigration and employment regimes (see also Gibson and Gray 2019; Sennett 2008).

In Mexico, many people worked within a system of "corporate paternalism" in which workers "ceded all effective authority to management" in exchange for "health, retirement pensions, and home ownership programs for the urban working class and lower middle class" (Hernández-León 2004, 429). A model for workers to have authority *and* health, retirement, and home ownership is needed. To the extent that immigrant employees attain greater authority on farms, they are likely to grow deeper local roots, turning Dairy City into more of a hometown for immigrant families. This would be an important guard against renewed waves of rural emigration. It could also be a tool for turning jobs parents don't want their children to have into careers youth might favorably contemplate. Currently, most dairy work is still considered respectable but largely undesirable. Farm ownership, or specializations in animal sciences, marketing, or finance might be a different story. So too would be sustainable farming. Expanding craft and dignity and translating it into more meaningful ownership or career paths for immigrant employees is crucial for building on growth.

CONCLUSION

In the early 2000s, the mayor of Dairy City organized a photo book of "all those persons who make [Dairy City] a better place to live." Over one hundred pages long, the book features photos of the owners and staff of local businesses, volunteer groups, and organizations. People with mostly German surnames appear on page after page, except, of course, for the two pages dedicated to the Bauer dairy. On these two pages, the photo and its caption feature people who recently arrived from Latin America. The caption recognizes the dairy for "setting production and innovation records." If the book were to be updated today, more than twenty years later, the photos would reflect the names and contributions of significant numbers of people who recently immigrated, largely from urban professional or commercial places in Mexico. Bauer and Pleasant Valley Dairy (PVD) farmers' efforts to promote dignity at work for people immigrating and making career changes have helped build a broader ecology of institutional growth than would have been possible without such efforts. The broader ecology of growth vis-à-vis immigrants supports farms in retaining immigrant employees and makes Dairy City a more viable and vibrant place to live for everyone.

In an interview with a local reporter that aired on television a few years ago, Wayne Bauer—the second eldest Bauer among four generations currently living on the farm—was asked what the secret to success in dairying is. He looked at the camera and said, "Surround yourself with good, quality people." He might have added, "and be good to them!" Wayne's comment recalls the dairy veterinarian who said, "In the industry we all have the same feed trucks, the same vaccines. What sets one operation apart from the other? It's the people, and it's the way they treat the animals" (Ford qtd. in Runyon 2016). What both comments miss is the way the firm is organized—how people are treated and what the social conditions of production are. Even if he did not say so explicitly, Wayne seemed to get this. He and his wife, Gail, were at the forefront of a craft-like managerial style on their farm. Of all the owner-managers, they hewed the most closely to this style, with positive effects for employees, the farm, and the community.

As the first people in their family to hire a significant number of farm employees, starting in the late 1990s, Wayne and Gail Bauer pursued a sociable version of craft-style work that embraces "collective communication" and "practices of cooperation" (Sennett 2008, 31, 37, 52; see also Crowley and Hodson 2014; Hodson 1999). The Bauers worked directly alongside employees and encouraged "frank" communication; such communication encourages the discovery and discussion of problems and creative solutions with ample employee input. Two decades later, Paloma regularly tells Owen Bauer (one of Wayne and Gail's sons) when his management practices are counterproductive and how to fix them, based on her mastery of farm operations and knowledge about how best to motivate and support people; Mateo disputes co-workers' diagnoses of cow illnesses and debates treatment, always with the goal of comforting and healing the cow; Humberto pitches strategic investments in tools based on his hands-on experience in the shop. He demonstrates how repair processes can be improved based on what he has learned from experience. These and other examples reflect Schwalbe's (2010) notion of "embodied skill," or knowledge gained through touch and movement, as well as thinking creatively about how to accomplish a task (Sennett 2008). This facilitates mastery in repair and improvisation in the face of challenges and surprises, which are common on large dairy farms. Such "collective craftsmanship" involves "plain speaking" and "speaking truth to power," encouraging people to identify and solve mistakes, instead of "passing them off" and allowing them to multiply (Sennett 2008, 31; Crowley and Hodson 2014; Schwalbe 2010).

Work at PVD was initially bureaucratically organized. Rigidity and hierarchy prevented the flow of information that would help people identify and solve problems. When problems worsened, people became frustrated with each other. Work was broken into smaller parts and was—as Schwalbe (2010, 109) characterizes work that lacks craft—"stultifying" rather than "enriching" (Mills 1956; Braverman 1974). Communication between employees, and between employees and managers, was limited. People mistrusted each other. Fortunately, when the lead manager, Peter, recognized the extent of the problems, he started listening more to employees. Based on their feedback, he sought ways to create more collaboration, work-life balance, and pathways for mobility. This has improved relationships at work. Employees who were formerly trapped in entry-level positions are getting more hands-on training in computer systems/software, herd management, and veterinary care. Peter was influenced by the Bauers in this, and he has influenced them in return.[1]

While the Bauers were at the forefront of craft-like managerial styles, Peter was more thoughtful about financial rewards for quality work and employment tenure. He created rewards for service. Peter was the first to open 401k accounts for full-time employees, buy employee health insurance, provide tickets to sporting events, and promote paid vacations. The Bauers now also offer health care, vision, dental, paid vacations, 401k after six months, and they continue to offer housing in the form of single-family homes in the center of Dairy City or nearby towns, as available. Hourly starting wages for a variety of positions at the Bauer farm range from $15 to $25, depending on experience and job tasks, and a series of raises begin at six months. The two farms have been converging in their labor practices and local institutional norms. Both farms have grown significantly since the early 2000s, outpacing the Hoffman farm, where Hans Hoffman has noted that he has "very low labor costs."

High labor costs on the Bauer and PVD farms raise a question similar to that posed by Plankey-Videla (2012, 191) in her study of a Mexican garment firm: Do high labor costs make the Bauer and PVD dairy farms uncompetitive in today's highly globalized dairy industry? Labor costs on the Bauer and PVD farms are significantly higher than they are/were on the Hoffman farm, and they are higher than on many other dairy farms that offer lower wages and few-to-no benefits (Keller 2019; Perez 2020; Sexsmith 2019). Like Plankey-Videla (2012), I find that the answer is a resounding no. Just as in "the high-end niche garment market where quality and turnaround are key," quality and efficiency in dairy farming are essential for success—these are achieved "not *in spite* of the increased cost of labor but *because of* it" (Plankey Videla 2012, 191).

Dairy farming is a volatile industry that magnifies the benefits of managerial practices promoting dignity at and beyond work.[2] Rather than responding to volatility with degrading labor practices that heighten instability, PVD and Bauer owner-managers used their managerial autonomy to organize work with dignity. The will and capacity to battle the elements and do dangerous work well, and safely, stems from such dignification, while public recognition and reward for the work further dignifies it (Bolton 2007; Ackroyd 2001; Sayer 2001; and Hodson 2001). For people who immigrated from abroad, making career changes in the process and finding little in the way of institutional support upon their arrival, dignity at work (Bolton 2007) encouraged many of them to stay. These decisions, however, were not made in a vacuum. The attractiveness of Bauer and PVD dairy jobs is negatively underscored by the perversity of US immigration policies that create "mixed immigration status" households with restricted mobility, and the difficult state of the US and global economy more generally. Good compensation and positive managerial practices at the dairies have encouraged long employment tenure of experienced workers. This has boosted production and supported local community institutional growth, reversing decades of decline. Additional growth moving forward will depend on employers continuing and deepening their commitments to workers, and governments fulfilling their responsibilities to vastly expand and uphold the rights of people who immigrate. While broader historical trends are currently moving in the opposite direction, degradation *is not inevitable*, nor should it be treated as such (see especially Pugh 2015).

Pugh (2015, 196) argues that treating the decline of work and community as inevitable shields employers (and governments) from responsibility for creating insecurity. People who immigrated to Dairy City fought notions of inevitability through their very movement—across borders, towns, and industries. They are leading the charge against so-called "inevitability," refusing to accept it. The threat of losing workers and their families has prompted the Bauers and PVD owner-managers to take responsibility for their employment practices. This stands in stark contrast to what is happening on other farms and across much of the US economy.

Charting Change

Drawing on Mills's sociological imagination, Davis (2009, xvii) argued that "the sociologist [is] like a mapmaker, describing large scale historical changes. . . and the social structures through which they [affect] individual lives." For the historical "transition from an agrarian to an industrial society," we could thus map or "link one person's move from farm to factory" with the larger currents of social change (Davis 2009, xvii). We can do the same for the intersections between one person's move from urban industrial Mexico to rural Kansas, and another person's move from a small to a large dairy farm in that same rural Kansas town. Charting these interactions provides insight into broader historical changes and how they are being rendered through social structures like those that developed on these two industrializing Dairy City farms.

The Bauer and PVD farms may seem like an odd choice for mapping broader historical change because they are atypical. However, as Stinchcombe (2002), Katz (2001), and Timmermans and Tavory (2012) point out, the strength of qualitative research is that it seeks to explain outliers instead of cases that cluster around the mean. In having to account for variations, we gain deeper insight; in this case, into vanishingly rare managerial efforts to boost production through dignified labor practices. A more typical case would be how former employees described the Hoffman farm. We would see the "lean" and degrading labor practices that have pervaded most firms in an era of accelerated finance capitalism. We would also see the degradation of community wrought by firms' disinvestment in employees and the places where they produce and sometimes sell. But even the idea of stable production in a community is atypical. More common for many US producers is constant relocation in the pursuit of ever lower costs of production, or constant dislocation and replacement of workers to undercut their bargaining power. In the Hoffman case, robots replaced people. The result of such "lean production" practices for

US communities is not stable economic or demographic growth based on employer commitments to workers (Crowley 2016), but rather new forms of poverty, degradation, and transience (Martin 2009; Stull, Broadway, and Griffith 1995). People who recently immigrated to Dairy City had no real intention of moving there or doing dairy work. For many, the road to this remote rural place started in a deindustrializing Mexico or war-torn, neoliberalizing Central America (as well as neoliberalizing Eastern Europe and South Africa in the early 2000s). People who moved from Mexico to Dairy City experienced the fall of peripheral Fordism and restructuring in Mexico. Peripheral Fordism was twice linked to a reimagining of global production. First, it was connected to the rise of "flexible specialization" (Bernard 2004; Shaiken 1995; Plankey-Videla 2012). Manufacturers used semiconductors to quickly retool plants, enabling them to make new products in response to changes in demand (Bernard 2004). This model was an inversion of historically supply-driven production (Bernard 2004; Plankey Videla 2012; Gereffi 1994). However, flexible managerial practices that initially encouraged teamwork and the development of multiple skill sets among relatively well-paid employees were subverted in the 1990s (Shaiken 1995). With growing global competition among producers and the constant threat of relocating production to other global sites, employers reduced their commitments to workers (Wright 2001; Bernard 2004, Hernández-León 2004).[3] Mexico began the same slide toward a service-based economy that the US was experiencing. With even less of a safety net in Mexico than the US, people in Mexico sought security in the US, where instability and inequality have been on the rise. This was also true for people in Central America who have been grappling with war-torn societies and restructuring (Garni and Weyher 2013; Menjívar 2011).

The evaporation of secure jobs and communities abroad forced prospective immigrants to make impossible choices. Seeking stable opportunities for themselves and their children, families moved to Dairy City. There, they found a place that has thus far avoided the transition to a "portfolio society," or what Pugh (2015) refers to as a "tumbleweed society." Both terms refer to the set of forces that displaced people abroad and accelerated lean and fragmented employment in the United States. The tumbleweed/portfolio society is organized by globalized finance and service: It is one in which employers have few fixed assets, weak bonds with employees, and little to no stake in local communities (Davis 2009; Sennett 2008; Pugh 2015).[4] Sennet (2008, 265) argues that this kind of society "is bulldozing the career path; jobs in the old sense of random movement now prevail . . . Craftsmanship seems particularly vulnerable to this possibility, since craftsmanship is based on slow learning and on habit." Slow learning and habit depend on job stability, but "long term attachments between employees and firms . . . are largely a thing of the past, with important consequences for individuals, households, and communities" (Davis 2009, 237; Pugh 2015).

Most bonds between employers and employees, as well as between companies and local communities, were severed by 1980s "chop shops" (Davis 2009). These chop shops were created by external shareholders who looked for companies in which managers were more loyal to employees than stock prices. They bought cheap shares in these companies, seized control, sold off physical company assets, and triggered a mass outsourcing of jobs (Davis 2009).

Companies that continue producing in the United States often use lean labor processes found in offshore production. They readily lay off workers, hire temporary or part-time employees who are ineligible for benefits, outlaw unions, recruit workers with the fewest rights or alternatives, surveil workers, and impose "strict task regimens" (Crowley and Hodson 2014; Davis 2009; Hodson 1999).[5] As production coordinated through networks of global contracts—facilitated by container shipping and telecommunications—generated a "global race to the bottom" in employment practices, a "lifetime of stable employment" became an "anachronism" (Davis 2009, x). This was true in Mexico, as well, where peripheral Fordism gave way to maquilas with high turnover rates and degrading labor practices (Hernández-León 2004; Bernard 2004; Davis 2009).[6] These processes have undermined hard-won gains of earlier labor and civil rights movements that sought to redress inequalities of gender, sexuality, race, class, and so on (Pugh 2015, 187; Hill 2021; Zeitlin and Weyher 2001).

With the US economy dominated by shareholder-owned corporations that prioritize shareholder profit over job stability (Davis 2009, v), upward mobility has declined, while inequality, student loan debt, and wage volatility have increased (Davis 2009; Tough 2023; Pugh 2015). Corporations have largely divested of their physical assets, community ties, and commitments to workers (Davis 2009; Sennett 2008). Brutal jobs have proliferated (Davis 2009). People's access to career-based employment has "been banished to civil servants and that sliver of academics with tenure" (Davis 2009, 3, 7), while "rewards for service have disappeared" (Sennett 2008, 35). Companies promote turnover to attract "fresher," less experienced, and more exploitable workers (Schwartzman 2013; Wright 2001). In this context, as workers' "experience accumulates, it loses institutional value" (Sennett 2008, 35). Workers may attempt to protect themselves from unemployment by developing a "portfolio" of skills that they can apply to any existing jobs, but as many scholars have found, in a "globalized marketplace" people are perpetually at risk of losing jobs to similarly skilled peers in other countries who are paid less for the same work (Sennett 2008, 35; Davis 2009; Tough 2023). In the United States, the "typical family is more likely to see income drop by half from one year to the next since the 1970s" (Davis 2009, 205–206; Ananat, Gassman-Pines, and Truskinovsky 2021). Pensions have disappeared, fewer jobs have health insurance, and housing costs are rising (Dougherty and Barbaro 2024). Health-related bankruptcies and evictions are also on the rise (Levey 2023; Desmond 2012). People and jobs are "tumbled" (Pugh 2015).

While instability spreads in the tumbleweed society (Pugh 2015), dairies still need permanent skilled employees. Dairy jobs may be less vulnerable to outsourcing than some craftwork that most people thought was safe, such as acting, writing, and even auto manufacturing—all of which are being additionally threatened by artificial intelligence (AI) (Kessler, Livni, and de la Merced 2023; Chmielewski 2023; Cox 2023);[7] however, dairy employment is almost never organized as "craft." When it is, as by degrees on the Bauer farm and PVD, employees are much more likely to have the time and resources to develop essential skills and avoid damaging turnover. Firms grow, adapt, and generate multiplier effects for individuals and communities when they craft dignity. And even with mechanization—as the Bauers begin implementing robots, for example—their craft-style labor practices will help people to move into the more technical, veterinary, mechanical, and human resources jobs that robots cannot perform (and which their incorporation emphasizes, both by eliminating more routine tasks and creating new demands). Since people moving into these jobs will have vast experience, they are best prepared to quickly identify the new sets of problems that will arise and to solve them in innovative ways (Sennett 2008). Employers will need to compensate tenure and expertise with growing rewards.

Having grown the farm and the community via efforts to retain employees, the Bauer trajectory is growth with people, even as it may now involve some degree of mechanization in milking jobs, where the most turnover has occurred in the past two decades. In addition, to the extent that the Bauers draw on milkers' experience to make the expanded operation successful, the farm will continue to grow. Milkers' experience makes them excellent designers. They have a strong feel for how tools—such as pumps, milk lines, tanks, and the parlors themselves—work (or fail).[8] They see how animals are faring and when they need additional care. To prevent tainted milk from getting into tanks, resulting in them being flushed or the farm penalized for high somatic cell counts when the milk is tested (each time it is collected), employees are encouraged to "[attend] to all cases—letting no exceptions slip through by carelessness or indifference" (Sennett 2008, 245). This means not a single cow mixed up; not a single line contaminated; not a single cow improperly treated. Collaboration, communication, and inclusion of all employees in the working of the organization—in true craft style—boosts "total quality control," prevents major losses, supports long employee tenure, and builds community (Sennett 2008).

Links Between Work and Community

Links between work and community are torn in the tumbleweed society (Pugh 2015; Davis 2009; Sennett 2008). When people's work experiences are highly fragmented, they are more likely to withdraw from social institutions, diminishing their social and political capital (Sennett 2008; Pugh 2015). This may be the result of unstable employment that forces people to constantly move or "scramble for work," the degradation of work that wears people down and strains social connection, and/ or the ways in which demoralizing work discourages or prevents people from being able to participate in voluntary associations, clubs, local institutions, and the like (Pugh 2015, 186; Sennett 2008; Gibson and Gray 2019). According to Sennett (2008, 36), while Putnam's *Bowling Alone* attributed the loss of social capital in the US to a "television culture and consumerist ethic," the true cause of people's withdrawal is "more directly tied to people's experiences at work." Employers also become less connected to and invested in local communities (Davis 2009).

In much of farming today, there is typically either lean production or few human workers at all. Crop farmers in western Kansas are increasingly farming without people (Gibson and Gray 2019). Their farms are technically growing, at least in size, but farmers rely on technology "to perform and reproduce their communities, which are becoming increasingly deterritorialized as competition in a scale-based game relocates members to other places" (Gibson and Gray 2019, 213). Farmers borrow large sums of money to buy sophisticated machinery—not unlike the Hoffmans with their robots. To recuperate the costs, they must farm as much land as possible, particularly as the price for their goods declines through monopsony (in which prices are determined by powerful implement dealers and retailers) and pursue "[ever] greater efficiencies" (Gibson and Gray 2019, 216; Hamilton 2008). When one farmer goes out of business, another farmer will try to buy the land, consolidating farms so that fewer people are farming. Farmers then rely on technology to communicate with people they used to interact with face-to-face. They conduct business and social life increasingly through technology (Gibson and Gray 2019).

Between 1920 and 2023, the number of farms and ranches in Kansas declined from 161,000 to 55,700 (Gibson and Gray 2019, 212; USDA 2024). As Gibson and Gray (2019, 221–225) explain, outmigration, both of former farmers and farmers' relatives who seek off-farm income, depresses the tax base of local communities: Dwindling tax bases undermine schools, which are the center of social life in many rural communities;

opportunities to "socialize and build shared memories" through sporting events and the performing arts are lost; families who need schools for their children and jobs must seek them elsewhere and may decide to live elsewhere as a result; as depopulation proceeds, there are also fewer people to volunteer, serve in local government, or run civic organizations. Farmers caught in these situations are often too busy to step into leadership or volunteer roles given their need to personally run larger operations with increasingly complex technology that they must manage (Gibson and Gray 2019). Ultimately, "the way farming has changed is to blame for the emptying of the countryside" (Gibson and Gray 2019, 217). This is because "success" depends on "owning a lot of land, and farm expansion depends on the financial crises and failures of other farmers" (Gibson and Gray 2019, 217). The resulting rending of the "social fabric of community . . . is not an unintended consequence, but rather a feature of capitalism—to break apart the social ties that bind people together so workers can be exploited more efficiently and with fewer threats to capital's profits" (Gibson and Gray 2019, 228 c.f. Davis 1992).

Many US dairy farmers have also had to consolidate to stay in business. However, in contrast to farmers who mechanize and decrease employment, they typically need *more* people to run the operation as they expand. Scholars have nonetheless found lean labor practices on several farms across the country (Keller 2019; Sexsmith 2019; Lloyd and Harrison 2012).[9] The Bauers and PVD managers, by contrast, adopted technologies that increase efficiencies, and they have scaled up their operations, but they have opted for more positive labor practices. They have sought to strengthen ties between people both on and off the farms.

Thus, in contrast to the tumbleweed society, the Bauers and PVD managers have created the conditions that facilitated the expansion of quality milk production *and* local community. Growing production bolstered employment, a local tax base, demand for local services, and local social life. The school is a prominent example. Before the Bauers and PVD managers recruited people to immigrate and stay in Dairy City, the school was on the brink of closing due to insufficient enrollment. The children of immigrant employees saved the school. And like the farming communities in Gibson and Gray's (2019) study before their recent rending, the school in Dairy City is the heart of local social life. Events five nights a week bring families together, providing entertainment and opportunities for connection. People are present to volunteer and serve. Families have access to jobs and schooling for their children. There are local professional opportunities in the school, nursing home, civic services, and local businesses that preserve middle rungs on ladders of mobility. Rather than becoming increasingly "deterritorialized" and "in trouble" (Gibson and Gray 2019), Dairy City has been growing. If it were to continue to grow, additional rungs on local ladders may emerge (Davis 2009).

Bringing Broader Public Attention to On-Going Structural Problems

As Gibson and Gray (2019, 229) argue, face-to-face interactions support social bonds that facilitate "a community critique of the conditions that give rise to struggle induced by forces beyond farmers' control." I would modify this to emphasize that these bonds also facilitate social critique more generally—of the conditions that foster other struggles generated by various forces beyond everyone's immediate control. More collective forms of critique also enable more collective (rather than individual) forms of struggle. And struggling collectively against the multiple forces of injustice impacting people is key to social change.

Unfortunately, many of the face-to-face interactions that have facilitated community critiques of unsustainable agriculture have neglected the people who do the work. Many people who work in US agriculture remain "in the shadows" (Keller 2019; Gray 2014). They may work on small or hard-to-reach farms and regularly move around to piece together stable employment, and/or they may be hidden by practices and provisions that shield farmers from public scrutiny. For example, consumers who meet farmers at farmers' markets, farm stands, or "pick your own fruit" farms (Gray 2014, 1), or through chefs who prepare foods they acquire from local farms, almost never interact meaningfully with people who work the farms. Gray (2014) and Guthman (2004) find that consumers' desires to opt out of factory farm systems in favor of a pastoral imaginary "conflate local, alternative, sustainable, and fair as a compendium of virtues against the demonized factory farm" (Gray 2014, 41). These consumers imagine that small local producers automatically uphold animal welfare, raise a diversity of crops, avoid hazardous chemicals, tend well to the land and environment, "and sustain regional foodsheds" (Gray 2014, 41). They *assume* that an "imagined bevy" of farm ethics extends to people and forget or neglect to ask about working conditions (Gray 2014; Guthman 2004). In reality, on several farms in New York, for example, scholars have found temporary labor camps with unsafe housing, lack of protective gear for workers, wage theft, intimidation, isolation, and paternalism/maternalism (Gray 2014; Keller 2019; Sexsmith 2019). Paternalism and maternalism refer to invasive practices among employers who use personal information and power to control workers. It is manipulation serving exploitation. Manipulation may include targeting immigrant workers who employers believe are unlikely to complain due to their restrictive immigration statuses (Gray 2014; Hondagneu-Sotelo 2007).

Public awareness of working conditions on both large and small farms is low (Gray 2014; Weil 2017). Weil (2017) finds this is by design. Several laws and regulatory exemptions specific to agriculture have shielded farms from public scrutiny, in many cases allowing abuses of people, animals, and the environment to accumulate and remain un- or under-reported, uninvestigated, and uncontested (Weil 2017; Piper 2020; Jameel and Sanchez 2023). In several states and at different times, these have included: "ag-gag" laws (the first was passed in Kansas in 1990, but it was struck down in a federal Kansas court in 2020) (Weil 2017; Piper 2020); mandatory reporting provisions for animal cruelty that "force liability and blame to fall entirely at the feet of low-income workers, barring efforts to show . . . abuse on the part of the [manager or] employer" (Weil 2017, 205); lack of "whistleblower protections for farmworkers under USDA jurisdiction," though Kansas does have some specific protections (Weil 2017, 205; FARM 2020); "right-to-farm" bills (Weil 2017); bills that aim to defund organizations that support animal welfare (e.g., a bill was proposed in Oklahoma, but failed in 2016) (Weil 2017; Pacelle 2016); "anti-terrorist" laws heightening prosecution of animal rights activists (Weil 2017); exemptions for farm animals from anti-cruelty provisions common in most states (Weil 2017); extra punitive anti-trespassing laws; special anti-defamation laws (Weil 2017); exemptions from provisions of labor laws, including some overtime and minimum pay provisions under the Fair Labor Standards Act (FLSA) and collective bargaining protections under the National Labor Relations Act (NLRA) (Kansas protects farmworkers from discrimination in hiring when they collectively bargain, but employers are not obligated to recognize employee unions or representatives) (Weil 2017; Gray 2014; NALC 2023); and limited oversight and enforcement by the FDA, USDA, and OSHA (Jameel and Sanchez 2023).[10]

Jameel and Sanchez (2023) find that people who die while working on small dairy farms in Wisconsin may not have their deaths adequately investigated. This is because some farms with fewer than eleven employees during the previous twelve months that do not provide housing have been shielded from Occupational Safety and Health Administration (OSHA) inspections (Jameel and Sanchez 2023; OSHA 2007). This dates back to the implementation (and renewal) of the congressional "small farms exemption" "to protect small family farms from government overreach (Jameel and Sanchez 2023). It's so ingrained in American agriculture that many dairy farmers assume that OSHA won't even try to go onto their property" (Jameel and Sanchez 2023, 16). Jameel and Sanchez (2023) report that in the cases of three dairy farm workers who died on small Wisconsin farms, OSHA officials went to the farms but left within an hour (Jameel and Sanchez 2023, 1). The authors argue that if the officials had spoken with law enforcement, "they might have learned that the farmers had readily talked with law enforcement officials about providing housing for their immigrant worker," which would have given OSHA jurisdiction (Jameel and Sanchez 2023, 3). Two of the cases that Jameel and Sanchez (2023) investigated involved dangerous work with equipment that had not been properly maintained or repaired, and the third involved a new employee being crushed by a herd (he had received very limited training). OSHA reportedly investigated five cases in which workers lived in temporary labor camps on the farms (Jameel and Sanchez 2023). "At least 17 workers—mostly immigrants—have died on Wisconsin dairy farms since 2009. Twelve of those deaths happened on farms with fewer than 11 workers. OSHA did not inspect eight of those 12, each time citing the small farms exemption" (Jameel and Sanchez 2023, 2).

People who work on small and/or remote farms and have restricted immigration statuses under a hostile US immigration regime may be especially isolated. This is also true for people working in domestic service jobs in cities (see especially Hondagneu-Sotelo 2007). Isolation and fear can make organizing difficult (Gray 2014; Keller 2019; Harrison and Lloyd 2012).[11] People may be unable to leave farms for meetings or to seek redress for labor, wage, safety, housing, and other violations (Gray 2014; Keller 2019). Employer surveillance may dissuade people from complaining to authorities for fear of retribution (Gray 2014; Keller 2019). With few rights or alternatives, and so much at stake, immigrants may be reluctant to speak up and challenge unfair practices. It also may be difficult for labor organizers to reach people in these situations, especially if workers move from farm to farm (McWilliams 1939 [1979]; Greenberg 2018; Gray 2014). Rural/geographic isolation or remoteness may also shield employers from public oversight (Gray 2014; Keller 2019). Public pressure for employers to improve their labor practices are unlikely when the public is unaware of what is happening.

Larger farms may be more visible and receive more public attention, which may facilitate organizing. "Across the United States, farmworker justice advocates have a long record of successfully targeting large scale agriculture and/or corporate food brands" involved in unscrupulous labor practices (Gray 2014, 134). Organizing national boycotts of food companies with recognizable brand names has helped raise wages for the produce growers and service providers that supply them (Gray 2014, 134). Gray (2014) gives the examples of farmworker justice campaigns in the Upper Midwest targeting Campbell and Heinz, and campaigns in Florida involving eleven major food companies, among others. However, as Gray (2014) points out, it is more difficult to organize workers who are not employed on large commodity farms or who don't produce goods sourced by major buyer/retailers. It is also more difficult to organize consumers in these cases.

Milk producers tend to employ people longer than crop farmers, which could facilitate organizing employees, but the organization of producer cooperatives may pose challenges to exerting consumer pressure.

Cooperatives tend to blend milk from several farms,[12] potentially making it difficult to trace which farm(s) the milk came from (unless it is from a local niche farmer, which places the farm back in the small farm category). For example, the Bauer and PVD farms are members of a cooperative that reports having over 10,000 members, meaning the cooperative distributes and markets milk from over 10,000 farms. Many milk producers across the country are incentivized to join large cooperatives to gain leverage in negotiating with powerful processors and retailers (Hamilton 2008; Kardashian 2012; Young 1990). The larger the cooperative, the more bargaining power producers have. Large cooperatives may also influence state and federal legislation. Boycotting milk from farms with poor labor practices that are members of large cooperatives would likely require boycotting all dairy products, because cooperatives typically distribute to processors and retailers that run dozens of labels. If the cooperative also contracts to provide dairy products to—for example—a school system, the boycott would likely need to include those outlets as well. Pressure from within cooperatives for all members to uphold healthy and positive labor practices is crucial.

Owners of large, industrialized dairies are, however, vulnerable to labor disputes that result in strikes. If employees walked off the job, the farms would rapidly be in jeopardy. Operating costs are high. Electricity, water, feed, medicine, and fuel are expensive. Cows that are not properly tended in a timely fashion can quickly become ill, and milk spoils fast. The farms would be unable to sell quality milk while being saddled with expenses for which owners are liable. It is unlikely that farmers would be able to find enough people with the necessary experience and skills to fill jobs, many of which are dangerous, dirty, and require attention around-the-clock. The Hoffman farm experienced this. Difficult labor conditions on the farm caused employee attrition and declining milk production.

Strikes among agricultural workers are only "allowed" in Kansas "during certain periods," defined as "critical production periods" (Farmworker Justice 2023; Farmers' Association for Responsible Management (FARM) 2020).[13] I was unable to find a specific definition of these time periods, but dairy farmers typically argue that critical production happens every day, all day, throughout the year. This is because many dairies operate 24 hours a day, 365 days a year. Lack of protection from employer retaliation may intimidate workers and prevent them from striking.

New Deal legislation infamously excluded most agricultural and domestic workers from its bill of rights (Gray 2014, 141). The exclusion was the result of the power of Southern Democrats who supported white supremacist politics to suppress the rights of Black people, many of whom worked in agriculture (Gray 2014, 49). Excluding agricultural and domestic workers means that "following the letter of the law can still result in extreme exploitation" (Gray 2014, 49). It replicates racialized systems of oppression. Some states have enacted legislation to protect farmworkers, but in Kansas, agricultural workers still tend to be excluded from minimum wage, overtime, rest and meal breaks, and maximum "hour or day" working hours protections (FARM 2020; FARM 2018; USDOL 2023).[14] Lack of protections for most workers in agriculture, paired with the danger and difficulty of the work, make many jobs especially brutal.

US immigration laws are also highly punitive and racialized (Golash-Boza and Hondagneu-Sotelo 2013; Golash-Boza 2015; Gonzales 2013).[15] It can take years and tens of thousands of dollars for people to adjust their statuses. Many people are denied eligibility for adjustment of status. People living in mixed immigration status households, even if they themselves have regularized immigration status, live in constant fear of being separated from family and losing substantial savings and investments in the US (Durand and Massey 2003; Massey, Durand, and Pren 2016; Massey 2020). Reflecting on the injustices of the US immigration system, Owen Bauer told me that a person he knows from South Africa had to wait ten years and pay $40,000 for citizenship. The person attained citizenship only after being forced to return to South Africa for a year, leaving his family behind in Dairy City. Owen shook his head and said, "The system is totally broken." Owen and Gail Bauer told me on several occasions how unfair the system is, how hard it is on immigrants, and how much they wish it would change.

While many dairy farmers support widely accessible paths to residency for immigrants (Ali 2022; Maddan, San Miguel, and Ynalvez 2022; Bustillo 2022),[16] some dairy owners exploit the few existing paths available to people who come from abroad to work on dairies. Perez (2019) found that several veterinarians trained in Mexico and promised high-level positions as animal scientists on US dairy farms have been tricked. They take large loans to travel to the US with special visas and are then pressed to work long hours for low pay for days on end, without breaks, on remote farms (Perez 2019). To leave, they would need another employer to sponsor them, but they are so isolated on the farms where they live—in substandard housing with no transportation—that they struggle to make the needed connections (Perez 2019). Fearful that they won't be able to pay travel debts and the costs of their education in Mexico, several people have remained on the farms hoping that conditions will improve (Perez 2019).

The interaction between lack of protection for farmworkers and restrictive immigration policy has long had the effect of (re)producing "a kind of indentured servitude" (Garcia 2020; Greenberg 2018; McWilliams 1939 [1979]). People who immigrate under temporary visa programs may become trapped by unscrupulous employers who exploit them (Garcia 2020; Greenberg 2018; Martin 2009). Employers who rely on labor contractors can further heighten immigrant workers' risks of exploitation. This is because labor contractors insulate agribusinesses from liability for labor practices and (as discussed) agricultural workers lack protections. According to Martin (2009, 80):

> Most farmers argue that relying on a contractor to get oranges picked is analogous to a home owner hiring a painter. Just as the home owner is not responsible for how the painter treats his workers, so the farmer is not responsible for the contractor's treatment of the crew. Grower Jim Griffiths summed up this attitude: "I wouldn't have the slightest idea who any of them [workers] were or where they are from. Theoretically, you can be fined or penalized for that [hiring unauthorized workers]. But it doesn't matter to me because I don't ever see them or know anything about them . . . The liability goes back to him."

Hundreds of contractors across the country have been charged with human trafficking and slavery for smuggling people into the United States and then holding them captive, forcing them to work off tens of thousands of dollars of "smuggling debts" (Martin 2009; Barrick, Lattimore, Pitts, and Zhang 2014). Further, since guest worker programs (H-2A/H-2B visas) require employers to provide housing and transportation, which many employers argue is "too expensive" (Gray 2014; Martin 2009; Barrick et al. 2014), many employers have sidestepped these programs in favor of recruiting unauthorized workers (McWilliams 1939 [1979]; Martin 2009).

Existing proposals to reform immigration policy for people working in agriculture, such as the Farm Workforce Modernization Act (FWMA), continue to give employers a great deal of power (Ali 2022; Garcia 2020; Familias Unidas por la Justicia). The emphasis of the bill is on the expansion of the H-2A Temporary Agricultural Program; however, Title I of the bill contains provisions for people currently in the United States who are undocumented and work in agriculture to adjust to lawful permanent status, a step toward citizenship, under certain conditions, including first attaining Certified Agricultural Worker (CAW) status (American Immigration Council (AIC) 2021). To qualify for CAW, people must show they worked in agriculture for at least 180 days during the past two years while also meeting additional requirements (AIC 2021). CAW provides temporary legal status for five-and-a-half years and may be renewed if the person "continued to work in agriculture at least one-hundred days per year" (AIC 2021). "All applicants for CAW status would have to pass criminal background checks and would be barred from the program for certain criminal convictions. Applicants would also have to be continuously present in the United States from the date the bill was introduced in Congress until the date they are granted CAW status" (AIC 2021).[17] People granted CAW status could

> adjust to lawful permanent resident (LPR) status if they engage in an additional period of agricultural work and pay a $1,000 fine. Farmworkers who have worked in agriculture in the United States for at least 10 years prior to the date of enactment of the bill could apply for LPR status if they work for at least four more years in agriculture while in CAW status. Farmworkers who have worked in agriculture for less than 10 years before enactment of the bill would have to work for at

least eight years more in agriculture while in CAW status before they could apply for LPR status (AIC 2021).

Since eligibility for any kind of immigration relief under FWMA depends largely on the employer, people who encounter unfair labor practices may be afraid to contest them for fear of losing eligibility for difficult-to-attain lawful immigration statuses. Some versions of the bill include record-keeping requirements regarding wages, housing, and transportation, as well as a means for suing employers, so that employees are not "shorted" (Bustillo 2022). The Farm Bureau has opposed worker protections (Bustillo 2022), but "the desperation of farm owners [to recruit immigrant employees], especially those in livestock and dairy agriculture in the West and Midwest, has pushed the Bureau toward neutrality to achieve passage of the bill" (Garcia 2022).

In their analysis of FWMA, Zoodsma, Dudley, and Minkhoff-Zern (2022) find that stakeholders' views of the proposed legislation vary. Whereas "grower advocacy" groups favor the expanded temporary worker provisions of FWMA, growers themselves tend to oppose them based on what they perceive to be costly and onerous program regulations (Zoodsma et al. 2022). Similarly, whereas worker advocacy groups that focus on policy and have little contact with workers tend to favor FWMA, advocacy groups that have direct contact with workers oppose the bill. The latter oppose the bill on the grounds that temporary worker programs—like those included in the FWMA—tend to lower wages for agricultural workers, make them more vulnerable to exploitation, and fail to provide reasonable or meaningful paths to residency and citizenship (Zoodsma et al. 2022; Garcia 2020). Worker advocacy groups that have direct contact with workers also criticize the bill's more general "complicated and limited pathway to citizenship that does not include all farmworkers who labored through the COVID-19 pandemic, makes e-verify mandatory in agriculture, and does not provide workers with a right to organize and collectively bargain without fear of retaliation" (Zoodsma et al. 2022, 9). Workers, in turn, are additionally concerned that the bill makes it difficult to move from farm to farm, secure long-term commitments from employers, and seek redress for discrimination and violations of housing and work contracts (Zoodsma et al. 2022). Reversing the vicious circle of exploitation caused by the interaction of discriminatory agricultural and immigration policies requires implementing protections for workers and creating clear and readily accessible pathways to residency and citizenship. Protections and pathways must be free of employer interference to be meaningful and to minimize opportunities for exploitation.

Inverting Dominant Models of Degradation

When the Bauers and PVD managers speak with reporters about the successes of their operations, they consistently credit employees. Treating people well enables them to care for the animals, which produces healthier milk and food (Jackson-Smith and Buttel 1998; Adcock et al. 2015; Rosson 2012).[18] The more vested people are in each other and in the food we produce and eat, the more likely people are to also care for the land, the environment, animals, and one another.

Dominant models of work and food production involve interlocking systems of degradation: Suppressing working conditions to suppress wages and food costs creates dangerous food systems (Patel 2012). People who are paid poorly in the new economy, dominated by low-wage service sector jobs, are forced to buy low-priced food. Demands for low-priced food propel politicians to reproduce policies in the name of so-called "food security" (Friedmann 1993). These policies sustain the "kind of indentured servitude" in agriculture that many scholars have documented (Garcia 2020; Gray 2014; Greenberg 2018).[19]

The Bauer and PVD cases show an inversion of the dominant models of degradation. Paying workers higher wages and treating them with dignity produces higher quality food that more people can afford. The more productive the farms, the more farmers can afford to increase workers' wages. This also holds true for the broader economy. The better the working conditions, the more productive the firm, the higher the wages, and the more people can afford quality goods. As Gray (2014,145) and Martin (2009) argue, raising the cost of produce by 3.6 percent—about $15 per year per household—would cover a 40 percent increase in wages.

The increased cost to households could be offset by reducing household food waste (Gray 2014, 145). It could also be offset by creating higher wages and better working conditions for people in all industries.

Ensuring dignity at work for employees requires the implementation and enforcement of legislation at state and federal levels that meaningfully protects workers and people who immigrate. There need to be mechanisms in place to ensure that revenue is regularly invested in workers. The runaway costs of shareholder profits across the economy play a significant role in degrading work in many industries. In contrast, the Bauers and PVD owner-managers demonstrate the extensive benefits of dignified labor practices to farms and communities. They used their managerial autonomy to invert dominant models of production, with pronounced benefits to their farms, employees, and the broader community. Their example should be backed by institutional mechanisms and replicated broadly.

That said, several problems remain on the Bauer and PVD farms that need to be addressed. Among them, and to foster ongoing growth in Dairy City, I have several recommendations. At the local level, families need dependable daycare for young children. Inadequate daycare is a problem that people in many industries and places around the US face. Dairy City is no exception. Greater representation of people who recently immigrated is also needed in local (and national) leadership positions. While recent immigrants are beginning to open their own small businesses in Dairy City, and many families are active at the school and in local social events and organizations, local civic leadership roles remain in the hands of people who did not recently immigrate. Increasing representation of a greater diversity of experiences would greatly enrich civic life. On the farms, the possibility of ownership stakes to stimulate profit sharing and innovation would benefit employees, farms, and the community.[20] Faster promotion into upper management positions is also key. This would guard against attrition and renewed waves of rural decline while further raising productivity and fostering household and community growth. In education, expansion of multilingual and intercultural programs would help honor the rich cultural history—and future—of the area. Currently, most programs are geared toward teaching English to Spanish speakers, though

English speakers would benefit enormously from expanded education in Spanish, and everyone would benefit from an expanded language program more generally (multiple languages and cultures).

The growth of firms, households, and communities is interconnected (Sennett 2008; Pugh 2015). The more that employers invest in and support employees through equitable and fair compensation and craft-like labor practices, the more productive their firms are. The more productive firms are, the greater the local tax base. The greater the local tax base, the more support local social institutions have, creating new opportunities for people who decide to reside there (Gray and Gibson 2019). These virtuous circles are created and sustained through immigration. Immigration is key to social, economic, and cultural (re)vitalization. There is no clearer evidence of this than rural towns like Dairy City that were once nearly blown off the map by homogenization and decline. Recent growth gives hope that places like Dairy City can continue re-diversifying and innovating. Confronting challenges of the future, including sustainable food systems and environment, will take extensive collaboration, energy, and creativity.

Crafting Dignity shows in detail how the quality of relations at and beyond work may be raised in reciprocal fashion, even in the face of multidimensional structural violences. Examining additional contexts in which employers who are pressured to replicate degrading practices instead resist them would help us to learn more about how to mend torn social fabrics in the face of adversity, as well as how to expand dignified labor practices that build healthier and more resilient communities at and beyond work. I have aimed to examine not just the effects of inclusive and sociable forms of craft-style management on the growth of community at work, but also the benefits that accrue to whole communities when dignified labor practices prevail. Sociable forms of craft-style management and dignified work are key to helping us build sustainable futures and communities (Sennett 2008). Learning more about how these dynamics emerge in additional contexts may help us to replicate them more broadly and inclusively.

The Dairy City region is an ancient immigrant destination (West 1998), and Dairy City itself is experiencing renewed immigration following recent farm consolidation. In this appendix, I provide fuller context for twenty-first-century immigration to Dairy City, as well as a more technical review of the recent restructuring of the US dairy industry that underscores local farmers' efforts to reignite immigration following decades of decline triggered by white settler colonialism. Rather than diversifying Dairy City, recent immigration has re-diversified the town. Such rediversification is crucial for building the ecology of growth I explore throughout the book. This appendix offers additional detail about how recent immigration patterns "renew" ancient destinations like Dairy City. My aim in providing such detail is to aid scholars in more fully capturing the nuances of interlinked patterns of migration over time, as well as their implications for contemporary power dynamics. In the same vein, I provide a more technical discussion of the recent period of dairy restructuring and its effects on US dairy farming. This discussion provides further context for the dynamics that emerged in Dairy City, as well as for questions about food (in)security, immigration, and social relations of production that I address throughout the book.

Ancient Destinations

As people speed through Kansas on interstate highways today, they may not realize that the land they traverse was part of the corridor that first welcomed humans to the continent more than ten thousand years ago (West 1998). Humans likely first entered North America by walking across a land bridge from Beringia to present-day Alaska and then southeast "between two towering blue walls of Pleistocene ice" (West 1998, 18). The eastern edge of the Rockies formed the western border of the corridor, reaching into present-day New Mexico, while a glacier that jutted south from the present-day Dakotas into eastern Kansas formed the eastern ridge (West 1998, 18). Early migrants pursued "wild horses, camels, pronghorn, deer, peccaries, bison, and mammoth" across the plains. They created seasonal settlements that eventually brought people together from all over the world, right in the geographical heart of what is today the United States, with Dairy City at its geographic core (West 1998).

"During the first five centuries of CE [the Common Era], central Kansas would have been one of the more interesting places in North America to watch the interactions among the continent's peoples and their ways" (West 1998, 27). It marked the heart of the "system of trade reaching from British Columbia to Florida and from New England to Baja California" (West 1998). This period also marked a moment of settlement mixed with circular migration across the plains, with people from mound-building and gardening societies establishing themselves on the plains long before contact with people from the Eastern Hemisphere (e.g., Spain, France, Britain) brought disease and disruption. A violent un-settling and "re-settling" of the plains ensued (West 1998, 27). Spanish explorers pushed from southwest to northeast beginning in 1541; French and then British explorers (the latter in 1763) moved in from the northeast, converging in Kansas, Nebraska, and eastern Colorado (West 1998; Turk 2005).

In the mid- to late nineteenth century, US railroad prospectors traveled to Germany to recruit new European immigrants. These prospectors spread news of a "plains-based Eden" in and around Dairy City (Turk 2005; Kansas Historical Society n.d.). High unemployment and political turbulence in Germany supplemented prospectors' propaganda, and many people crossed the Atlantic to try their luck at farming the plains. German immigrants arrived in Dairy City as 200,000 amateur gold seekers trekked through from the Eastern United States (West 1998). Gold seekers sought fortunes to the west, in the Rockies (West 1998). To aid the traveling gold seekers and grow their farms, German settlers built footbridges, raised and traded fresh cattle for prospectors' exhausted animals, and sold supplies at outposts in Dairy City: "Anyone who could start a toll bridge or a ferry, or lay in a stock of whiskey, crackers, and herring, trade in foot-sore cattle and start a ranch, could get rich" (Kansas Historical Society, n.d.; see also West 1998, 256).

European immigrants were aided in raising farms on the plains via the Pacific Railroad Act, the Homestead Act, and the Morrill Act, which "promoted transportation, cultivation of land, and higher education, respectively" (Billings 2012, 699), but only for people who were either citizens or "eligible for citizenship" in the new nation-state; i.e., they were racialized white (Ngai 2004). A few years after President Lincoln signed the Homestead Act, Sofia Newcomb travelled by train to Dairy City to claim four homesteads. She and her three children built a four-room house at the corner of four homesteads—one room on each parcel. Kansas Historical Society documents claim the train eliminated the "difficulty of wading through tunnels of shoulder-high prairie grasses" to navigate terrain unmarked by trees or mountains. It also came at great cost to Native American and Mexican American peoples. The arrival of the train marked the end of thousands of years of cyclical migrations among diverse groups of Native American peoples. The train tracks, which ran through what became the center of Dairy City, were likely laid and maintained by Mexican Americans and people from Mexico who were displaced by economic depression in Mexico (Blue 2021, 191) and/or violently repressive working conditions in US border states (Blue 2021, 192; Montejano 1987). People who worked laying and maintaining the tracks were called "*traqueros*" (Blue 2021). The rail lines they laid aided the rise of cattle and meatpacking across the Midwest. Meatpacking industries have often been located along rail lines to support the transportation, slaughter, and sale of cattle (or meat products and inputs). Although Dairy City farmers who descended from European homesteaders developed creameries and egg-packing plants that shipped millions of dollars' worth of goods all the way to Hawaii, they did not engage in meatpacking.

After "breaking" the prairie and raising their farmsteads, European settlers began selling surplus food to soldiers stationed at military forts across Kansas and Nebraska (West 1998; Kansas Historical Society, n.d.).

Soldiers at these forts "cleared the way" for additional gold seekers and settlers by violently driving Indigenous peoples off the homelands that had sustained them for generations (West 1998; Sides 2006). Indigenous peoples had been annually migrating in a circular fashion for thousands of years, camping near the Rockies in the winter and hunting, foraging, and trading across the plains in the summer (West 1998; Sides 2006). US military campaigns were paired with "buffalo safaris," in which people from the East Coast hunted buffalo for sport (decimating the herds), terminating a whole way of life (West 1998). Now Indigenous groups were cut off from their food sources and trade routes. They faced genocide, forced removals to reservations, and child abduction (Alatidd 2022; Department of the Interior and Bureau of Indian Affairs 2022). The federal government, in collaboration with some religious organizations, abducted Native American children and sent them to boarding schools where they faced forced assimilation and many children were tortured and killed (Alatidd 2022; Department of the Interior and Bureau of Indian Affairs 2022).

European immigration to and through Dairy City persisted until about 1930 (Turk 2005; Kansas Historical Society n.d.). After that, there was a sixty-year lull in immigration—long enough for most people to forget that generation after generation of white European farmers inherited or bought into property originally acquired through Homestead Acts. Although immigration from Mexico to Kansas took off again after the 1970s, most of the people who immigrated from Mexico during this time moved to meatpacking towns in other parts of the state. It wasn't until 1999 that immigration to Dairy City resumed in earnest.

Some people who came to Dairy City in the early 2000s were from South Africa and Romania, but the vast majority of people who immigrated—sometimes via large US cities—were born in Mexico. Their immigration is distinct from white European settler colonialism. The Latinx/e population today constitutes about 22 percent of the population. The non-Hispanic white population declined by 9 percent between 2000 and 2010 (and the total non-Latinx/e population by 15 percent), but non-Hispanic white residents continue to outnumber people from all other ethnic and racial backgrounds (US Census Bureau 2016, 2024).

Restructuring: Going Big to Stay in Business

In the early aughts, the Bauers, Hoffmans, and Pleasant Valley Dairy (PVD) owners expanded their operations in order to save them. They were not alone. From 1970 to 2006, the number of dairy farms in the United States declined by 88 percent, but the number of farms with 2,000 or more cows doubled (Kardashian 2012).[1] According to MacDonald et al. (2016), herd sizes grew 1,000 percent between 1987 and 2012, and dairy farms with $5 million or more in sales currently account for 72 percent of production in the United States.

Two sets of factors compelled most US dairy farmers to scale up their operations. First is their need to negotiate with large and powerful processors, retailers, truckers, and feed/farm implement suppliers (Hamilton 2008). Second is their need to reduce the costs of production by creating economies of scale (Hendrickson et al. 2001; Shields 2010; MacDonald et al. 2018, 2020). Creating economies of scale became increasingly significant in the aftermath of a severe price shock in 2008 (Kardashian 2012).

In the early 2000s, global markets created high prices for milk, which encouraged many US farmers to expand production as much and as fast as possible. Droughts in Australia and New Zealand suppressed global milk supply while demand for milk in China rose with income (Kardashian 2012). Milk prices are also determined by milk orders markets, which are linked to futures markets and financial trading. By 2006, milk prices climbed to $24 per hundredweight (the measure for milk volume) and stayed high for over two years (Kardashian 2012, 4). US dairy farmers borrowed heavily to boost production by expanding and improving their herds (Kardashian 2012).

Just as US farmers were filling out their expensive new herds, the 2005 US Energy Bill promoting ethanol production began to inflate corn prices (Kardashian 2012; Hamilton 2008). Feed costs rose steeply. Europe eliminated quotas on milk production while Russia embargoed European milk. This increased global milk supply while intensifying competition between US and European producers for shrinking global markets. As droughts in Australia and New Zealand ended, producers there ramped up production, creating a glut. As a result, "from December 2008 to June 2009, milk prices dropped 50%, which constituted the largest single drop since the great depression" (Kardashian 2012, 5, 6). This is when Owen and Nelson bought shares in the Bauer farm and began taking over management.

In 2008, China, which had been buying large quantities of US milk, suddenly halted imports after milk-based melamine poisoning sickened 300,000 people, mostly children (Kardashian 2012, 5). Fears about milk's safety spread to the United States, suppressing the domestic market. Global milk supply outpaced demand by ever-growing margins. Prices continued their downward spiral as the US economy entered a recession (Kardashian 2012). Farmers were producing more milk than ever before, but feed costs soared while milk prices plunged. Many farmers had to borrow money to service their loans and pay employees they had hired while prices were high (Kardashian 2012). They also had expensive electric bills for running milk pumps and refrigerated tanks on increasingly high-tech farms (Kardashian 2012). Meanwhile, fuel costs for transporting milk kept rising, as did the costs of producing feed for hungry heifers (Kardashian 2012). Thousands of farmers were suddenly unable to feed their cows, pay their employees, service their loans, or acquire new loans to service the original loans (Kardashian 2012). Many farmers were forced to cull their cows, putting their farms permanently out of business (Kardashian 2012; Sexsmith 2019; Laughton 2015, 2017).

The Bauers weathered the 2008 crisis by producing their own feed. At PVD, Peter bought feed under contract from farm owners. Peter decided to mix bran into silage to generate a consistently higher-protein feed that reduced the amount of silage he required. This stabilized nutrition for cows, which allowed them to produce more milk. He also invested in better storage silos and packing techniques to preserve feed and reduce purchases. The PVD board granted Peter more autonomy to decide how to manage costs. The Hoffmans experimented with different breeds of dairy cows to increase milk yield while holding production costs stable.

Dairy consolidation reached a tipping point in the early 2010s. Whereas 50 percent of US dairy cows were in herds smaller than 140 in 1997, by 2012 more than 50 percent of cows were in herds larger than 900 (Clay et al. 2020, 37; MacDonald, Cessna, and Mosheim 2016). At the same time, the number of dairy farms in the United States continued to decline. By 2017, there were an estimated 40,000 US dairy farms, down from 640,000 in 1970 (Clay et al. 2020, 37). Before the late 1990s, US dairy farmers typically worked exclusively with their relatives. By the late 1990s, most US dairy farmers had begun turning to immigrant employees (Adcock et al. 2015; Mercier 2014; Panikkar and Barrett 2021).

Some dairy farmers decided to sidestep the "mega-farm" trend by pursuing niche production (e.g., "farm to table") or producing organic milk, but they represented less than a quarter of the US milk market (Kardashian 2012, 229). Niche and organic milk farmers hoped to fetch high prices in wealthy urban markets, but to get higher prices, farms must typically be located close by (DuPuis 2002). In addition, farmers who undertake niche production often process, bottle, *and* transport their milk—difficult and expensive undertakings individually, and especially in conjunction (DuPuis 2002). If too many farmers compete for a small number of wealthy consumers, then falling prices due to stiff competition may drive some niche farms out of business (DuPuis 2002; Kardashian 2012; Hamilton 2008).

Organic milk garners higher prices than "regular" milk, but organic milk production has largely been coopted by large processors and re-tailers, driving down the price and making its production prohibitively expensive (DuPuis 2002; Kardashian 2012). While organic milk is often conceived of as "ethical" or "sustainable," "sustainable" dairy farming often reproduces racial, ethnic, and class-based inequalities by promot-ing concerns for the environment over workers (Gray 2014, Sbicca 2015, Guthman 2014). Strategies for reducing labor costs by employing vulner-able immigrant workers have been documented on many "sustainable" farms (Sbicca 2015; Gray 2014).

Dairy City's farmers are located too far from large cities to pursue niche production, but their remoteness (perversely) facilitates industrial-style production. The closer big farms are to large populations, the more sus-ceptible they are to complaints about water and air pollution. In Califor-nia, residents who live close to large dairies are enacting laws to regulate emissions of air pollutants. Soil disturbances on farms release small "par-ticulate matter" that can cause respiratory distress and lung disease (Kardashian 2012). Many residents also protest dangerous exposure to nitrogen oxide from large manure lagoons and ammonia from the animal feed (silage) that farmers store and feed to cattle (Kardashian 2012). Dairy farmers in California have responded to some of these struggles by selling their farmland at high prices to suburban developers and buying cheaper land farther away from large populations (Gilbert and Wehr 2003; Kardashian 2012). Urban sprawl continues, however, forcing California's dairy farmers to move ever farther afield (Gilbert and Wehr 2003). Since there are many sunk capital costs in dairy farms—including the barns, tanks, pumps, lagoons, and silos (Gilbert and Wehr 2003; Kardashian 2012), perpetually moving is a losing proposition. In Dairy City, farms are so remote that they face little resistance from people opposed to having large, industrial dairy operations in their backyards. As people in some Kansas meatpacking towns say, the cows "smell like money" (Ruiz 2017). This may perversely enable environmental and health problems to expand in rural areas.

Dairy City farmers have invested hundreds of thousands of dollars in large new milking parlors, self-removing milk pumps, and large refrigerated storage tanks. They buy sex-selective semen and artificially inseminate cows that they confine in barns with bedded stalls on land that they have long owned. They work with nearby university agricultural extension agents to gear animal husbandry toward raising the highest-yield dairy cows, thus joining the ranks of farmers who collectively coax 190 billion pounds of milk from 9 million cows annually—versus 120 billion pounds from 25.6 million dairy cows in 1944 (Kardashian 2012).

Every day, Dairy City farmers ship tens of thousands of gallons of milk to a dairy cooperative in Kansas City. Kansas City is the home of the country's largest cooperative. The larger the cooperative, the greater its negotiating power with both processors and retailers. Cooperatives also pressure state and federal legislators to protect producers' interests, largely via farm bills that guarantee prices and markets, and sometimes by committing governments to buying milk and dairy goods for reduced-price lunches at public schools or to promoting the sale of milk through SNAP. Milk producers like the Bauers, Hoffmans, and PVD owner-managers work together with other farm owners via cooperatives that they co-own. They are stronger together.

Dairy farmers in Kansas have local and state political support for their operations. The Kansas Department of Agriculture (KDA) even tries to recruit farmers from the East and West Coasts, emphasizing that farmers facing environmental challenges in California and New York can find peace in Kansas, where environmental laws are relatively lax and the sparsely populated state is flush "with wide open spaces" (KDA, n.d.). On its website, which automatically launches with dramatic synthesized music and a voice-over narrative, KDA brags, "Kansas is home to a robust and stable agricultural economy, where ag is the number one industry in the state. A vast portion of our agricultural strength comes from all our large commercial feed-yards (nearly one-third of all the beef finished and processed in the USA is right here in western Kansas), which laid the groundwork for our dairies' success." Several dairying families have moved to Kansas to take advantage of these "amenities." One university agricultural extension agent helped several families relocate from both Pennsylvania and the West Coast to Kansas. He said that when these families previously tried to expand their farms on either coast, they had to break them up into several smaller operations. In Kansas, by contrast, they consolidated. Now, in southwest Kansas, home to the state's largest dairies, twenty-five families own and operate thirty-six large dairies. Some farmers have gone across state lines to acquire existing farms rather than start from scratch, which is more expensive, because new farms require larger capital investments.

NOTES

Introduction

1. To protect participants' confidentiality, I use pseudonyms for all people and places.

2. This estimate includes the people who immigrated with employees (i.e., partners and/or a variety of relatives), as well as some people who had to find housing outside of Dairy City but work and send their kids to school in Dairy City. Per the farmers' memories, people from Eastern Europe came from Kurdistan, Czechoslovakia, and, primarily, Romania.

3. See also Schwartzman (2013); Stanley (1994); Stull, Broadway, and Griffith (1995); Ribas (2016); Martin (2009); Keller (2019); Harrison and Lloyd (2012); Lichter (2012); Greenberg (2018).

4. This methodological framework is informed by Desmond's (2014) relational ethnography. See also Becker (1996).

5. A general note on language throughout the book: Language is dynamic. I tried to take great care in how I used both language and terminology throughout. My learning continues.

6. This farm's owner-managers declined to participate. Evidence of this farm's practices is thus from interviews with former employees, other area farmers and farming experts, people familiar with the farm, and secondary data sources (published statements the farmers gave to reporters and people who work in the dairy industry). My understanding and characterization of Hoffman farm practices is based on interviews with my interlocutors and the secondary data sources. The Hoffman farm was not a fieldsite. Evidence of the other two farms, however, includes observation and farm owners' and managers' participation. See the methods section for details.

7. See Shulte and Tranel (n.d.); Holloway, Bear, and Wilkinson (2014); Driessen and Heutinck (2015); Jacobs and Siegford (2012).

8. Developing embodied skill involves "slow learning" and "heightened awareness of how materials respond to our efforts to make them comply with our designs" (Schwalbe 2010, 109; Sennet 2008).

9. Owen and Nelson Bauer had replaced hourly pay with pay per shift, which eliminated overtime. Employees complained and Owen relented (see Chapter 3).

10. When workers do organize, agribusinesses typically seek newly "suppressed

racial minority groups" to displace workers with greater bargaining power but still limited citizenship rights (McWilliams 1939 [1979], 111, 118; Ngai 2004; Ribas 2016; Martin 2009; Schwartzman 2013; Blue 2014; Griffith and Kissam 1995; Bonacich 1972; Garcia 2020; Gray 2014; Greenberg 2018; King 2012; McWilliams 1939 [1979]; Ribas 2016).

11. Typifying these trends, carcass "disassembly" (meatpacking) plants mechanize, deskill, and flexibly relocate production to perpetually reduce labor costs (Bonanno and Constance 2001; Edwards 1979; Huffman and Miranowski 1996; McMichael 2013; Schwartzman 2013; Stanley 1994; Stull et al. 1995). When companies cannot offshore production, they relocate to rural, anti-union states where thousands of newly displaced workers from large US cities and other countries are constantly "imported" or "inshored" to provide low-wage labor (Schwartzman 2013; Champlin and Hake 2006; Ribas 2016; Gray 2014). They target immigrants with restricted legal rights, few alternative sources of employment, and an orientation to making and saving more money than they could in their countries of origin (Schwartzman 2013; Ribas 2016; Lichter 2012). Managers then regulate workers' movements to shave seconds off their production times, penalizing them for delays while both triggering mistakes and discouraging reporting (Edwards 1979, 12; see also Crowley and Hodson 2014; Ribas 2016; Schwartzman 2013; Stull et al. 1995; Kandel and Parrado 2005; Bonacich 1972; Bonanno and Constance 2001; Champlin and Hake 2006; Friedland 1980; Huffman and Miranowski 1996; McMichael 2013; Garni 2018).

12. Managing in the shadows obscures unscrupulous labor practices that may include paternalism/maternalism, which refer to employers isolating, monitoring, and manipulating people to steal unpaid labor from them while pressuring them to work constantly (Rollins 1985; Gray 2014; Keller 2019; Sexsmith 2019; Harrison and Lloyd 2012; Hondagneu-Sotelo 2007). In these cases, farm owners invade workers' private lives to acquire personal information they can use to control them (Gray 2014). They seek to separate workers from their families, believing that isolated employees have few "distractions" from work (Sexsmith 2019; Keller 2019; Garcia 2020; Greenberg 2018; McWilliams 1939 [1979]; Martin 2009; Keller 2019; Gray 2014).

13. The degradation of work entails standardizing the labor process across sites and monitoring workers using software that tracks employees' every move, including bathroom breaks (Davis 2009). Automation and division of labor impede employee autonomy and collaboration (Schwartzman 2013). Temporary work arrangements enable firms to reduce benefit and salary commitments to

workers, and to lay off workers during down times. Insecure employment and uncertainty for workers proliferates (Kalleberg 2018). See also McMichael (2013); Gray (2014); Weil (2017); Piper (2020); Jameel and Sanchez (2023); Pacelle (2016); Gray (2014); Perez (2020); Keller (2019); Sexsmith (2019); Harrison and Lloyd (2012); Garni (2018).

14. See also Bernard (2004), Hernández-León (2004), Babb (2003); Plankey-Videla (2012); Shaiken (1995); Garni and Weyher (2013); Casanova (2019).

15. See also Gómez Cervantes, Alvord, and Menjívar (2018). Many immigrants encounter more structural violences when lifetime career employment is replaced with increasingly brutal jobs that pay little and offer few chances for advancement (Pugh 2015; Davis 2009; Sennet 2008). Affording homes, educations, and the necessities of life is difficult for a growing number of people (Davis 2009; Tough 2023; Emmons, Kent, and Ricketts 2018). The precarity of work is matched by the precarity of community (Pugh 2015; Gibson and Gray 2019).

16. Keller (2019); Baker, Kades, Kolodinsky, and Belarmino (2021); Gray (2014); Donato, Tolbert, Nucci, and Kawano (2007); Farmer and Moon (2009); Kochhar, Suro, and Tafoya (2005); Zúñiga and Hernández-León (2005); Millard and Chapa (2001); Kandel and Cromartie (2001).

17. Gouveia, Carranza, and Cogua (2005, 23) characterize Nebraska as a "re-emerging destination" to account for Mexican immigration at the beginning of the twentieth century. When I refer to ancient destinations, I follow West (1998) in recognizing how these places have been destinations for thousands of years.

18. In many cases people moved through major US cities.

19. See also Keller (2019); Zúñiga and Hernández-León (2005).

20. Return migration risks family separation in the face of restrictive immigration policies that create "mixed immigration status" households and limited mobility.

21. The 1.5 generation refers to people who immigrated as children.

22. For recent data on education and housing costs compared with compensation, see Tough (2023); Emmons, Kent, and Ricketts (2018); Bureau of Labor Statistics (2023); Pew Research Center (2023).

23. See also Bureau of Labor Statistics (2022).

24. See also Bureau of Labor Statistics (2022). The more that employers construct turnover to undercut workers, the more that people's job paths become characterized by "random movement" rather than a career (Sennet 2008, 265; Pugh 2015; Davis 2009; Bureau of Labor Statistics 2022; Pew Research Center 2023).

25. See also Pew Research Center (2023) and Bradsher (2023).

26. See also Tough (2023) and Pew Research Center (2023).

27. See also Gray (2014) and Wright (2001).

28. See also Shields (2010); MacDonald et al. (2018); MacDonald et al. (2020); and MacDonald, Cessna, and Mosheim (2016). See also Jackson-Smith and Buttel (1998) for precursors to this pattern.

29. US dairy farming is polypolistic and oligopsonistic, meaning that there are many producers but few cooperatives, processors, or retailers. Processors and retailers have substantial market power (Hamilton 2008; Kardashian 2012; Young 1990).

30. See also Garni (2018).

31. See also Perez (2020) and Jameel and Sanchez (2023).

32. See also Harrison and Lloyd (2012).

33. See also Davis (2009).

34. See also Rubin and Brody (2011).

35. While the concept of craftwork implies sociality via communication and learning, Sennet's (2008) emphasis on "sociable" or "collective" craftsmanship also means people working together. I avoid the term "craftsmanship" because nearly half the people working on the farms in Dairy City are women. "Craft-like" or "craft-style" work are more inclusive.

36. See also Lucas (2015) and Casanova (2019).

37. Bolton (2007, 2011) distinguishes dignity *in* work from dignity *at* work. She argues that dignity in work refers to respect for workers at and beyond the worksite, while dignity at work involves dignified work conditions. These dynamics, however, are deeply intertwined. For clarity, I use the term dignity at work to include both sets of dynamics (see also Hodson 2001).

38. See also Jacobs and Siegford (2012).

39. If milk becomes infected and accidentally enters the milk stream, employees must flush and clean large tanks, and the milk is lost. Employees have to treat sick cows carefully because if they medicate a cow who does not heal, she may either not be sold, or she will be sold at a reduced rate, making it difficult for famers to recuperate the costs of feeding, sheltering, and treating cows who are unable to produce (Kardashian 2012). Non-compliance with rules about medicating culled cows may cost farmers their contracts with auction or slaughterhouses (Kardashian 2012). See also Garni (2018).

40. I somewhat modify or obscure the precise size to protect confidentiality.

41. This represents a 2,450 percent increase between 2000 and 2010, and double that between 2000 and 2020 (US Census Bureau 2016, 2024).

42. I use somewhat modified ranges for herd sizes to protect farmers' internal confidentiality. Farmers are often able to identify one another by herd size. Obscuring details such as herd size makes it difficult for farmers and others to identify them.

43. See also Becker (2001); Katz (1997, 2001); Timmermans and Tavory (2012); Falcone (2018); and Duneier (2001).

44. See also Fortun (2001) and Schmalzbauer (2014).

45. I somewhat generalize the date to protect confidentiality.

46. Part-time employees typically fill in for full-time workers when the latter request time off, but also sometimes provide seasonal help when harvests or other tasks temporarily increase.

47. See also Roscigno, Yavorsky, and Quadlin (2021). Included in my meaning of "dynamics" here is degree.

48. This methodology is informed by Becker (2001) and by the framework Desmond (2014) proposes for relational ethnography (see also Becker 1996; Davis 2009, xvii on Mills's sociological imagination).

Chapter 1. Not-So-New Immigrant Destinations

1. For example, Vega's (2015) earliest point of reference is 1950. Hirschman and Massey (2008) and Zúñiga and Hernández-León (2005) primarily refer back to nineteenth-century immigration, though Zúñiga and Hernández-León (2005: xii) also briefly note "Mexican-origin" communities in the Southwestern United States that "predate the arrival of Euro Americans."

2. Gouveia, Carranza, and Cogua (2005, 23) use the term "re-emerging destination" to account for Mexican immigration to Nebraska at the beginning of the twentieth century. Their point of reference is still much later than mine, which I base primarily on the work of West (1998).

3. Until the mid- to late twentieth century, most milk was produced on integrated family farms where farmers raise cows in addition to other livestock and crops (DuPuis 2002).

4. High-volume milk producers tend to win the best contracts (Hamilton 2008).

5. Truckers prefer to collect as much milk from as few farms as possible to reduce mileage and the number of stops they make (Hamilton 2008). The Bauers produce their own feed, but not all dairy farmers do (e.g., PVD purchases feed).

6. See also Perez (2020).

7. It also diverges from previous research indicating that lone immigrants are

usually favored over families in new destinations, as individuals are characterized as having a "low impact" on the economy and local social institutions, and where they typically live in segregated communities (Zúñiga and Hernández-León 2005; Donato et al. 2005, 88; Keller 2019; Sexsmith 2019; Hirschman and Massey 2008).

8. Mutual pressure to improve labor practices is reminiscent of how some twentieth-century "heads of local businesses were more likely than not to be acquainted with each other, through serving on the same corporate and non-profit boards and through membership in the same social clubs. Dense networks made it easier to maintain local standards of good corporate behavior" (Davis 2009, 196, 237).

9. See also Donato, Stainback, and Bankston III (2005).

10. Whereas many of the immigrant employees interviewed on dairy farms in the Midwest and East Coast lacked personal transportation (Keller 2019; Sexsmith 2019), families who immigrated to Dairy City during the past twenty-five years have at least one car. Almost everyone drives. In one notable exception, Elena, who had never driven because she either lived in cities with public transportation or other people drove her, said she had several hair-raising experiences learning how to drive in Dairy City. She started driving slowly around town a couple of years ago, which was comfortable for her until winter came and the roads got icy. She spent hours practicing. Elena has gained confidence, but she still resists driving under stressful conditions.

11. See also Ali (2022); Garcia (2020); Familias Unidas por la Justicia; and American Immigration Council (AIC) (2021).

12. See also Gray (2014); Donato et al. (2005); and Zúñiga and Hernández-León (2005).

13. Farmers mentioned both H-2A and H-2B visas to me but seemed unclear about the distinction and which had been more prevalent. Farmers' interactions with H-2 visas seemed to have been short-lived. They particularly disliked the temporary labor arrangements, preferring permanent employees.

Chapter 2. Risky Business

1. I paraphrase Humberto here because he said this to me over the phone—I was jotting notes as he spoke but not tape-recording the conversation.

2. See also Bonanno and Constance (2001); Huffman and Miranowski (1996); McMichael (2013); Stanley (1994); Stull et al. (1995); Champlin and Hake (2006); and Lichter (2012).

3. See also Bonanno and Constance (2001); Huffman and Miranowski (1996); McMichael (2013); Stanley (1994); Stull et al. (1995); Champlin and Hake (2006); and Lichter (2012).

4. I borrow this framework from Desmond (2014, 554) and Becker (2001).

5. See also Harrison and Lloyd (2012).

6. This manager had passed away. Ramiro said that he liked the new lead manager, but not the secretary.

7. Nidia also took a job at PVD. Ramiro, Nidia, and their children stayed for about thirteen years. They left a few years ago to spend time with family in Mexico.

8. "Naturally occurring affordable housing" refers to older or less well-maintained units with rents that are low due to poor the condition of the unit (Dougherty and Barbaro 2024).

9. See also Casanova (2019); Rubin and Brody (2011); and Crowley and Hodson (2014).

10. See also Keller (2019) and Harrison, Lloyd, and Kane (2009).

11. See also Harrison and Lloyd (2012); Keller (2019); and Maloney and Eiholzer (2017).

12. According to INEGI (2024), 79 percent of the national population lives in urban areas, which INEGI counts as consisting of at least 2,500 inhabitants. Bada and Fox (2022) argue that 2,500 is too low a threshold for rurality, and they adjust it to 5,000, re-estimating that 25 percent of the population lives in rural areas; however, two of three states in which the greatest number of people in Mexico live in rural areas also have the highest urban majorities—or people living in cities with more than 15,000 people. Those states are Veracruz and Estado de Mexico (Bada and Fox 2022), and they are places of origin for several people who immigrated to Dairy City—specifically, from Mexico City and a city of over 15,000 people less than fifty miles from the state capital of Veracruz.

13. People who immigrated to Dairy City originally came from at least eight states in Mexico where the urban populations range from a low of 62 percent to a high of 87 percent (INEGI 2024). Even by adjusted definitions of rural versus urban, the populations of all eight states live in majority urban municipalities (Bada and Fox 2022).

14. Per Zúñiga and Hernández-León's (2005, 255) call to examine "intragroup differences" that tend to be obscured by "homogeneity in national origins" of immigrants to "new destinations."

15. See also Bonanno and Constance (2001); Edwards (1979); Huffman and

Miranowski (1996); McMichael (2013); Schwartzman (2013); Stanley (1994); Stull et al. (1995); Champlin and Hake (2006); Ribas (2016); and Gray (2014).

Chapter 3. Organizing Work

1. See also Crowley and Hodson (2014); Edwards (1979); and Stinchcombe (1959).

2. See also Crowley and Hodson (2014); Edwards (1979); and Stinchcombe (1959).

3. See also Kandel and Parrado (2005).

4. Portions of this chapter first appeared in Garni (2018). They are used with permission of *Rural Sociology*/Wiley & Sons, from "Crafting Mass Dairy Production: Immigration and Community in Rural America," *Rural Sociology*, Volume 83, Issue 2, 2018; permission conveyed through Copyright Clearance Center, Inc.

5. See also Hodson (1999, 2001) and Rubin and Brody (2011).

6. If the organization of work constantly changes, however, then repetition is interrupted, and the "anchor of experience" needed for skill development never emerges (Sennet 2008).

7. Raises within positions are automatic after completing three, six, twelve, and eighteen months, and then every six months until a regular (elevated) salary is reached, at which point employees get additional raises every twelve months. The first set of raises was $4 per shift (50 cents per hour), and then $2 per shift, plus paid vacations. Recently, the farm switched back to wages by the hour instead of by shift. Starting minimum wages currently tend to range from $15 to $25 per hour, depending on the job responsibilities. Full-time employees also receive benefits. Various positions are compensated differently, with herding starting at the lowest remuneration and equipment maintenance at the highest. The Bauers print their job salaries and raise schedules for employees.

8. See also Hodson (2001) and Sennett (2008) on craft and pride in work.

9. Whereas relational competency refers to managers treating employees as whole human beings (minding their family ties and desires for work-life balance) and setting realistic expectations for employee performance, operational competency involves listening to employees, taking their advice, and providing reliable information (Rubin and Brody 2011, 470).

10. See also Edwards (1979).

11. Ramiro, by contrast, said he really liked working at PVD, though he often clashed with the farm secretary.

Chapter 4. Brokering Trust

1. I use the term institutions broadly here to include businesses, organizations, and service providers.

2. The education experts I consulted about this argue that students should advance to the next grade, regardless. See also Bowman-Perrott, Herrera, and Murry (2010).

3. See also Gibson and Gray (2019) on the centrality of schools in rural communities.

4. There are only one of each.

5. I avoid saying anything more about the speaker because although he said he wanted to emphasize his points for Zaira to record for the study, he expressed a broader sense of fear about the situation for immigrants in other parts of Kansas and the US.

6. *Americano/a* is the term participants used to refer to people who are white and were born in the United States. "American," however, encompasses the whole Western Hemisphere, and even if it were confined to the United States, "American" does not mean "white," as participants' usage implies. Americans are multiethnic and multiracial.

7. Some people also previously qualified for vouchers for limited health care through the Kansas Statewide Farmworkers' Health Program (KSFHP).

8. Within a seventy-five-mile radius, people can also access several migrant health centers and charity hospitals if they need surgery or urgent care. There are also two centers in towns sixty miles away that provide all services in one stop—vision, dental, behavioral, and primary care, and they both have interpreters on staff.

Chapter 5. My Farm Is Your Farm?

1. See also Baker, Kades, Kolodinsky, and Belarmino (2021); Fox, Fuentes, Valdez, Purser and Sexsmith (2017); Harrison and Lloyd (2011); Keller (2019); and Maloney and Eizholzer (2017).

2. The reason most jobs in rural labor markets are terrible is because farming corporations have replicated the "lean flexibility" pervading other US industries (common in US agriculture for well over a century) (e.g., McWilliams 1939 [1979]; Schwartzman 2013; Blue 2012; Griffith and Kissam 1995; Lichter 2012).

3. See also Kochhar, Suro, and Tafoya (2005); Sexsmith (2019); Harrison and Lloyd (2011); Keller (2019); Baker et al. (2021); and Gray (2014, 63). Financialization enabled large corporate employers to consolidate their power

over workers despite centuries of resistance (McWilliams 1939 [1979]; Chavez 1991; Martin 2009; King 2012; Gray 2014).

4. The USDA (2022, 10) found that more people moved into farmwork as "employment in the non-farm economy declines."

5. When insurance markets in countries of origin fail, particularly in the midst of restructuring and other crises, people often migrate internationally to secure income in more stable labor markets. These migrations are a means for people to independently "insure" against health problems and livelihood and asset losses (Massey et al. 1998; De Haas et al. 2019).

6. Hernández-León (2004, 429, 441) defines "red-unions" as "pro-government."

7. Crossa (2022, 12) found that the prevailing maquila wage in Mexico in 2021 was 141 pesos per day, or $7 USD. That wage is higher than the average prevailing wage in other parts of Mexico (Crossa 2022).

8. See also Anner (2011); Garni and Weyher (2013); and Patel (2012).

9. Referencing research by Lowell Ricketts, William Emmons, and Ana Hernández Kent at the Federal Reserve Bank of St. Louis, Tough (2023, 2) defines "the college wealth premium" as a measure of the wealth (assets minus debts) that "a typical college graduate [accumulates] over their life span, compared with that of a typical high school graduate."

10. The costs of education in the United States are becoming prohibitive, replicating inequality to an alarming degree. "By late 2010 aggregate student loan debt had surpassed credit card debt . . . with over $800 billion in loans outstanding" (Davis 2009, viii). And "in 2020, 60.7 percent of outstanding student loans had a higher balance than when they were first issued" (Beamer and Steinbaum 2023; Nilaj, Pinto, Steinbaum, and Beamer 2023). This is especially true for "female, Black, and Hispanic" students who face disadvantages in education and US labor markets. Meanwhile, political support for redressing such inequalities and making college more affordable and accessible has waned (Tough 2023).

11. Minkoff-Zern (2019, 2) found that the US Agricultural Census undercounts Hispanic and Latinx/e farm owners, discounts non-white Latinx/e farm owners, and fails to determine how many Hispanic and Latinx/e farm owners are first-generation immigrants.

12. PVD has been focused on experimenting with improved feed sources, converting waste (methane) into energy and improving the quality of milk parlors.

13. See also Hsu and Bustillo (2023); McKinley and Ferré-Sadurní (2023).

14. "As fewer young immigrants are entering agriculture, the average age of

immigrant farmworkers is rising" (USDA 2018, 6). In 2006, the average age of US- and foreign-born agricultural workers was just under 36; in 2019 it was 41.6; in 2024, the average age of US-born workers was 35 (USDA 2024).

15. White workers, older workers, workers with higher degrees, and people who work in public or private sector manufacturing have the longest job tenures; by contrast, people who work in hospitality, people with less than a high school diploma, people who are Black, Hispanic, women, and young have the shortest job tenures (Bureau of Labor Statistics 2022, 1). Food service workers have the shortest median tenure, at 1.6 years, while those in the public sector have the longest, at 6.8 years (compared with 3.7 for private industry) (BLS 2022).

16. See also Pew Research Center (2023).

Conclusion

1. The convergence of managerial practices between the two farms reflects the long-standing closeness of business operators in the area. The success of one business is bolstered by that of another. When growth is based on positive labor practices, employer pressure to conduct business responsibly grows (Davis 2009).

2. See Bolton (2007), Ackroyd (2001), Sayer (2001), and Hodson (2001).

3. See also Babb (2003); Plankey-Videla (2012).

4. Previously, companies attained corporate status via state legislatures that considered their applications on a "case-by-case basis" (Davis 2009, 8). The primary criterion was large investment in public works. Once incorporated, companies were regarded as an "institution endowed with responsibilities" (Davis 2009, 196). Commercial banks that loaned money to corporations were "geographically constrained to operate in a single state or city" and "they became uniquely tied to the wellbeing of the local business community and took a lead in guiding local philanthropy" (Davis 2009, 196). Loans were drawn from local deposits from other local businesses. The health of one business was integral to that of another (Davis 2009, 196).

5. See also Kandel and Parrado (2005).

6. See also Pugh (2015).

7. See also Beckett and Paul (2023).

8. Sennett (2008) gives the example of the difference between architects who get into the field to develop their designs versus those who use "computer assisted design" (CAD). The former anticipate problems based on experience, and they use their experience to make corrections and improvements. The latter often fail

to anticipate and thus create a cascade of problems for which they have little experience to draw on to fix them.

9. See also Perez (2020).

10. Despite these exemptions and protections for farmers, farmers in Gray's (2014, 84–86) study complained that they were overregulated. See also Zoodsma et al. (2022) and Jameel and Sanchez (2023).

11. See also Hondagneu-Sotelo (2007).

12. Per my interviews, milk from each farm is tested when truckers collect it to ensure consistent high quality across farms—farmers are paid for the volume of high-quality milk they produce, measured in part by "somatic cell counts" indicating whether the cows had infections or not. Milk of similar quality across farms is later blended.

13. While several organizations represent migrant farmworkers in Kansas, these are typically geared toward seasonal crop workers. I did not encounter any efforts to organize workers in or around Dairy City.

14. According to the Kansas Department of Labor (2023), "all employees not covered by the Federal Fair Labor Standard Act must be paid Kansas minimum wage." Many dairy employees are covered by the FLSA, though there may be exceptions if employees are performing a mix of agricultural and non-agricultural work in the same week (FARM 2018).

15. See also Gómez Cervantes, Alvord, and Menjívar (2018).

16. See also Garcia (2022).

17. The criminalization of immigration means that behaviors not previously categorized as criminal are being treated as criminalized and very minor charges can now make people ineligible for adjustment of status (Abrego, Coleman, Martínez, Menjívar, and Slack 2017; Menjívar, Cecilia, Gómez Cervantes, and Alvord 2018; Hondagneu-Sotelo 2007; Golash-Boza and Pierrette Hondagneu-Sotelo 2013; Armenta 2018).

18. See also Runyon (2016).

19. See also McWilliams (1939 [1979]); Ribas (2016); Martin (2009); Schwartzman (2013); Chavez (1991); King (2012).

20. There is "some" form of ownership occurring, through "bonus checks" when above-average profits occur, for example. However, much of this remains "rhetorical"—talk of "ownership" or "your farm," without possibility of real "ownership." Shifting from rhetorical to material would make a real difference.

Appendix

1. See also Hendrickson et al. (2001); Shields (2010); MacDonald et al. (2018); MacDonald et al. (2020).

REFERENCES

Abrego, Leisy, Mat Coleman, Daniel E. Martínez, Cecilia Menjívar, and Jeremy Slack. 2017. "Making Immigrants into Criminals: Legal Processes of Criminalization in the Post-IIRIRA Era." *Journal on Migration and Human Security* 5, 3: 694–715.

Ackroyd, Stephen. 2007. "Dirt, Work, and Dignity." In *Dimensions of Dignity at Work*, ed. Sharon Bolton, 30–51. Oxford: Elsevier.

Adcock, Flynn, David Anderson, and Parr Rosson. 2015. "The Economic Impacts of Immigrant Labor on U.S. Dairy Farms: A Report Prepared for the National Milk Producers' Federation." College Station: Texas A&M AgriLife Research, Center for North American Studies, September 9. nmpf.org/files/immigration-survey-090915.pdf.

Alatidd, Jason. 2022. "Native American Boarding Schools in Kansas Supported US Land Grab and Forced Cultural Assimilation." *Topeka Capital-Journal*, May 12.

Ali, Safia Samee. 2022. "Farmers Push for Immigration Reform to Counter Labor Shortages and Rising Food Prices." *NBC News*, September 5.

Alvarez, Linda. 2019. "No Safe Space: Neoliberalism and the Production of Violence in the Lives of Central American Migrants." *Journal of Race, Ethnicity, and Politics* 5: 4–36.

Amaral-Phillips, Donna. 2014. "Management of Fresh Dairy Cows Critical for a Dairy's Profitability." Lexington, KY: Extension. Accessed July 28, 2016: articles.extension.org/pages/69058/management-of-fresh-dairy-cows-critical-for-a-dairys-profitability.

American Immigration Council (AIC). 2021. "Farm Workforce Modernization Act of 2021 Factsheet." Accessed November 3, 2023: americanimmigrationcouncil.org/research/farm-workforce-modernization-act-2021.

Ananat, Elizabeth O., Anna Gassman-Pines, and Yulya Truskinovsky. 2021. "Increasing Instability and Uncertainty among American Workers." In *Who Gets What?: The New Politics of Insecurity*, eds. Frances McCall Rosenbluth and Margaret Weir, 307–328. Cambridge: Cambridge University Press.

Ankele, John, and Anne Macksoud. 2001. *The Global Banquet: Politics of Food* [video recording]. New York: Old Dog Productions.

Anner, Mark. 2011. "The Impact of International Outsourcing on Unionization and Wages: Evidence from the Apparel Export Sector in Central America." *ILR Review* 64, 2: 305–322.

Armenta, Amada. 2017. *Protect, Serve, and Deport: The Rise of Policing as Immigration Enforcement*. Berkeley: University of California Press.

Babb, Sarah. 2003. *Managing Mexico: Economists from Nationalism to Neoliberalism*. Princeton: Princeton University Press.

Bada, Xóchitl, and Jonathan Fox. 2022. "Persistent Rurality in Mexico and 'the right to stay home.'" *The Journal of Peasant Studies* 49, 1: 29–53.

Baker, Daniel, Jini Kades, Jane Kolodinsky, and Emily H. Belarmino. 2021. "Dairy Is Different: Latino Dairy Worker Stress in Vermont." *Journal of Immigrant and Minority Health* 23: 965–975.

Barrick, Kelle, Pamela K. Lattimore, Wayne J. Pitts, and Sheldon X. Zhang. 2014. "Labor Trafficking Victimization among Farmworkers in North Carolina: Role of Demographic Characteristics and Acculturation." *International Journal of Rural Criminology* 2, 2: 225–243.

Beamer, Laura, and Marshall Steinbaum. 2023. "America's Student Loans Were Never Going to Be Repaid." *New York Times*, Opinion, July 13.

Becker, Howard S. 1996. "The Epistemology of Qualitative Research." In *Ethnography and Human Development: Context and Meaning in Social Inquiry*, eds. R. Jessor, A. Colby, and R. Shweder, 53–72. Chicago: University of Chicago Press.

Becker, Howard S. 2001. "Epistemology of Qualitative Research." In *Contemporary Field Research: Perspectives and Formulations,* ed. Robert Emerson, 53–71. Long Grove, IL: Waveland Press.

Beckett, Lois, and Kari Paul. 2023. "'Bargaining for Our Very Existence': Why the Battle over AI Is Being Fought in Hollywood." *The Guardian*, July 22.

Bernard, Mitchell. 1994. "Post-Fordism, Transnational Production, and the Changing Global Political Economy." In *Political Economy and the Changing Global Order*, eds. Richard Stubbs and Geoffrey Underhill, 216–229. New York: St. Martin's Press.

Billings, Roger D. 2012. "The Homestead Act, Pacific Railroad Act and Morrill Act." *Northern Kentucky Law Review* 39, 4: 699–736.

Blue, Ethan. 2014. *Doing Time in the Depression: Everyday Life in Texas and California Prisons*. New York: New York University Press.

Blue, Ethan. 2021. *The Deportation Express: A History of America through Forced Removal*. Berkeley: University of California Press.

Bolton, Sharon C. 2007. "Dignity In and At Work: Why it Matters." In

Dimensions of Dignity at Work, ed. Sharon C. Bolton, 1–16. Oxford: Elsevier.

Bonacich, Edna. 1972. "A Theory of Ethnic Antagonism: The Split Labor Market." *American Sociological Review* 37, 5: 547–559.

Bonanno, Alessandro, and Douglas H. Constance. 2001. "Corporate Strategies in the Global Era: The Case of Mega-Hog Farms in the Texas Panhandle Region." *International Journal of Sociology of Agriculture and Food* 9, 1: 5–28.

Bowman-Perrott, Lisa J., Socorro Herrera, and Kevin Murry. 2010. "Reading Difficulties and Grade Retention: What's the Connection for English Language Learners?" *Reading & Writing Quarterly* 26, 1: 91–107.

Bradsher, Keith. 2023. "China's E.V. Threat: A Carmaker That Loses $35,000 a Car." *New York Times,* October 5.

Broadway, Michael J., and Donald D. Stull. "Meat Processing and Garden City, KS: Boom and Bust." *Journal of Rural Studies* 22, 1: 55–66.

Braverman, Harry. 1974. *Labor and Monopoly Capital: The Degradation of Work in the Twentieth Century.* New York: Monthly Review Press.

Bureau of Labor Statistics. 2023. Accessed October 1, 2023: bls.gov/ooh/construction-and-extraction/plumbers-pipefitters-and-steamfitters.htm.

Bureau of Labor Statistics. 2022. Employee Tenure Summary. Accessed October 1, 2023: bls.gov/news.release/pdf/tenure.pdf.

Bustillo, Ximena. 2022. "The Senate Is Nearing a Deal on Immigration that Could also Lower Food Prices." *National Public Radio,* July 18.

Carr, Patrick J., Daniel T. Lichter, and Maria J. Kefalas. 2012. "Can Immigration Save Small-Town America? Hispanic Boomtowns and the Uneasy Path to Renewal." *The Annals of the American Academy of Political and Social Science* 641, 1: 38–57.

Casanova, Erynn Masi de. 2019. *Dust and Dignity: Domestic Employment in Contemporary Ecuador.* Ithaca: ILR Imprint of the Cornell University Press.

Champlin, Dell, and Eric Hake. 2006. "Immigration as Industrial Strategy in American Meatpacking." *Review of Political Economy* 18, 1: 49–70.

Chavez, Leo. 1991. *Shadowed Lives: Undocumented Immigrants in American Society.* New York: Harcourt College Publishers.

Chmielewski, Dawn. 2023. "Actors Decry 'Existential Crisis' over AI-Generated 'Synthetic' Actors." *Reuters,* July 21.

Clay, Nathan, Tara Garnett, and Jamie Lorimer. 2020. "Dairy Intensification: Drivers, Impacts and Alternatives." *Ambio* 49: 35–48.

Cornelius, Wayne, and David Myre. 1998. *The Transformation of Rural Mexico:*

Reforming the Ejido Sector. La Jolla, CA: Center for US-Mexico Studies, University of California, San Diego.

Costa, Daniel, Josh Bivens, Ben Zipperer, and Monique Morrissey. 2024. "The U.S. Benefits from Immigration but Policy Reforms Needed to Maximize Gains." Economic Policy Institute. October 4. Accessed November 24, 2024: epi.org/publication/u-s-benefits-from-immigration.

Cox, Joseph. 2023. "'Disrespectful to the Craft': Actors Say They're Being Asked to Sign Away Their Voice to AI." *Vice*, February 7.

Cross, John A. 2006. "Restructuring America's Dairy Farms." *Geographical Review* 96, 1: 1–23.

Crowley, Martha. 2016. "Neoliberalism, Managerial Citizenship Behaviors, and Firm Fiscal Performance." *A Gedenkschrift to Randy Hodson: Working with Dignity*, 28: 213–232. Bingley: Emerald Group Publishing Limited.

Crowley, Martha, and Randy Hodson. 2014. "Neoliberalism at Work." *Social Currents* 1, 1: 91–108.

Cruise, James, and Thomas Lyson. 1991. "Beyond the Farmgate: Factors Relating to Agricultural Performance in Two Dairy Communities." *Sociologia Ruralis* 56, 1: 41–55.

Davis, Gerald. 2009. *Managed by the Markets: How Finance Reshaped America.* New York: Oxford University Press.

de Haas, Hein, Stephen Castles, and Mark J. Miller. 2019. *The Age of Migration: International Population Movements in the Modern World.* London: Bloomsbury Publishing.

Department of the Interior and Bureau of Indian Affairs. 2022. "Federal Indian Boarding School Initiative Investigative Report." May. bia.gov/sites/default/files/dup/inline-files/bsi_investigative_report_may_2022_508.pdf.

Desmond, Matthew. 2012. "Eviction and the Reproduction of Urban Poverty." *American Journal of Sociology* 118, 1: 88–133.

Desmond, Matthew. 2014. "Relational Ethnography." *Theory and Society* 43: 547–549.

Donato, Katharine, Melissa Stainback, and Carl Bankston III. 2005. "The Economic Incorporation of Mexican Immigrants in Southern Louisiana: A Tale of Two Cities." In *New Destinations: Mexican Immigration in the United States,* eds. Víctor Zúñiga and Rubén Hernández-León. New York: Russell Sage Foundation: 76–102.

Donato, Katharine, and Charles M. Tolbert II, Alfred Nucci, and Yukio Kawano. 2007. "Recent Immigrant Settlement in the Nonmetropolitan United States: Evidence from Internal Census Data." *Rural Sociology* 72, 4: 537–559.

Dougherty, Conor, and Michael Barbaro. 2024. "How the Cost of Housing Became So Crushing: The Roots of the Property Crisis Run Deep and Have Proved Very Hard to Fix." The Daily Podcast. *New York Times*, September 24.

Douphrate, David. 2014. "Worker Health and Safety on US Dairy Farms." Austin: University of Texas School of Public Health. Accessed September 23, 2018: ncfh.org/uploads/3/8/6/8/38685499/worker_health_and_safety_on _us_dairy_far ms.pdf.

Driessen, Clemens, and Leonie F. M. Heutinck. 2015. "Cows Desiring to Be Milked? Milking Robots and the Co-Evolution of Ethics and Technology on Dutch Dairy Farms." *Agriculture and Human Values* 32: 3–20.

Duneier, Mitchell. 1999. *Sidewalk*. New York: Farrar Straus & Giroux.

DuPuis, Melanie. 2002. *Nature's Perfect Food: How Milk Became America's Drink*. New York: New York University Press.

Durand, Jorge, and Douglas Massey. 2003. "The Costs of Contradiction: US Border Policy 1986–2000." *Latino Studies* 1: 233–252.

Edwards, Richard. 1979. *Contested Terrain: The Transformation of the Workplace in the Twentieth Century*. New York: Basic Books.

Emerson, Robert M., Rachel I. Fretz, and Linda L. Shaw, eds. 2011. *Writing Ethnographic Fieldnotes*. Chicago: Chicago University Press.

Emmons, William R., Ana H. Kent, and Lowell R. Ricketts. 2018. "Is College Still Worth It? The New Calculus of Falling Returns." Center for Household Financial Stability. Federal Reserve Bank of St. Lous. Accessed October 1, 2023: stlouisfed.org/-/media/project/frbstl/stlouisfed/files/pdfs/hfs/is-colle ge-worth-it/emmons_symposium.pdf.

Equipo Maíz. 2004. *¿Cómo Quedó el TLC?* San Salvador: Asociación Equipo Maíz.

Falcone, Jessica. 2018. *Battling the Buddha of Love: A Cultural Biography of the Greatest Statue Never Built*. Ithaca: Cornell University Press.

Farmer, Frank L., and Zola K. Moon. 2009. "An Empirical Examination of Characteristics of Mexican Migrants to Metropolitan and Nonmetropolitan Areas of the United States." *Rural Sociology* 74, 2: 220–240.

Farmers Assuring Responsible Management (FARM). 2020. "Human Resources Legal Factsheet: Kansas." Accessed October 29, 2023: nationaldairyfarm.com /wp-content/uploads/2020/07/Kansas-Fact-Sheet-2020-Update-Q2.pdf.

Farmers Assuring Responsible Management (FARM). 2018. "Federal Human Resources Legal Factsheet." Accessed October 29, 2023: nationaldairyfarm .com/wp-content/uploads/2018/10/Federal-LegalFactsheet.pdf.

Fleming, Crystal M., Michèle Lamont, and Jessica S. Welburn. 2012. "African

Americans Respond to Stigmatization: The Meanings and Salience of Confronting, Deflecting Conflict, Educating the Ignorant and 'Managing the Self.'" *Ethnic and Racial Studies* 35: 400-417.

Fox, Carly, Rebecca Fuentes, Fabiola Ortiz Valdez, Gretchen Purser, and Kathleen Sexsmith. 2017. *Milked: Immigrant Dairy Farmworkers in New York State*. New York: Workers' Center of Central New York and Worker Justice Center of New York.

Fortun, Kim. 2001. *Advocacy after Bhopal: Environmentalism, Disaster, New Global Orders*. Berkeley: University of California Press.

Fine, Lisa M. 2006. *The Story of Reo Joe: Work, Kin, and Community in Autotown, U.S.A.* Philadelphia: Temple University Press.

Friedland, William H. 1980. "Technology in Agriculture: Labor and the Rate of Accumulation." In *The Rural Sociology of Advanced Societies*, eds. Frederick H. Buttel and Howard Newby, 201–214. Montclair, NJ: Allanheld, Osmun & Co.

Friedmann, Harriet. 1993. "The Political Economy of Food: A Global Crisis." *New Left Review* 197: 29–57.

Garcia, Angela. 2010. *The Pastoral Clinic: Addiction and Dispossession along the Rio Grande*. Berkeley: University of California Press.

Garcia, Matt. 2022. "The Unlikely Supporters of a Bill That Would Increase Guest Workers." *Washington Post*, December 14.

Garni, Alisa. 2018. "Crafting Mass Dairy Production: Immigration and Community in Rural America." *Rural Sociology* 83, 2: 244–269.

Garni, Alisa, and L. Frank Weyher. 2013. "Dollars, 'Free Trade,' and Migration: The Combined Forces of Alienation in Postwar El Salvador." *Latin American Perspectives* 40, 5: 62–77.

Geertz, Clifford. 1973. *The Interpretation of Cultures*. New York: Basic Books.

Gereffi, Gary. 1994. "The Organization of Buyer-Driven Global Commodity Chains: How US Retailers Shape Overseas Production Networks." *Commodity Chains and Global Capitalism*: 95–122.

Gibson, Jane W., and Gibson J. Gray. 2019. "The Price of Success: Population Decline and Community Transformation in Western Kansas." In *In Defense of Farmers: The Future of Agriculture in the Shadow of Corporate Power*, eds. Jane Gibson and Sara Alexander, 211–232. Lincoln: University of Nebraska Press.

Gilbert, Jess, and Kevin Wehr. 2003. "Dairy Industrialization in the First Place: Urbanization, Immigration, and Political Economy in Los Angeles County, 1920–1970." *Rural Sociology* 68: 467–491.

Gillespie, Jeffrey, Eric Njuki, and Angel Terán. 2024. "Structure, Costs, and

Technology Used on U.S. Dairy Farms." (Report No. ERR-334). US Department of Agriculture, Economic Research Service.

Golash-Boza, Tanya. 2015. "Targeting Latino Men: Mass Deportation from the USA, 1998–2012." *Ethnic and Racial Studies* 38, 8: 1221–1228.

Golash-Boza, Tanya, and Pierrette Hondagneu-Sotelo. 2013. "Latino Immigrant Men and the Deportation Crisis: A Gendered Racial Removal Program." *Latino Studies* 11, 3: 271–292.

Goldbaum, Christina. 2019. "Trump Crackdown Unnerves Immigrants, and the Farmers Who Rely on Them." *New York Times*, March 18.

Gómez Cervantes, Andrea, Daniel Alvord, and Cecilia Menjívar. 2018. "'Bad Hombres': The Effects of Criminalizing Latino Immigrants through Law and Media in the Rural Midwest." *Migration Letters* 15, 2: 182–196.

Gonzáles, Alberto. 2013. *Reform Without Justice: Latino Migrant Politics and the Homeland Security State*. Oxford: Oxford University Press.

Gouveia, Lourdes, and Rogelio Saenz. 2000. "Global Forces and Latino Population Growth in the Midwest: A Regional and Subregional Analysis." *Great Plains Research*: 305–328.

Gouveia, Lourdes, Miguel Carranza, and Jasney Cogua. 2005. "The Great Plains Migration: Mexicanos and Latinos in Nebraska." In *New Destinations: Mexican Immigration in the United States,* eds. Víctor Zúñiga and Rubén Hernández-León. New York: Russell Sage Foundation: 23–49.

Gray, Margaret. 2014. *Labor and the Locavore: The Making of a Comprehensive Food Ethic*. Berkeley: University of California Press.

Greenberg, Michael. 2018. "In the Valley of Fear." *New York Review of Books* 65, 20, December 12. nybooks.com/articles/2018/12/20/in-the-valley-of-fear.

Griffith, David, and Ed Kissam. 1995. *Working Poor: Farmworkers in the United States*. Philadelphia: Temple University Press.

Guthman, Julie. 2004. *Agrarian Dreams: The Paradox of Organic Farming in California*. Berkeley: University of California Press.

Hamilton, Shane. 2008. *Trucking Country: The Road to America's Wal-Mart Economy*. Princeton: Princeton University Press.

Harrington, Lisa, Max Lu, and David E. Fromm. 2010. "Milking the Plains: Movement of Large Dairy Operations into Southwestern Kansas." *The Geographical Review* 100, 4: 538–558.

Harrison, Jill Lindsey, and Sarah E. Lloyd. 2012. "Illegality at Work: Deportability and the Productive New Era of Immigration Enforcement." *Antipode* 44: 365–385.

Harrison, Jill Lindsey, and Sarah E. Lloyd. 2013. "New Jobs, New Workers, and New Inequalities: Explaining Employers' Roles in Occupational Segregation by Nativity and Race." *Social Problems* 60, 3: 281–301.

Harrison, Jill, Sarah Lloyd, and Trish O'Kane. 2009. "Overview of Immigrant Workers on Wisconsin Dairy Farms." *Changing Hands: Hired Labor on Wisconsin Dairy Farms*, Briefing 1.

Hegeman, Roxana. 2018. "Immigrants Say Working at Kansas Ranch Was 'Like Slavery.'" *Topeka Capital-Journal*, March 7.

Hendrickson, Mary, William D. Heffernan, Philip H. Howard, and Judith B. Heffernan. 2001. "Consolidation in Food Retailing and Dairy." *British Food Journal* 103: 715–728.

Hernández-León, Rubén. 2004. "Restructuring at the Source: High-Skilled Industrial Migration from Mexico to the United States." *Work and Occupations* 31, 4: 424–452.

Hill, Laura Warren. 2021. *Strike the Hammer: The Black Freedom Struggle in Rochester, New York, 1940–1970*. Ithaca: Cornell University Press.

Hirschman, Charles, and Douglas Massey. 2008. "Places and Peoples: The New American Mosaic." In *New Faces in New Places: The Changing Geography of American Immigration*, ed. Douglas Massey, 1–21. New York: Russell Sage Foundation.

Hodson, Randy. 1999. "Management Citizenship Behavior: A New Concept and an Empirical Test." *Social Problems* 46, 3: 460–478.

Hodson, Randy. 2001. *Dignity at Work*. Cambridge: Cambridge University Press.

Holloway, Lewis, Christopher Bear, and Katy Wilkinson. 2014. "Re-capturing Bovine Life: Robot-Cow Relationships, Freedom, and Control in Dairy Farming." *Journal of Rural Studies* 33: 131–140.

Holloway, Lewis, Christopher Bear, and Katy Wilkinson. 2014b. "Robotic Milking Technologies and Renegotiating Situated Ethical Relationships on UK Dairy Farms." Agriculture and Human Values 31 (2014): 185–199.

Hondagneu-Sotelo, Pierrette. 2007. *Doméstica: Immigrant Workers Cleaning and Caring in the Shadows of Affluence*. Berkeley: University of California Press.

Howard, Hilary, and Christopher Flavelle. 2024. "How Climate Disasters Are Making Mobile Homes a Huge Risk." *New York Times*, October 14. nytimes.com/2024/10/14/climate/mobile-homes-hurricanes.html.

Hsu, Andrea, and Ximena Bustillo. 2023. "As These Farmworkers' Children Seek a Different Future, Who Will Pick the Crops?" *National Public Radio*, July 28.

Huffman, Wallace E., and John A. Miranowski. 1996. "Immigration, Meat

Packing, and Trade: Implications for Iowa." Iowa State University Economic Staff Paper Series 285. Ames, IA: Iowa State University. Accessed March 2, 2016: lib.dr.iastate.edu/econ_las_staffpapers/282.

Instituto Nacional de Estadística y Geografía (INEGI) [National Institute of Statistics and Geography]. 2024. Población Rural y Urbana. cuentame.inegi.org .mx/poblacion/rur_urb.aspx?tema=P.

International Labor Organization and World Bank. 2024. "Employment in Agriculture (% of Total Employment) (Modeled ILO Estimate)—Mexico and United States." data.worldbank.org/indicator/SL.AGR.EMPL.ZS?location s=MX and data.worldbank.org/indicator/SL.AGR.EMPL.ZS?locations=US.

Jackson-Smith, Douglas, and Frederick H. Buttel. 1998. "Explaining the Uneven Penetration of Industrialization in the U.S. Dairy Sector." Staff Paper No. 2, Program on Agricultural Technology Studies. Madison: University of Wisconsin–Madison. Accessed April 3, 2016: pats.wisc.edu/pubs/60.

Jacobs, J. A., and J. M. Siegford. 2012. "Invited Review: The Impact of Automatic Milking Systems on Dairy Cow Management, Behavior, Health, and Welfare." *Journal of Dairy Science* 95, 5: 2227–2247.

Jameel, Maryam, and Melissa Sanchez. 2023. "Dairy Workers on Wisconsin's Small Farms Are Dying. Many of Those Deaths Are Never Investigated." *ProPublica*, October 25.

Jordan, Miriam. 2020. "Farmworkers, Mostly Undocumented, Become 'Essential' During Pandemic." *New York Times*, April 2.

Johnson, Kenneth M., and Daniel T. Lichter. 2020. "Metropolitan Reclassification and the Urbanization of Rural America." *Demography* 57, 5: 1929–1950.

Kalleberg, Arne L. 2011. *Good Jobs, Bad Jobs: The Rise of Polarized and Precarious Employment Systems in the United States, 1970s to 2000s.* New York: Russell Sage Foundation.

Kandel, William, and John Cromartie. 2004. *New Patterns of Hispanic Settlement in Rural America.* No. 99. US Department Agriculture, Economic Research Service.

Kandel, William, and Emilio A. Parrado. 2005. "Restructuring of the US Meat Processing Industry and New Hispanic Migrant Destinations." *Population and Development Review* 31, 3: 447–471.

Kane, Mike. 2023. "America's Farms Are Facing a Serious Labor Shortage." *National Public Radio*, July 30.

Kansas Department of Agriculture. N.D. "Dairy in Kansas: The Premier Dairy Frontier." Accessed November 25, 2023: dairyinkansas.com.

Kansas Historical Society. N.D.

Kansas Statewide Farmworker Health Program (KSFHP). 2024. Accessed November 2024: kdhe.ks.gov/356/Kansas-Statewide-Farmworker-Health -Progr.

Kardashian, Kirk. 2012. *Milk Money: Cash, Cows, and the Death of the American Dairy Farm*. Lebanon, NH: University of New Hampshire Press.

Katz, Jack. 1997. "Ethnography's Warrants." *Sociological Methods Research* 25, 4: 391–423.

Katz, Jack. 2001. "A Theory of Qualitative Methodology: The Social System of Analytic Fieldwork." In *Contemporary Field Research: A Collection of Readings*, ed. Robert Emerson, 127–148. Long Grove, IL: Waveland Press.

Katz, Jack. 2004. "On the Rhetoric and Politics of Ethnographic Methodology." *The ANNALS of the American Academy of Political and Social Science* 595,1: 280–308.

Katz, Jack. 2012. "The Expanding Warrants of Ethnographic Research." *The Annals of the American Academy of Political and Social Science* 642, 1: 258–275.

Keller, Julie. 2019. *Milking in the Shadows: Migrants and Mobility in America's Dairyland*. New Brunswick, NJ: Rutgers University Press.

Keller, Julie C., Margaret Gray, and Jill L. Harrison. 2017. "Milking Workers, Breaking Bodies: Health Inequality in the Dairy Industry." *New Labor Forum* 26, 1: 36–44.

Kendi, Ibram X. 2016. *Stamped from the Beginning: The Definitive History of Racist Ideas in America*. London: Hachette UK.

Kessler, Sarah, Ephrat Livni, and Michael J. de la Merced. 2023. "Tech Fears Are Showing Up on Picket Lines." *New York Times*, September 16.

King, Gilbert. 2012. *Devil in the Grove: Thurgood Marshall, the Groveland Boys, and the Dawn of a New America*. New York: HarperCollins.

Kochhar, Rakesh, Roberto Suro, and Sonya Tafoya. 2005. "The New Latino South: The Context and Consequences of Rapid Population Growth." Pew Research Center, Policy Commons. Accessed March 2022: policycommons .net/artifacts/628939/the-new-latino-south/1610253.

Kruse, Douglas L. 2002. *Research Evidence on Prevalence and Effects of Employee Ownership. The National Center for Employee Ownership*, February 13. nceorb .org.

Laca, Anna-Lisa. 2020. "Covid-19 Recession Likely to Cause Milk Prices to Reflect 2008." *Dairy Herd Management*, March 17.

Laughton, Chris. 2015. *Northeast Dairy Farm Survey, 2014*. Farm Credit East.

Laughton, Chris. 2017. *Northeast Dairy Farm Survey, 2016*. Farm Credit East.

Le Guin, Ursula K. 1974. *The Dispossessed: An Ambiguous Utopia*. New York: Harper and Row.

Levey, Noam. 2023. "Medical Debt Nearly Pushed this Family into Homelessness. Millions More Are at Risk." *National Public Radio*, September 11.

Lichter, Daniel. 2012. "Immigration and the New Racial Diversity in Rural America." *Rural Sociology* 77, 1: 3–35.

Linthicum, Kate. 2023. "Dream Interrupted: As Gang Violence Soars in Mexico, Migrants in U.S. Rethink Plans to Go Home." *Los Angeles Times*, July 18.

Lobao, Linda, and Katherine Meyer. 2001. "The Great Agricultural Transition: Crisis, Change, and Social Consequences of Twentieth Century US Farming." *Annual Review of Sociology* 27, 1: 103–124.

MacDonald, James M., Jerry Cessna, and Roberto Mosheim. 2016. "Changing Structure, Financial Risks, and Government Policy for the U.S. Dairy Industry." Economic Research Report 205. United States Department of Agriculture.

MacDonald, James M., Robert A. Hoppe, and Doris Newton. 2018. "Three Decades of Consolidation in U.S. Agriculture." Economic Information Bulletin 189. United States Department of Agriculture Economic Research Service.

MacDonald, James M., Jonathan Law, and Roberto Mosheim. 2020. "Consolidation in U.S. Dairy Farming." A report summary from the Economic Research Service. United States Department of Agriculture, July. ers.usda.gov /publications/pub-details/?pubid=98900.

Maddan, Sean, Claudia San Miguel, and Marcus A. Ynalvez. 2016. "The Link Between Consumer Prices, Labor Costs, and Immigration in the U.S." *American Business Immigration Coalition*, July 11. aboutbgov.com/3WC.

Madrid, Cori. 2009. "El Salvador and the Central American Free Trade Agreement: Consolidation of a Transnational Capitalist Class." In *The Nation in the Global Era: Conflict and Transformation*, ed. Jerry Harris, 79–100. Leiden: Brill.

Maloney, Thomas R., and Libby Eiholzer. 2017. "Workforce Issues and the New York Dairy Industry: Focus Group Report." Department of Applied Economics and Management, College of Agriculture and Life Sciences. Ithaca: Cornell University.

Maloney, Thomas R., and David C. Grusenmeyer. 2005. *Survey of Hispanic Dairy Workers in New York State* 640–2016–42914.

Manglos-Weber, Nicolette. 2018. *Joining the Choir: Religious Membership and Social Trust Among Transnational Ghanaians*. Oxford: Oxford University Press.

Marrow, Helen. 2012. *New Destinations Dreaming: Immigration, Race, and Legal Status in the Rural American South*. Palo Alto, CA: Stanford University Press.

Martin, Philip. 2009. *Importing Poverty? Immigration and the Changing Face of Rural America*. New Haven: Yale University Press.

Massey, Douglas. 2020. "Immigration Policy Mismatches and Counterproductive Outcomes: Unauthorized Migration to the U.S. in Two Eras." *Comparative Migration Studies* 8, 21: 1–27.

Massey, Douglas S., Joaquin Arango, Graeme Hugo, Ali Kouaouci, and Adela Pellegrino. 1999. *Worlds in Motion: Understanding International Migration at the End of the Millennium*. Oxford: Clarendon Press.

Massey, Douglas S., Jorge Durand, and Karen A. Pren. 2016. "Why Border Enforcement Backfired." *American Journal of Sociology* 121, 5: 1557–1600.

McCorkel, Jill A., and Kristen Myers. 2003. "What Difference Does Difference Make? Position and Privilege in the Field." *Qualitative Sociology* 26, June: 199–231.

McKinley, Jess, and Luis Ferré-Sadurní. 2023. "New York Employers Are Eager to Hire Migrants They Can't." *New York Times*, September 9.

McMichael, Philip. 2013. "Value Chain Agriculture and Debt Relations: Contradictory Outcomes." *Third World Quarterly* 34, 4: 671–90.

McWilliams, Carey. 1939 [1979]. *Factories in the Field: The Story of Migratory Farm Labor in California*. Berkeley: University of California Press.

Menjívar, Cecilia, and Shannon Drysdale Walsh. 2017. "The Architecture of Feminicide: The State, Inequalities, and Everyday Gender Violence in Honduras." *Latin American Research Review* 52, 2: 221–240.

Menjívar, Cecilia, Andrea Gómez Cervantes, and Daniel Alvord. 2018. "The Expansion of 'Crimmigration,' Mass Detention, and Deportation." *Sociology Compass* 12, 4: e12573.

Mercier, Stephanie. 2014. "Employing Agriculture: How the Midwest Farm and Food Sector Relies on Immigrant Labor." *The Chicago Council on Global Affairs*. Accessed March 9, 2016: thechicagocouncil.org/sites/default/files/Midwest_Ag_final.pdf.

Merton, Robert. 1987. "Three Fragments from a Sociologist's Notebooks." *Annual Review of Sociology* 13: 1–28.

Millard, Ann V., and Jorge Chapa. 2004. *Apple Pie and Enchiladas: Latino Newcomers in the Rural Midwest*. Austin: University of Texas Press.

Mills, C. Wright. 1956. *White Collar*. New York: Oxford University Press.

Minkoff-Zern, Laura-Anne. 2019. *The New American Farmer: Immigration, Race, and the Struggle for Sustainability*. Cambridge: MIT Press.

Minkoff-Zern, Laura-Anne. 2017. "Race, Immigration and the Agrarian Question: Farmworkers Becoming Farmers in the United States." *The Journal of Peasant Studies* 45, 2: 389–408.

Mizrachi, Nissim, Israel Drori, and Renee R. Anspach. 2007. "Repertoires of Trust: The Practice of Trust in a Multinational Organization amid Political Conflict." *American Sociological Review* 72, 1: 143–165.

Molzahn, Cory, Viridiana Ríos, and David A. Shirk. 2012. "Drug Violence in Mexico: Data and Analysis through 2011." San Diego: Trans-Border Institute, University of San Diego.

Montejano, David. 1987. *Anglos and Mexicans in the Making of Texas, 1836–1986.* Austin: University of Texas Press.

National Agricultural Law Center (NALC). 2023. "Collective Bargaining Rights." Accessed October 26, 2023: nationalaglawcenter.org/collective-bargaining-rights-for-farmworkers.

National Agricultural Statistics Service (NASS). 2020. United States Department of Agriculture. Accessed December 30, 2023: nass.usda.gov.

Ngai, Mae. 2004. *Impossible Subjects: Illegal Aliens and the Making of Modern America.* Princeton: Princeton University Press.

Nilaj, Eduard, Sérgio Pinto, Marshall Steinbaum, and Laura Beamer. 2023. "The Repayment Pause and the Continuing Crisis of Non-Repayment." Millennial Student Debt Series, 12. Jain Family Institute. jainfamilyinstitute.org/wp-content/uploads/2023/06/MSD-12-Repayment-Pause-6.15.23.pdf.

Ocejo, Richard E. 2017. *Masters of Craft: Old Jobs in the New Urban Economy.* Princeton: Princeton University Press.

Occupational Safety and Health Administration. 2007. *Small Farming Operations and Exemption from OSHA Enforcement Activities.* osha.gov/laws-regs/standardinterpretations/2007-07-16.

Pacelle, Wayne. 2016. "Oklahoma Bill to Defund Animal Welfare Organizations Dies a Merciful Death." *Huffington Post,* April 12.

Paige, Jeffery. 1998. *Coffee and Power: Revolution and the Rise of Democracy in Central America.* Cambridge: Harvard University Press.

Panikkar, Bindu, and Mary-Kate Barrett. 2021. "Precarious Essential Work, Immigrant Dairy Farmworkers, and Occupational Health Experiences in Vermont." *International Journal of Environmental Research and Public Health* 18, 7: 3675–3695.

Patel, Raj. 2012. *Stuffed and Starved: The Hidden Battle for the World Food System.* Brooklyn: Melville House.

Perez, Maria. 2020. "Wisconsin's Diary Industry Would Collapse without the

Work of Latino Immigrants—Many of them Undocumented." *Milwaukee Journal Sentinel,* November 12.

Perez, Maria. 2019. "American Farms Recruit Mexican Veterinarians for Jobs as Animal Scientists—but the Real Work Is Milking Cows and Cleaning Pens for Low Pay." *Milwaukee Journal Sentinel,* December 4.

Pérez Monterosas, Mario. 2003. "Las Redes Sociales de la Migración Emergente de Veracruz a los Estados Unidos." *Migraciones Internacionales* 2, 1: 136–160.

Perkowski, Mateusz. 2015. "Cows, Farmers Adapt to Robotic Dairy Systems." *Capital Press,* October 29.

Pew Research Center. 2023. "Which Workers Are More Exposed to AI on Their Jobs?" Pew Research Center, July 26. pewresearch.org/social-trends/2023 /07/26/which-u-s-workers-are-more-exposed-to-ai-on-their-jobs.

Piper, Kelsey. 2020. "Kansas's Ag-Gag Law Has Been Ruled Unconstitutional. *Vox,* January 23.

Plankey-Videla, Nancy. 2012. *We Are in This Dance Together: Gender, Power, and Globalization at a Mexican Garment Firm.* New Brunswick: Rutgers University Press.

Provine, Doris Marie, Monica W. Varsanyi, Paul G. Lewis, and Scott H. Decker. 2016. *Policing Immigrants: Local Law Enforcement on the Front Lines.* Chicago: University of Chicago Press.

Pugh, Allison. 2013. "What Good Are Interviews for Thinking about Culture? Demystifying Interpretive Analysis." *American Journal of Cultural Sociology* 1: 42–68.

Pugh, Allison. 2015. *The Tumbleweed Society: Working and Caring in an Age of Insecurity.* Oxford: Oxford University Press.

Putnam, Robert. 2000. *Bowling Alone: The Collapse and Revival of American Community.* New York: Simon & Schuster.

Ribas, Vanessa. 2016. *On the Line: Slaughterhouse Lives and the Making of the New South.* Berkeley: University of California Press.

Roscigno, Vincent J., Jill E. Yavorsky, and Natasha Quadlin. 2021. "Gendered Dignity at Work." *American Journal of Sociology* 127, 2: 562–620.

Rollins, Judith. 1985. *Between Women: Domestics and their Employers.* Philadelphia: Temple University Press.

Rosenbloom, Raquel. 2022. "A Profile of Undocumented Agricultural Workers in the United States." Center for Migration Studies of New York, August 30. cmsny.org/agricultural-workers-rosenbloom-083022.

Rosson, Parr C. 2012. "Regional Views on the Role of Immigrant Labor on U.S.

and Southern Dairies." *Journal of Agricultural and Applied Economics* 44, 3: 269–277.

Rosson, Parr C., Flynn Adcock, Dwi Susanto, and David Anderson. 2009. "The Economic Impacts of Immigration on U.S. Dairy Farms." A Report Prepared for the National Milk Producers' Federation. College Station: Texas A&M Agrilife Research, Center for North American Studies. Accessed February 18, 2016: nmpf.org/files/file/NMPF%20Immigration%20Survey%20Web.pdf.

Rotz, C. Alan, C. U. Coiner, Kathy J. Soder. 2003. "Automatic Milking Systems, Farm Size, and Milk Production." *Journal of Dairy Science* 86, 12: 4167–4177.

Rubin, Beth A., and Charles J. Brody. 2011. "Operationalizing Management Citizenship Behavior and Testing Its Impact on Employee Commitment, Satisfaction, and Mental Health." *Work and Occupations* 38, 4: 465–499.

Ruiz, Zaira. 2017. "Smells like Money: Mexican Employee Endurance in a Southwest Kansas Meatpacking Plant." M.A. Thesis. Manhattan: Kansas State University.

Runyon, Luke. 2016. "Gigi the Cow Broke the Milk Production Record. Is That Bad for Cows?" *National Public Radio,* Morning Edition, March 18.

Salamon, Sonya. 1995. *Prairie Patrimony: Family, Farming, and Community in the Midwest.* Chapel Hill: University of North Carolina Press Books.

Sayer, Andrew. 2007. "What Dignity at Work Means." In *Dimensions of Dignity at Work*, ed. Sharon Bolton, 17–20. Oxford: Elsevier.

Sbicca, Joshua. 2015. "Food Labor, Economic Inequality, and the Imperfect Politics of Process in the Alternative Food Movement." *Agriculture and Human Values* 32: 675–687.

Scheper-Hughes, Nancy. 1995. "The Primacy of the Ethical: Propositions for a Militant Anthropology." *Current Anthropology* 36, 3: 409–430.

Schmalzbauer, Leah. 2014. *The Last Best Place?: Gender, Family, and Migration in the New West.* Stanford: Stanford University Press.

Schneider, Leighton. 2020. "Dairy Farmers Dumping Milk amid COVID-19: Pandemic's Impact on the Dairy Industry." *NBC News,* April 21.

Schuenemann, Gustavo M. 2012. *Calving Management in Dairy Herds: Timing of Intervention and Stillbirth.* Columbus: Ohio State University Extension. Accessed May 23, 2016: ohioline.osu.edu/factsheet/VME-29.

Schuenemann, Gustavo M., S. Bas, A. A. Barragan, and J. D. Workman. 2014. "Management and Training of Dairy Personnel with Emphasis on Teamwork and Performance." Proceedings, 50th Florida Dairy Production Conference.

Gainesville, TN. Accessed May 23, 2016: dairy.ifas.ufl.edu/dpc/2014/Schu enemann.pdf.

Schulte, Kristen, and Larry Tranel. 2016. "The Economics of Automatic Milking Systems." Iowa State University Extension, August 2. extension.iastate.edu /dairyteam/sites/www.extension.iastate.edu/files/dairyteam/Economics%20of%20 Automatic%20Milking%20Systems_V2%200.pdf.

Schwalbe, Michael. 2010. "In Search of Craft." *Social Psychology Quarterly* 73, 2: 107–111.

Schwartzman, Kathleen C. 2013. *The Chicken Trail: Following Workers, Migrants, and Corporations across the Americas*. Ithaca: Cornell University Press.

Sennett, Richard. 2008. *The Craftsman*. New Haven: Yale University Press.

Sewell, Summer. 2012. "'It's Five Years since a White Person Applied': The Immigrant Workforce Milking America's Cows." *The Guardian*, July 25.

Sexsmith, Kathleen. 2019. "Decoding Worker 'Reliability': Modern Agrarian Values and Immigrant Labor on New York Dairy Farms." *Rural Sociology* 84, 4: 709–735.

Shaiken, Harley. 1995. "Lean Production in a Mexican Context." In *Lean Work: Empowerment and Exploitation in the Global Auto Industry*, ed. Steve Babson, 247–259. Detroit: Wayne State University Press.

Shields, Dennis A. 2010. "Consolidation and Concentration in the U.S. Dairy Industry." Congressional Research Service, 7–5700. Washington, DC. Accessed February 10, 2016: crs.gov.R41224.

Shiva, Vandana. 2001. *Stolen Harvest: The Hijacking of the Global Food Supply*. London: Zed Books.

Sides, Hampton. 2006. *Blood and Thunder: The Epic Story of Kit Carson and the Conquest of the American West*. New York: Penguin Random House.

Simnitt, Skyler, and Philip Martin. 2022. "U.S. Fruit and Vegetable Industries Try to Cope with Rising Labor Costs." United States Department of Agriculture Economic Research Service. ers.usda.gov/amber-waves/2022.

Small, Mario Luis. 2009. "'How Many Cases Do I Need?' On Science and the Logic of Case Selection in Field-Based Research." *Ethnography* 10, 1: 5–38.

Small, Mario Luis. 2006. "Neighborhood Institutions As Resource Brokers: Childcare Centers, Interorganizational Ties, and Resource Access among the Poor." *Social Problems* 53, 2: 274–292.

Smith-Howard, Kendra. 2014. *Pure and Modern Milk: An Environmental History since 1900*. Oxford: Oxford University Press.

Sommer, Judith E., Robert A. Hoppe, Robert C. Green, and Penelope J. Korb.

1998. "Structural and Financial Characteristics of U.S. Farms, 1995: 20th Annual Family Farm Report to the Congress." Agricultural Services Information Bulletin 746. Washington, DC.

Stanley, Kathleen. 1994. "Industrial and Labor Market Transformation in the U.S. Meatpacking Industry." In *The Global Restructuring of Agro-food Systems*, ed. Philip McMichael, 129–144. Ithaca: Cornell University Press.

Stinchcombe, Arthur L. 2000. "Social Structure and Organizations." *Economics Meets Sociology in Strategic Management* 17: 229–259.

Stinchcombe, Arthur L. 1959. "Bureaucratic and Craft Administration of Production: A Comparative Study." *Administrative Science Quarterly* 4, 2: 168–187.

Stinchcombe, Arthur L. 2005. "Methods for Sociology and Related Disciplines." *The Logic of Social Research*: 1–21.

Stull, Donald D., Michael J. Broadway, and David Griffith. 1995. *Any Way You Cut It: Meat Processing and Small Town America*. Lawrence: University Press of Kansas.

Sutton, Kelsea Kenzy. 2013. "The Beef with Big Meat: Meatpacking and Antitrust in America's Heartland." *South Dakota Law Review* 58: 611.

Tilly, Charles. 2010. "Cities, States, and Trust Networks." In *Contention and Trust in Cities and States*, 1–16. Dordrecht: Springer Netherlands.

Thorne, Barrie. 1980. "You Still Takin' Notes? Fieldwork and Problems of Informed Consent." *Social Problems* 27, 3: 284–297.

Timmermans, Stefan, and Iddo Tavory. 2012. "Theory Construction in Qualitative Research: From Grounded Theory to Abductive Analysis." *Sociological Theory* 30, 3: 167–186.

Tough, Paul. 2023. "Americans Are Losing Faith in the Value of College. Whose Fault Is That?" *New York Times Magazine*, September 5.

Turk, Eleanor. 2005. "Germans in Kansas." *Kansas History: A Journal of the Central Plains* 28: 44–71.

Tweed, Thomas A. 2006. *Crossing and Dwelling: A Theory of Religion*. Cambridge: Harvard University Press.

United States Census Bureau. 2016. American Fact Finder. Accessed June 2, 2016: factfinder.census.gov.

United States Census Bureau. 2024. Accessed November 28, 2024: factfinder.census.gov.

United States Department of Agriculture (USDA). 2024a. Farm Labor. ers.usda.gov/topics/farm-economy/farm-labor.

USDA. 2024b. Dairy. ers.usda.gov/data-products/chart-gallery/gallery/chart

-detail/?chartId=101405; ers.usda.gov/topics/animal-products/dairy/backgr ound.

USDA. 2024c. Kansas Farm Numbers. nass.usda.gov/Statistics_by_State/Kan sas/Publications/Economic_Releases/Farm_Numbers/2023/KS-farmnum2 302.pdf.

USDA 2022. U.S. Agricultural Census 2022. Hispanic Producers. nass.usda.gov /Publications/Highlights/2024/Census22_HL_HispanicProducers.pdf.

United States Department of Labor. 2023. State Minimum Wage Laws. Accessed August 7, 2023: dol.gov/agencies/whd/minimum-wage/state.

Valentine, Brent Eric. 2005. "Uniting Two Cultures: Latino Immigrants in the Wisconsin Dairy Industry." Working Paper No. 121, Center for Comparative Immigration Studies, University of California, San Diego, La Jolla, CA. Accessed May 9, 2016: citeseerx.ist.psu.edu/viewdoc/download?doi510.1.1.474. 7978&rep5rep1&type5pdf.

Vega, Sujey. 2015. *Latino Heartland: Of Borders and Belonging in the Midwest.* New York: New York University Press.

Wakayama, Brady. 2020. "Dairy Farms Thriving during Coronavirus Pandemic." *KRQE*, March 16.

Waldinger, Roger, and Michael I. Lichter. 2003. *How the Other Half Works: Immigration and the Social Organization of Labor.* Berkeley: University of California Press.

Wamsley, Laurel. 2024. "Mortgage Rates Were Supposed to Come Down. Instead, They're Rising. Here's Why." *National Public Radio*, October 18.

Weil, Sonia. 2017. "Big-Ag Exceptionalism: Ending the Special Protection of the Agricultural Industry." *Drexel Law Review* 10: 183.

West, Elliot. 1998. *The Contested Plains: Indians, Goldseekers, and the Rush to Colorado.* Lawrence: University Press of Kansas.

Wright, Melissa. 2001. *Disposable Women and Other Myths of Global Capitalism.* New York: Routledge.

Young, Brigitte. 1990. "Does the American Dairy Industry Fit the Meso-Corporatist Model?" *Political Studies* 38: 72–82.

Zeitlin, Maurice, and L. Frank Weyher. 2001. "'Black and White, Unite and Fight': Interracial Working-Class Solidarity and Racial Employment Equality." *American Journal of Sociology* 107, 2: 430–467.

Zoodsma, Anna, and Mary Jo Dudley, Laura-Anne Minkhoff-Zern. 2021. "National Food Security, Immigration Reform, and the Importance of Worker Engagement in Agricultural Guestworker Debates." *Journal of Agriculture, Food Systems, and Community Development* 11, 4: 139–151.

Zuboff, Shoshana. 1989. *In the Age of the Smart Machine: The Future of Work and Power*. New York: Basic Books.

Zúñiga, Víctor, and Rubén Hernández-León, eds. 2005. "Introduction." In *New Destinations: Mexican Immigration in the United States*. New York: Russell Sage Foundation.

Zahniser, Steven, Edward Taylor, Thomas Hertz, and Diane Charlton. 2018. Farm Labor Markets in the United States and Mexico Pose Challenges for U.S. Agriculture, EIB-201, U.S. Department of Agriculture, Economic Research Service, November.

INDEX

wages, 4, 140
    affordability and, 118, 158–159
    competition and, 5, 135
    consumption and, 158–159
    cuts and, 47
    deductions and, 37
    higher for night shifts at PVD, 62
    labor organizing and, 151–152, 157–158
    maquilas and, 122, 129
    overtime paid, 5, 37
    overtime withheld, 36, 72, 151, 154, 172n9
    pay structure and, 178n7
    raises and, 4–5, 76
    search for improved, 118, 122, 126,
        129, 136

suppression and, 4, 9, 45, 118, 157–158
    unpaid, 6, 172n12
West, Elliot, 7, 24–25, 45, 161–164
white settler colonialism, 25, 161
World War II women workers, 1, 5
work-life balance, 4–5, 20, 50, 52, 57, 66,
    82, 140, 178n9
Wright, Melissa, 6, 8, 143, 145, 174n27, 202

Zúñiga, Víctor, 7, 14, 21, 36, 47–48, 50,
    52, 65, 173n16, 173n19, 175n1, 176n7,
    176n12, 177n14, 188, 191, 203

www.ingramcontent.com/pod-product-compliance
Lightning Source LLC
Chambersburg PA
CBHW030328270326
41926CB00010B/1544